Using FTP

Quick Start to Internet Success!

The best DOS and Windows FTP sites

Go to this FTP address	Look in this directory	What you'll find
ftp.cica.indiana.edu	/pub/pc/win3	The premier Windows shareware site. It's mirrored by many other sites.
oak.oakland.edu	/SimTel/win3	Another huge collection of Windows shareware.
oak.oakland.edu	/SimTel/msdos	Huge collection of MS-DOS shareware.
ftp.ncsa.uiuc.edu	/Web/Mosaic/Windows	Home of Mosaic.
ftp.ncsa.uiuc.edu	/Web/Mosaic/Windows/viewers	Helper applications for Mosaic.
ftp.ncsa.uiuc.edu	/Web/html/Windows	Shareware HTML utilities.
ftp.cdrom.com	/pub/os2	Collection of files for OS2 users.
ftp.cdrom.com	/pub/doom	Collection of software and documents for use with the game Doom.
ftp.cdrom.com	/pub/gutenberg	Project Gutenberg mirror.
ftp.cso.uiuc.edu	/pc/pcmag	*PC Magazine* files.
ftp.microsoft.com	/bussys	LAN software, Mail, SQL, and Winsocks.
ftp.microsoft.com	/deskapps	Access, Excel, PowerPoint, Word, Office, and games.
ftp.microsoft.com	/developr	The Microsoft Developer's Network.
ftp.microsoft.com	/peropsys	DOS and Windows software.
ftp.mcp.com	/pub/que/net-cd	Copies of the software that's on the CD included in bestselling Que books.
ftp.qualcomm.com	/quest/windows/eudora	Eudora e-mail manufacturer.
ftp.utas.edu.au	/pc/trumpet	Home of Trumpet Winsock and News Reader.
ftp.law.cornell.edu	/pub/LII/Cello	Home of the Cello WWW browser.
boombox.micro.umn.edu	/pub/gopher	Big Gopher archive with documentation and software.
titan.ksc.nasa.gov	/pub/win3/winvn	Home of the WinVN newsreader.

201 W. 103rd Street • Indianapolis, IN 46290 • (317) 581-3500
Copyright© 1995 Que Corporation

To connect to an FTP site with Anarchie:

1 Double-click on an FTP site from the Bookmark list.

Or choose Get from the FTP menu, enter the FTP address, and click List.

2 Anarchie presents you with a list of files.

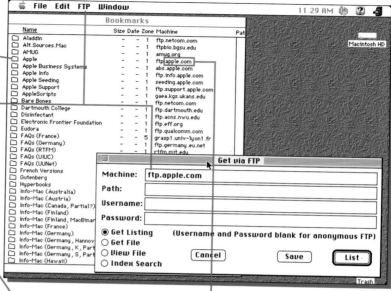

The domain name of the FTP server

To retrieve a listed file with Anarchie:

1 Double-click the desired file. (The file is transferred and appears as an icon on your Desktop.)

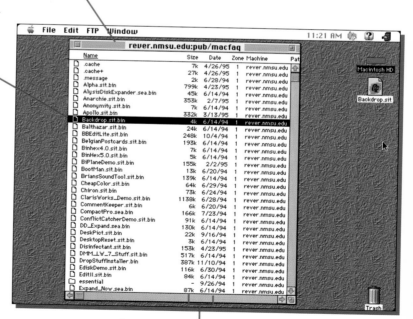

Shows the size of the file and when it was last updated

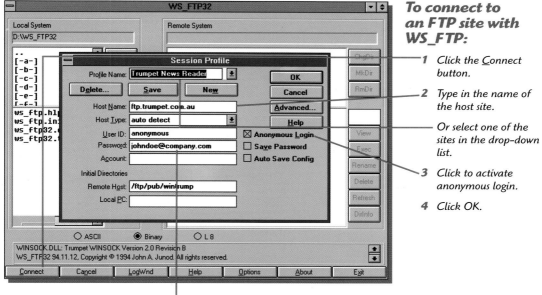

To connect to an FTP site with WS_FTP:

1 Click the Connect button.

2 Type in the name of the host site.

— Or select one of the sites in the drop-down list.

3 Click to activate anonymous login.

4 Click OK.

You should use your e-mail address as a password when accessing anonymous FTP sites.

Current local directory   Current remote directory

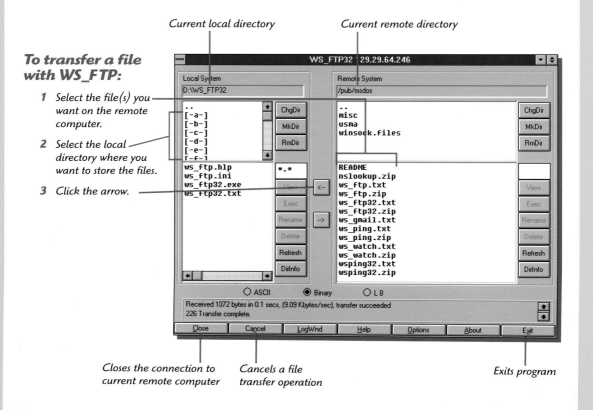

To transfer a file with WS_FTP:

1 Select the file(s) you want on the remote computer.

2 Select the local directory where you want to store the files.

3 Click the arrow.

Closes the connection to current remote computer

Cancels a file transfer operation

Exits program

The best Macintosh FTP sites

Go to this FTP address	Look in this directory	What you'll find
sumex-aim.stanford.edu	/info-mac	The best Mac software site anywhere.
sumex-aim.stanford.edu	/info-mac/AntiVirus	AntiVirus software.
sumex-aim.stanford.edu	/info-mac/Application	Application software.
sumex-aim.stanford.edu	/info-mac/Communication	Telecommunications software.
sumex-aim.stanford.edu	/info-mac/Compress-Translate	File compression utilities.
sumex-aim.stanford.edu	/info-mac/Font	More fonts than you'll ever use.
sumex-aim.stanford.edu	/info-mac/Game	Mac games.
sumex-aim.stanford.edu	/info-mac/Graphic	Graphic utilities.
sumex-aim.stanford.edu	/info-mac/Sound	Sound utilities and files.
ftp.hawaii.edu	/mirrors/info-mac	Mirror of the sumex-aim.stanford.edu/info-mac site.
mrcnext.cso.uiuc.edu	/pub/info-mac	Mirror of the sumex-aim.stanford.edu/info-mac site.
grind.isca.uiowa.edu	/mac/infomac	Mirror of the sumex-aim.stanford.edu/info-mac site.
mac.archive.umich.edu	/mac	Another huge site!
mac.archive.umich.edu	/mac/util/network	Networking utilities.
mac.archive.umich.edu	mac/util/comm	Communications utilities.
archive.orst.edu	/pub/mirrors/archive.umich.edu/mac	Mirror to the mac.archive.umich.edu site.
ftp.ncsa.uiuc.edu	/Web/Mosaic/Mac	Main NCSA Mosaic program.
ftp.ncsa.uiuc.edu	/Web/Mosaic/Mac/Helpers	Programs to use with Mosaic to view pictures and movies, listen to sounds, view PostScript, and more.
wuarchive.wustl.edu	/systems/mac/macintosh	Macintosh software divided into over two dozen directories.
wuarchive.wustl.edu	/systems/mac/info-mac and /systems/mac/umich.edu	Mirrors of the Info-Mac and UMich archives.
ftp.cdrom.com	/pub/gutenberg	Mirror of the Project Gutenberg files.
ftp.mcp.com	/pub/que/macnet-cd	Copies of much of the software that's on MacNetCD included with *Special Edition Using the Internet with Your Mac*.
ftp.mcp.com	/pub/software/Macintosh	More Macintosh software, primarily from Macmillan's Hayden imprint, which specializes in Macintosh topics.
ftp.qualcomm.com	/quest/mac/eudora	Eudora manufacturer.
amug.org	/amug	Arizona Macintosh User's Group.
ftp.apple.com	/dts	Apple's software FTP site.
boombox.micro.umn.edu	/pub/gopher	Big Gopher archive with documentation and software.

Using

FTP

PLUG YOURSELF INTO...

THE MACMILLAN INFORMATION SUPERLIBRARY™

Free information and vast computer resources from the world's leading computer book publisher—online!

FIND THE BOOKS THAT ARE RIGHT FOR YOU!

A complete online catalog, plus sample chapters and tables of contents give you an in-depth look at *all* of our books, including hard-to-find titles. It's the best way to find the books you need!

- **STAY INFORMED** with the latest computer industry news through our online newsletter, press releases, and customized Information SuperLibrary Reports.

- **GET FAST ANSWERS** to your questions about MCP books and software.

- **VISIT** our online bookstore for the latest information and editions!

- **COMMUNICATE** with our expert authors through e-mail and conferences.

- **DOWNLOAD SOFTWARE** from the immense MCP library:
    - Source code and files from MCP books
    - The best shareware, freeware, and demos

- **DISCOVER HOT SPOTS** on other parts of the Internet.

- **WIN BOOKS** in ongoing contests and giveaways!

TO PLUG INTO MCP: ➔ WORLD WIDE WEB: **http://www.mcp.com**

GOPHER: gopher.mcp.com

FTP: ftp.mcp.com

Using
FTP

Mary Ann Pike
Noel Estabrook

que

Using FTP

Copyright© 1995 by Que® Corporation.

Library of Congress Catalog No.: 95-69232

ISBN: 0-7897-0238-X

97 96 95   6 5 4 3 2 1

Interpretation of the printing code: the rightmost double-digit number is the year of the book's printing; the rightmost single-digit number, the number of the book's printing. For example, a printing code of 95-1 shows that the first printing of the book occurred in 1995.

Publisher: *Roland Elgey*

Associate Publisher: *Stacy Hiquet*

Publishing Director: *Brad R. Koch*

Managing Editor: *Sandy Doell*

Director of Marketing: *Lynn E. Zingraf*

Credits

Acquisitions Editor
Beverly M. Eppink

Product Director
Jim Minatel

Production Editor
Chris Nelson

Editors
Danielle Bird
Noelle Gasco

Technical Editors
Discovery Computing

Acquisitions Assistant
Ruth Slates

Operations Coordinator
Patty Brooks

Editorial Assistant
Andrea Duvall

Book Designer
Sandra Schroeder

Cover Designer
Dan Armstrong

Production Team
Steve Adams
Chad Dressler
Amy Durocher
Karen Gregor
Bob LaRoche
Paula Lowell
G. Alan Palmore
Kaylene Riemen
Clair Schweinler
Brenda Sims
Michael Thomas
Scott Tullis

Indexer
Rebecca Mayfield

Composed in *ITC Century*, *ITC Highlander*, and *MCPdigital* by Que Corporation.

About the Authors

Mary Ann Pike has a B.S. in electrical engineering and an M.A. in professional writing from Carnegie-Mellon University. She has experience in software design and development, and is currently working as a technical writer at the Software Engineering Institute at Carnegie-Mellon University. She has authored several other Que Internet books, including *Special Edition Using the Internet*, Second Edition, *Using Mosaic*, and *Special Edition Using the World Wide Web and Mosaic*. Several of her books have won awards from the Society for Technical Communication.

Noel Estabrook is currently a faculty member of the College of Education at Michigan State University after having obtained degrees in Psychology, Education, and Instructional Technology. He is heavily involved in delivering Internet training and technical support to educators, professionals, and laymen. He also runs his own training business part-time in addition to writing. Most recently, he has been involved in authoring on the Web and coauthored Que's *Using UseNet Newgroups*. He can be contacted at **noele@msu.edu**.

Acknowledgments

I would like to thank my husband Tod for the technical and emotional support that gets me through these projects. In addition, I would like to thank John Junod, the author of WS_FTP, for providing me with technical information about WS_FTP. Finally, I would like to thank the crew at Que that works so hard to produce a fine product.

Mary Ann Pike

To my wife, Anita, for putting up with another long stretch of deadlines and 70-hour weeks (maybe I'll take a break now!) and to my Lord Jesus Christ, Who makes it all possible.

Noel Estabrook

Trademarks

We'd Like to Hear from You!

As part of our continuing effort to produce books of the highest possible quality, Que would like to hear your comments. To stay competitive, we *really* want you, as a computer book reader and user, to let us know what you like or dislike most about this book or other Que products.

You can mail comments, ideas, or suggestions for improving future editions to the address below, or send us a fax at (317) 581-4663. For the online inclined, Macmillan Computer Publishing has a forum on CompuServe (type **GO QUEBOOKS** at any prompt) through which our staff and authors are available for questions and comments. The address of our Internet site is **http://www.mcp.com** (World Wide Web).

In addition to exploring our forum, please feel free to contact me personally to discuss your opinions of this book: I'm **jminatel@que.mcp.com** on the Internet.

Thanks in advance—your comments will help us to continue publishing the best books available on computer topics in today's market.

Jim Minatel
Product Development Specialist
Que Corporation
201 W. 103rd Street
Indianapolis, Indiana 46290
USA

Contents at a Glance

{Table of Contents}

What is anonymous FTP?

see page 18

Chapter 3: The Nuts and Bolts of FTP

What you need to use FTP

see page 29

Chapter 4: FTP Concepts and Culture

Simple Archie searches

see page 69

Part II: Transferring Files with Windows

Chapter 5: Connecting to FTP Sites with WS_FTP

The WS_FTP window
see page 78

Chapter 6: Getting and Sending Files

How to
download
files

see page 93

Chapter 7: Adding Sites to WS_FTP's List

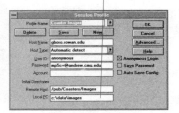

Chapter 8: Finding Files with WSArchie

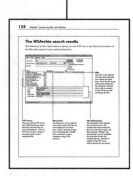

The WSArchie search results
see page 128

see page 128

Part III: FTP for Macintosh

Chapter 10: Connecting to FTP Sites with Anarchie

Chapter 11: Getting and Sending Files

*Up close with the Bookmark
list and Archie windows
see page 161*

Chapter 12: Adding Bookmarks in Anarchie

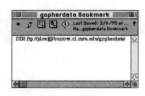

Chapter 13: Finding Files with Anarchie

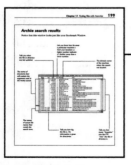

*Archie search results
see page 199*

Part IV: FTP and Archie from the Command Line

Chapter 14: Text-Based Access to FTP

Chapter 15: Archie Searches from a Command Line

*Transferring
a file to your
command–
line account*

see page 222

Part V: FTP from the World Wide Web

Chapter 16: FTP Access through Mosaic and Netscape

Part VI: The Best FTP Resources

Chapter 17: The Best Sources of Software and Computing Information

Windows software

see page 262

Chapter 18: FTP Sites Just for Fun

Internet and general computing resources

see page 276

Business and finance sites

see page 291

Movies and entertainment
see page 293

Fun and unusual sites
see page 299

Part VII: Indexes

Introduction

If you're buying this book, you probably have an idea of what the Internet is. Maybe you've done some traveling on the Information Superhighway, but you're still at a loss about how to find the "exits" that have interesting resources.

The Internet is a treasure trove of information. There are thousands of computers on the Internet, with hundreds of thousands of files on them. You can find everything from programs that help you balance your checkbook to recipes for coconut macadamia cookies. And it's all free for the taking.

The good news is, it's easy to get these files. Transferring files between computers is one of the things the Internet was designed to do. You can use FTP (File Transfer Protocol), one of the oldest services on the Internet, to copy programs and files from distant computers to your own.

You used to have to know arcane UNIX commands to use FTP. It took tons of typing just to get to the directory you were looking for. Now the Internet is more accessible to the masses. People have developed easy-to-use graphical interfaces for all the Internet services, including FTP. Transferring a file now is as easy as pointing and clicking.

Of course, it's still not utopia. There's no main index of FTP sites to help you find the files you're looking for. However, the Archie service lets you look for files on FTP sites. Like FTP, Archie used to require incantations to get it to work. Now there are graphical interfaces that let you look for files by filling out a simple form.

What do we cover in this book?

This book has these main goals:

- To explain to you what FTP and Archie are, and to show you what FTP can do for you. We tell you how to install the Archie and FTP software (if you need it) and give you a quick look at the FTP interfaces for some of the popular online services and Internet service providers.

- To show you how to use Windows Archie and FTP programs to find the files you want and transfer them to your computer. You'll learn how to use FTP to download all of those great files just waiting for you on the Net.

- To show you how to use Macintosh Archie and FTP programs to find the files you want and transfer them to your computer. There's a lot of Macintosh software on the Net, as well as pictures and text files that can be viewed by anyone.

- To show you how to use the UNIX command-line interface for Archie and FTP. Many people still use a command-line account for their Internet access.

- To tell you how to use FTP through the World Wide Web (WWW). We explain how you can get files off FTP sites using the WWW, one of the newest Internet services.

- To provide you with a starting place for your Internet exploration. We've included some of the best Macintosh and Windows software sites in this book, as well as sites with collections of interesting and useful files.

FTP is one of the oldest, yet most useful, services the Internet provides. Now that you can point and click to get to the files you want and download them to your computer, FTP is even more appealing than it was when it first became available.

What makes this book different?

This book is a complete reference for FTP, including the Windows, Macintosh, and UNIX command-line interfaces. It even tells you how to get to FTP sites using one of the newest Internet services, the World Wide Web. If you're the type of person who likes to keep your hard disk full, *Using FTP* will show you how to do just that. Even if you've used the Internet for years, you might not be aware of what's waiting for you at FTP sites. This book shows you where to find things and how to get them.

We wrote this book for everyone—people who have just started using computers, and those who have been on the Internet for years. As long as you can use your mouse, you have all the technical background you need.

This book uses plain English to tell you how to use one of the most basic Internet services. You'll learn the best way to use the different FTP interfaces to get what you need, without having to speak a dialect of computerese.

How do I use this book?

This book is not meant to be read from cover to cover. There are sections that cover using FTP from Windows, Macintosh, and UNIX, so unless you use all three operating systems, you won't need to read all those sections.

Most of you will want to read the first and last sections of the book. The first four chapters explain what FTP is and how it works. Of course, you might not really care about that—you just want to use it! If you just want to jump in feet first, by all means go right to the part written for the operating system you're using. You'll probably want to check out the last two chapters, which tell you about some of the places where you can go to find the stuff you want.

How this book is put together

There are a number of different FTP interfaces, but the underlying concepts for using FTP are the same for all of them. What this book tries to do is first give you an understanding of how FTP works. Then, once you have that basic knowledge, you learn how to use FTP from a popular Windows interface, a popular Macintosh interface, and the UNIX command line. The book is divided into parts that cover these major topics. Each part contains chapters that give you easy-to-follow, step-by-step instructions. This book also includes tips on the best way to do things and answers a lot of specific questions you might come up with.

Part I: FTP—What? How? Huh?

Chapter 1 gives you a quick introduction to the Internet and explains what FTP is. Chapter 2 introduces Archie and gives you some idea of what else you can do with FTP, besides download the latest version of your favorite game. Chapter 3 tells you what you need to use FTP and gives you a quick look at a number of different FTP interfaces. Chapter 4 discusses the underlying FTP concepts that are common to all interfaces.

Part II: Transferring Files with Windows

Here's where you learn the nitty-gritty of how to get to FTP sites and get the files you want. This part concentrates on how you use the popular Windows FTP interface WS_FTP. Chapter 5 tells you how to connect to FTP sites and get to the directories you want. Chapter 6 tells you how to download (and upload, if you have privileges) files. Chapter 7 tells you how to set up WS_FTP to quickly access the sites that you visit most. Chapter 8 introduces WSArchie, a Windows Archie client that lets you look for files on FTP sites. Chapter 9 discusses how to us WS_FTP from sites that are trying to protect themselves from unwanted intrusion, and talks about some of the more advanced FTP commands.

Part III: FTP for Macintosh

In this part, you'll learn how to use Anarchie, a popular Macintosh program that combines FTP and Archie. Chapter 10 tells you how to set up Anarchie, connect to predefined FTP sites, and get to the directories you're interested in. Chapter 11 tells you how to download (and upload, if you have privileges) files. Chapter 12 explains how to add the sites you use most to the predefined list of sites by using bookmarks. Chapter 13 tells you how to use Anarchie to find the files you want.

Part IV: FTP and Archie from the Command Line

UNIX was one of the early operating systems on the Internet. Many of the computers that connect to the Net still use UNIX, so Chapter 14 tells you how to do FTP the old-fashioned way: from the UNIX command line, using all of those arcane commands to connect to sites and transfer files. Chapter 15 shows you how to connect directly to one of the Archie servers on the Net and do your searches right at the source.

Part V: FTP from the World Wide Web

Chapter 16 shows you FTP from the World Wide Web, using Mosaic and Netscape, two of the most popular Web applications in use today. You might not want to bother using an FTP application if you have access to the World Wide Web.

Part VI: The Best FTP Resources

Archie won't tell you about a lot of the FTP sites because it doesn't know about them. Chapters 17 and 18 give you some places to go to find some of the more interesting and more unusual FTP resources. Chapter 17 contains information about some of the largest software repositories on the Net where you can find both Macintosh and Window software. It also tells you where to go to get general computing and Internet resources. Chapter 18 is a collection of some of the fun and unusual information you can find at FTP sites.

Part VII: Indexes

The final part contains an Action Index of useful tasks and features. This index points you to where these tasks are covered in the book. The Indexes part also contains a standard topic index that lets you quickly find the information you need throughout the book.

Information that's easy to understand

This book contains a number of special elements and conventions to help you find information quickly—or skip stuff you don't want to read right now.

Bold type indicates new terms and stuff that you have to type. Internet addresses also appear in bold: for example, **ftp.mcp.com**. UNIX and DOS commands and messages displayed on-screen appear in a `special computer typeface`.

If you see two keys separated by a plus sign, such as Ctrl+X, that means to press and hold the first key, press the second key, and then release both keys.

❶ (Tip)

Tips either point out information often overlooked in the documentation or help you use your software more efficiently, for example, by providing a shortcut. Some tips help you solve or avoid problems.

✱ {Note}

Notes contain additional information or "reminders" of important information you might want to know.

✖ <Caution>

Cautions alert you to potentially dangerous consequences of a procedure or practice, especially if it could result in serious or even disastrous results, such as the loss or corruption of data.

Q&A

What are Q&A notes?

Cast in the form of questions and answers, these notes provide you with advice on ways to avoid or solve common problems, or answer common user questions.

 Plain English, please!

These notes explain the meanings of technical terms or computer jargon. **99**

Sidebars are interesting nuggets of information

Sidebars provide interesting, nonessential reading, side-alley trips you can take when you're not at the computer or when you just want some relief from "doing stuff." Here you might find more technical details, funny stories, personal anecdotes, or interesting background information.

Part I:

FTP—What? How? Huh?

The What's of FTP

Ever wondered what FTP is all about and what it's like? If you have, this chapter's for you!

The fact that you decided to get this book indicates that you probably already know something about the Internet and may even be "cruising." However, it also means that you want to know more about the capabilities and possibilities of the Internet—primarily, how to use FTP.

How does it really work? What's out there? Where is it? What's the best way to get it? These are all questions you probably asked yourself before you decided to get a book with the answers. Well, you picked the right one. We've designed this book to help you become an expert at finding, retrieving, and using files available on the Internet through the use of FTP. This chapter gives you some basic information to get you started.

What is the Internet?

As you can probably guess, a complete answer to this question takes up a whole book by itself. But there are some basics that you should be aware of, if you aren't already.

The **Internet** is primarily a network of networks. Thousands of machines throughout the world are connected together using phone lines, fiber optics, and other technologies to create an interconnected "web" of computers.

To help you visualize this, just think of your phone company. Even though there may be main offices, switching stations, and the like, a phone company would be useless (and in fact probably wouldn't exist) if there weren't individual phones in constant use everywhere. Think of the computers that make up the Internet as those telephones. Even though there are main "hubs" throughout the Internet, its real power and accessibility comes from all the individual computers out there that have come online.

Despite the predictions of some that computers and the Internet were nothing more than a passing fad, nothing could be further from the truth. The Internet is here to stay and is slowly becoming part of everyday modern life (see fig. 1.1).

Fig. 1.1
Read a newspaper, pick a wine, or buy some software. Whatever you do in the course of your day, the Internet wants to be part of it.

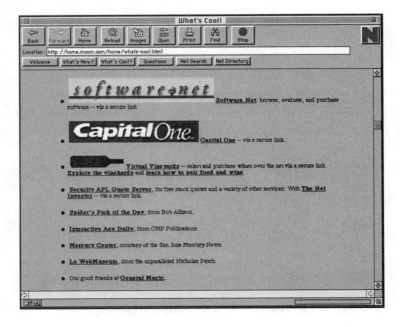

It is increasingly difficult to read a magazine or newspaper, or watch an evening of television without mention of the **Information Superhighway**. In fact, some cable companies have recently been licensed to offer Internet services. It probably won't be long before you can answer your e-mail while watching HBO!

Although this book focuses on a particular capability of the Internet, there are many other commonly used resources. E-mail, Gopher, News, the World Wide Web, and FTP are among the most popular. This book covers FTP in detail, but it's important to be aware of the other resources, as well.

E-mail

E-mail is probably used more than anything else on the Internet. E-mail fulfills a variety of needs and performs a diverse number of functions.

E-mail is most often used for exchanging messages between individual users on the Internet. These messages can contain personal or business information or correspondence, among other things. Most e-mail systems also allow users to attach files to their messages so that they can send documents and even executable programs.

E-mail can also provide communication between groups of users. E-mail mailing lists are set up so that many people with a common need or interest can share information without having to send out a lot of individual messages.

Gopher

Developed at the University of Minnesota, **Gopher** was probably the first "user-friendly" Internet resource. You can access information such as files, documents, and programs through Gopher, as well as connections to thousands of machines throughout the world.

The difference between Gopher and other access programs is that Gopher provides an easy-to-use, menu-driven interface for the user. Rather than type complicated commands to perform functions or receive files, you simply enter a number or click your mouse to select the desired menu item. Gopher does the rest.

News

UseNet News is also becoming a very popular resource on the Internet. News basically takes the place of the mailing list. Instead of having group discussions take place through a series of messages via e-mail, UseNet News is distributed through clients that deposit the messages in **newsgroups**. Each group has a particular topic or focus. For instance, one newsgroup about dogs is **rec.pets.dogs.misc**.

Users use a **news client** both to read messages and to post their own messages to newsgroups. To access a newsgroup, you simply subscribe to it, much as you would subscribe to a magazine, only electronically. Once subscribed, you can participate in discussions, gather information, or simply browse the news of the day.

The World Wide Web

The **World Wide Web** (often referred to as **WWW**) is the hottest new kid on the block. Think of WWW as "Gopher with guts." It is a similar resource to Gopher, only, instead of being menu driven, it's graphically driven. Accessing different WWW sites and resources is as simple as clicking a highlighted word or picture (see fig. 1.2).

Fig. 1.2
The WWW interface. To access any of the resources on this WWW site, just click the icon for the desired destination.

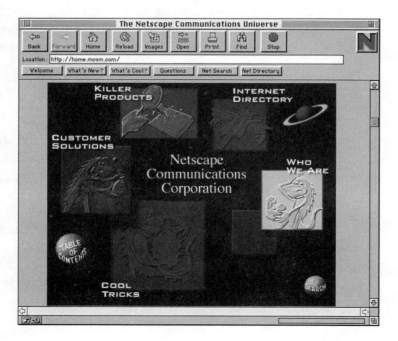

In addition to having access to all of the available WWW services, you can also access FTP, Gopher, News, e-mail, and other resources through the World Wide Web. WWW shows promise of being the Internet interfact of the future. It is easy to use, powerful, and highly interactive.

What is FTP?

The year is 2010. You tram over to the local library. As you go down its aisles of books, videos, CDs, power tools, and everything else imaginable, you fill your cart with items. But remember—this is 2010 and this is a special library. As you grab that bestseller off the shelf, another one magically appears to take its place. The same thing happens with everything else you check out. Not only that, but there are no due dates—what you take, you keep. What's more, everybody contributes; this library might even contain a few of your works!

Sounds pretty idealistic, doesn't it? Well, take heart, such a library already exists on the Internet, and it's called **FTP**. Some machines on the Internet are dedicated **electronic libraries**. Each library contains files of text, graphics, and software tools that you can read, view, and use on your computer. Like our futuristic library, there are no due dates because you keep what you take (although there is occasionally a small fee for doing so). You can even contribute to the holdings of a particular library.

We'll take a closer look at exactly what these libraries are like in the next section, "What is an FTP site?" First, however, let's talk a little more about FTP.

FTP (**File Transfer Protocol**) is a fast, efficient, and reliable way to transfer information. It was one of the first Internet services developed to allow users to transfer files from one place to another. This service is designed to let you connect your **local** machine to a **remote** computer on the Internet, browse through the files and programs that are available on the computer, and then retrieve those files to your computer.

Plain English, please!

> **Local** and **remote** are two words you see a lot in this book, but they are very simple to understand. A local machine is your computer—after all, you can't get any more local than your desktop. A remote machine is one that you access remotely via a modem or network. **"**

FTP uses a **client-server** relationship to work effectively. You use a program on your computer (the client) to connect to a remote machine (the server). You are, in effect, the FTP site's customer. The site is there literally to "serve" you by providing you with text files, software, system utilities and a myriad of other resources (see fig 1.3).

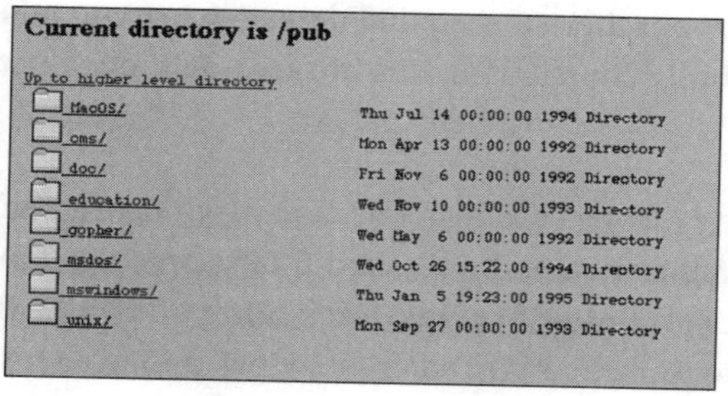

Fig. 1.3
FTP sites offer all sorts of useful material. This site contains files for use on Macintosh, DOS, and Windows computers, as well as information on education and Gopher.

```
Current directory is /pub

Up to higher level directory
 MacOS/          Thu Jul 14 00:00:00 1994 Directory
 oms/            Mon Apr 13 00:00:00 1992 Directory
 doc/            Fri Nov  6 00:00:00 1992 Directory
 education/      Wed Nov 10 00:00:00 1993 Directory
 gopher/         Wed May  6 00:00:00 1992 Directory
 msdos/          Wed Oct 26 15:22:00 1994 Directory
 mswindows/      Thu Jan  5 19:23:00 1995 Directory
 unix/           Mon Sep 27 00:00:00 1993 Directory
```

What is an FTP site?

Those libraries we referred to earlier are commonly called **FTP sites**. Each site is its own self-contained electronic library containing information, files, and applications on everything imaginable. You don't really *take* files from FTP sites, you *copy* them from the FTP site to your own computer through the use of a modem (or other network connection) and FTP software.

" *Plain English, please!*

> **FTP sites** are computers that are set up for the transfer of files, information, and applications through the use of **File Transfer Protocol** (FTP). With the help of a computer, modem, and software that "speaks" the language of FTP, you can access hundreds of FTP sites around the world. **"**

FTP sites offer trillions of bytes of information—too much to mention in one book. There are, however, some basic types of information available that are briefly mentioned here:

- **Text files**. An infinite variety. Get a copy of the lyrics to your favorite Bob Dylan song, grab a copy of *Alice in Wonderland*, or get the latest wisdom on good manners on the Internet.

- **Multimedia files**. Pictures, 3D renderings, stereograms (you know, those stupid things you have to stare at for 45 seconds before you can see them?), even movie clips. See Arnold tell you, "I'll be back" right on your computer, or perhaps look at a picture of Waikiki.

- **Applications**. From e-mail programs, to FTP programs, to programs that will help you balance your checkbook, software of every type, flavor, and color is available with FTP.

Of course, there are hundreds of variations of these three basic categories. Hopefully, they give you an idea of the types of resources that you have instant access to with FTP.

Mirror, mirror, on the wall

Have you ever tried to win one of those radio call-in contests? It's not easy, is it? And the reason it isn't easy is because there are probably 100 people trying to get in and only 4 phone lines to get in to. Let's face it, those contests are popular; everybody wants to win something.

Something similar happens with FTP sites. Some FTP sites have become so well known and so popular, everybody wants to get on them to access all the great stuff. Needless to say, there are a lot of "busy signals."

To alleviate this problem, many FTP sites have **mirrors**. A mirror is just what it sounds like—a copy of the original. When an FTP site is mirrored, that means there is a copy of it on another FTP site. This helps to make some of the more popular information easier to get to. It's a way of having two phone numbers to dial the same phone.

What is anonymous FTP?

Unfortunately, as great as a lot of the information out there is, it's not always available to everybody. Many FTP sites are set up for a specific purpose or for a particular group of users. This succeeds in restricting access to some of the available resources.

The good news is, there are lots and lots of sites out there that are available to everybody. These sites are referred to as **anonymous** FTP sites. They are called that because they don't require users to identify themselves in order to access the site. Rather, you're invited in as their "guest" to browse and retrieve files as you wish.

✱ {Note}

Just because an FTP site is an anonymous site does not necessarily mean it has unlimited access. A site may limit the number of anonymous users during business hours, restrict anonymous users to particular areas, or not allow the downloading of certain files from their sites. Keep in mind that free instant access may not let you take all the candy in the candy store when you want to take it (see fig. 1.4).

Fig. 1.4
Many FTP sites like this one restrict use to certain times of the day and to a particular number of users to access their files.

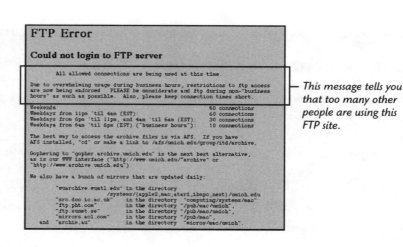

This message tells you that too many other people are using this FTP site.

The wide range of files available on anonymous FTP sites means that there really is something there for everyone—from the novice to experienced programmers.

FTP for beginners

Beginners usually start out using FTP for simple things. Text and graphics files are usually the first things beginners look for on FTP sites. There is no greater thrill than to download that first picture and see it appear on-screen —just like bringing home that first book from the library when you were a kid. Of course, that also means that you'll probably be downloading some software to view the picture with.

Beginning users also experiment with some of the more basic programs that they find as they cruise around the Net. Perhaps it will be a program to collect and organize phone numbers on your computer. Or maybe a utility to help arrange recipes electronically. These are just a few examples of the many files that users often begin with.

FTP for intermediate users

Intermediate users, as well as advanced users, often continue to locate and download the types of files that beginners do, but they usually take it a step further. Perhaps they find a utility that allows them to transpose pictures into a unique formation, or maybe they locate some multimedia files that require more advanced hardware.

There are also utilities for users that are simple programs designed to help users work faster and better. Utilities to compress and encode files and others that expedite certain commonly used functions are popular for more advanced users who can take advantage of them.

FTP for advanced users

In addition to all the uses mentioned in the preceding two sections, advanced users can utilize FTP even further. You can often find patches and updates that help current programs work better. (Sometimes these small pieces of software that help to enhance existing software require some programming to work.)

There are also a host of utilities and programs for those who use operating systems such as UNIX, AIX, and Solaris. These files don't benefit the average Windows or Macintosh user, but can be of great help to advanced programmers.

What this book teaches you

FTP is a very powerful tool that can be confusing and even frustrating if you don't have the right tools to help you. This book is designed to give you the know-how to use other tools to make FTP useful and easy. This book explains:

- **FTP clients.** These programs let you use FTP. From free to commercially available software, these programs help you get what you want. This book introduces you to a number of FTP clients, including the best ones for Windows and Macintosh.

- **FTP processes.** How does FTP work? This book explains directories and shows you how to find files, what different types of files do, and what you can do with files.

- **FTP issues.** These include such issues as security, the best uses for FTP, and some of the intricacies and shortcuts of FTP.

- **FTP sites.** You learn about the best and hottest FTP sites available for just about any information you want or need.

This book teaches you everything you need to know about FTP: how to use it on your desktop computer with the best tools available.

2 The How's of FTP

In this chapter:

- When is FTP good for distributing information within our company?
- Can FTP help get information to our customers?
- So, what does Archie do and how does it work?
- The limits of Archie searches

You can do a lot more with FTP than just pick up shareware and Internet statistics.

A t first you might just think of FTP as a way of getting into those "libraries" out on the Internet. After all, you want copies of a lot of the stuff that's in those libraries. But FTP is actually a lot more useful than that. Its main feature is the ability to move information, and that opens up a lot of possibilities.

Also, sometimes when you want to use FTP to pick up software or documents, it can be daunting trying to find a specific document or program. With all that information at hundreds of anonymous FTP sites around the world, how do you find what you want? **Archie** is a service that helps you look for stuff and tells you where you can get it. But Archie does have its limitations (don't we all?).

Some of the ways you can use FTP

As we explained in Chapter 1, FTP is often used to make "libraries" of software or documents available. Anyone can connect to these sites and get copies of the software or documents for themselves. But you can use FTP in more creative ways. For example, FTP gives you a way of exchanging data between geographically distant parts of a company, or you can use it to make time-critical information available to clients.

Move information within your company

Say your company has divisions spread all over the country, and they all need to share information. You could set up an FTP site at one division and store all of your information there. Anyone who needed to get access to data files or programs could connect to this FTP server to pick them up. In the same way, anyone who needs to put information at the site for others to use can upload files.

A perfect example of this is the way Que and I exchange information for the books I'm working on. There is a Macmillan FTP site that has a section specifically for Que authors. When I've finished working on a chapter, I connect to the FTP site and upload the chapter to the Que authors part of the server. They take the chapter, edit it, and then put it back on the FTP server for me to download and address the questions they had in their editing.

This type of FTP site is usually not set up for anonymous use. You would have to log in to a personal account on the FTP server rather than log in as an anonymous user. You don't need a special FTP client to log in to personal accounts—any of the programs described in this book will let you log in to personal accounts on an FTP server.

Get information to your customers

What if your company frequently needs to get information to its customers who are spread out around the country (or even the world)? How can you provide information to your customers without having to spend big bucks on customer service personnel to answer questions and send out promotional material?

One of the things you might do is set up an FTP server that contains promotional materials, technical notes, and even software bug patches for your products. With the number of businesses and individuals on the Internet expanding at a phenomenal rate, many companies are starting to do just this to get information out to their customers.

For example, Microsoft has an anonymous FTP site (**ftp.microsoft.com**) where you can find a number of different things:

- Product support phone numbers for every Microsoft product
- Software, including bug fixes, updated drivers, utilities
- Information about Microsoft products

Security and FTP

You probably don't think about it, but when you send data from one computer to another over the Internet, you can't be sure that someone isn't "listening" to your data. Because of the way the Internet works, there are a number of points where others could get access to your data.

When you connect to another computer using FTP, information going between your computer and the remote computer can follow a path that moves over many different networks. Since you have no control over these networks, you have no idea who is connected to these networks, or who may be watching the information going over the network. Someone who wants to watch the information flowing over a network needs to have a computer connected directly to that network.

While it is rare for information to be monitored over the Internet, it makes sense to protect important information (by using **encryption encoding**, for example) before transferring it using FTP. There are several different commercial encryption products available to let you encrypt and decrypt your data.

Another example of a company that has created an FTP server as a resource for its customers is Frame Technology. Its main product is FrameMaker, a desktop publishing application. Frame Technology has set up an FTP server (**ftp.frame.com**) to make it easy for its customers to get a wide variety of information about its products. On this FTP server, you can find:

- An area for customers to leave problem files for technical support

- Areas for documentation, technical notes, product data sheets, training information, press releases, newsletters, FrameMaker **FAQs**

- An area containing filters to translate files from other applications to FrameMaker's format

- An area for customers to leave templates, tip files, etc., as resources for others

❝ *Plain English, please!*

FAQ stands for Frequently Asked Questions. FAQs are documents that contain answers to common questions that are asked about a topic. **❞**

Meet Archie—how to find files

Let's continue with our analogy of anonymous FTP servers as libraries. What if you had this great collection of libraries, but no catalog to tell you where they were, or what they had in them? You'd never be able to use any of the information that was available to you. Most Internet resources are like this. Lots of great stuff, but no way to find it.

A few years ago, someone came up with the idea of having a service that would keep track of some of the information on the Internet—particularly, information available at anonymous FTP sites. They decided to call this service **Archie**. (Don't ask me why... I know how to use these things, but I don't know *all* of the Internet folklore.)

How Archie works

The way the Archie system works is that there are a number of servers (perhaps 20) around the world that provide the Archie service. These servers let you do searches through a database of file information. The servers' databases have information about all of the files on the anonymous FTP servers that have registered with the Archie system.

So, the way the system works is that every so often (every few months), the Archie servers check with the registered FTP sites to update their databases of file information. They ask each FTP server for a complete list of what files it has and all the information for every file. For each file in its database, the Archie server has information about:

- The name of the file

- What FTP server it lives on

- What directory you can find it in

- How big it is

- What the protection on the file is

- When it was last modified

How do you get the Archie server to give you information about a file? Well, you can use Telnet to log in to an Archie server and request information about a particular file. Or, you can send your request to a server from an Archie client running on your machine. The Archie server will search through its database, looking to see if any of the registered servers have the file that you requested. If it finds the file, the Archie server gives you all the information it has about the file.

The Archie server will also tell you when it last got an update from that FTP server. This can be important information because, like everything else on the Internet, FTP servers may change frequently. Servers may be taken out of service, or they may have their directory structure completely revised. So if the Archie server's last update from an FTP server was more than a month ago, there's a good possibility that the file (or the server!) may no longer be there.

Once you've got the search results back from the Archie server, you can connect to one of the FTP servers that has the file you want and retrieve a copy of the file.

Archie's limitations

So, it would seem that Archie is a great solution for finding the location of files on the Internet. But, as is so often the case, things aren't really as great as they seem at first glance. There are a number of reasons why Archie isn't as helpful as it might be.

First of all, Archie limits you to searching for files by name. You've got to know the file name (or at least part of the file name) in order to find anything. So, if you're looking for a particular game, or document about a particular topic, you won't find it unless you know the file name it's stored under.

Another problem with Archie is that the Archie databases are always somewhat out of date. The Archie servers only talk to any individual FTP server a few times during the year (maybe 4–6 times) to find out what its file structure looks like. Lots of things may have happened to the server since the last time Archie talked to it (including the server's having been renamed or completely removed from the Internet). The file may have been removed from the FTP server, or a new version of the file may have been placed on the server.

Is there anything I can do if the FTP server that had the file I wanted has disappeared, or if the file is gone from the server?

If you can't even connect to the machine that used to have the file, you can try sending mail to the postmaster at the FTP server's site. To figure out how to send mail to the postmaster, remove the machine name (the leftmost part) from the FTP server's address and use that as the postmaster's address. For example, if you can't connect to the machine bitsy.mit.edu, send mail to postmaster@mit.edu. Tell the postmaster what you're looking for, and ask if there is still an anonymous FTP server that provides the information.

If it's a matter of not being able to find a file where it used to live on a server, there are a couple of things you can do. One thing is to look around the server for informational files (often called README, readme.txt, index.txt, etc.). If the directory structure of a server has changed, there is often information about where files have moved. If informational files are not of any help, you can send mail to the postmaster to ask if the file is still around. If you do this, you may have to wait a while for a response, because postmasters are usually very busy with systems administration work, and finding files for random people on the Internet isn't one of their high-priority tasks.

 (Tip)

> When you're trying to figure out which server to get a file from, pick one that Archie has updated recently in its database to have a better chance of finding the file there.

There are a number of very large anonymous FTP servers on the Internet that make huge numbers of shareware programs available. Archie won't be able to find anything for you at any of these big FTP software repositories. None of these sites (or a number of other large, popular sites) are registered with the Archie servers. They aren't registered because most people know about them anyway, and they're too busy as it is. If you want to see if a file exists at one of these sites, you just have to go to the site and look around. (See Chapters 17 and 18 for information about big software repositories and other popular FTP servers.)

Lots of smaller sites also are not registered with the Archie servers. So, just because you don't find a file you're looking for doesn't mean it isn't available on an anonymous FTP server somewhere. If you know someone who has the file you want, you may have to ask them where they got it. Or, there may be a discussion group (like a UseNet newsgroup or a mailing list) that might have information about the location of the types of files you're looking for. Just keep your eyes open and keep a list of references to FTP servers you come across in your wanderings on the Internet.

(Tip)   UseNet newsgroups give you access to a wealth of information on very specific topics. Post a message asking for relevant FTP servers to a newsgroup that discusses the topic you're interested in.

3 The Nuts and Bolts of FTP

In this chapter:

- What do I need to use FTP?

- A little information about FTP programs

- What are some common Windows and Macintosh FTP interfaces?

- And how about some of the FTP interfaces that online services use?

FTP is available for any type of computer and any type of Internet account. No two FTP interfaces are exactly alike, but they all let you transfer files.

FTP is one of the oldest services on the Internet. The basic idea of FTP is to let you upload or download files between your machine and another machine on the Internet. Originally, the only way to use FTP was by entering cryptic text-based commands at your operating system prompt. Now, there are many graphical interfaces that allow you to use FTP from Windows, a Macintosh, or many of the commercial online services such as CompuServe or America Online.

What you need to use FTP

Your computer must be connected to the Internet for you to use FTP directly. You have a permanent Internet connection if your computer is directly connected to a network that is part of the Internet. You can get a temporary connection to the Internet if you dial in to your Internet account using **SLIP** or **PPP**. Once you're connected to the Internet, all you need is FTP software to upload and download files.

Plain English, please!

SLIP (Serial-Line Internet Protocol) and **PPP (Point-to-Point Protocol)** are two communication protocols, or sets of standards, that let you connect your computer to a network over standard phone lines.

SLIP/PPP or network access

The best type of connection is one where your computer is permanently connected to a network that is part of the Internet. You're most likely to have a direct connection to the Internet if you work for a large company, a university or school system, or the federal government. Usually, only places that want to connect relatively large numbers of computers to the Internet (more than 50, say) have their own permanent network connection.

If you have only a few computers where you work, or if you want to connect your home computer to the Internet, you will probably do so using SLIP or PPP. To do this, you must get an account with a provider that offers SLIP or PPP service. You must then run SLIP or PPP software on your computer (the provider usually supplies the software you need). You use this software and a modem to dial in to your Internet account, and once you connect to your account, your computer is connected to the Internet.

You can use any of the Internet services (such as FTP) directly from your computer once you are connected to your SLIP or PPP account. The only disadvantage is that with most SLIP/PPP providers you don't have a permanent Internet address that allows you to offer Internet services (for example, you can't set up an anonymous FTP server that allows people to retrieve files from your computer).

An FTP program

Once you have your computer connected to the Internet, you can get access to the thousands of FTP sites that exist on the Net. All you need is the software that lets you send the FTP commands.

How do you find this software? There are a number of ways you can get it:

- The software that you use to connect to the Internet may have come with an FTP program.

- If you have a direct network connection, your network administrator should be able to give you an FTP program to use on your computer.

- If you have a SLIP or PPP connection, your Internet account provider may be able to give you the software.

- There's the ever popular method of asking a friend who has an FTP program to give you a copy. (Be sure to pay the registration fees if it's shareware.)

- Or there may be a professional society or user group that you belong to that has a library of shareware and freeware.

Once you have a basic FTP program, you can use it to look through FTP servers for other FTP programs.

FTP with shareware, freeware, and public domain software

A lot of Internet software was created while the network was still research oriented. Software that was developed as part of a research project was distributed by its authors to anyone who needed it. Much of this older Internet software is difficult to use because the authors were mostly technical researchers who didn't want to spend a lot of time designing nice user interfaces. They just wanted something that worked and didn't care how arcane the commands were.

As more people have become connected to the Net, software authors have created programs with friendly interfaces for old Internet services. The authors of these programs often distribute them for free or a nominal cost since the programs are written as a hobby, not as a commercial venture.

You can find many of these free and almost-free programs at FTP sites around the Net. There are a number of free or shareware graphical interfaces for FTP itself, for both Windows and Macintosh.

Windows software

Most Windows interfaces for FTP have similar features. You specify the FTP server you want to connect to, and the account name and password used to connect to that server in a connection dialog box. The main window of the FTP application has an area that shows the current directory on your computer (including a list of files in that directory). You can navigate to the directory where you want to transfer files to or from. There is also an area in the window that shows you the current directory on the server (again, including a list of files in that directory), and that lets you navigate to the desired directory on that server. Command buttons enable you to copy the files to and from the server; some buttons may even let you do things like remove files or limit the types of files you see in the directory listings. Try different FTP programs until you find one with features that you particularly like.

Share, free, public—What's the difference?

There are big repositories of noncommercial software at many FTP servers on the Internet. Most of this software is developed by people for personal use. If the developers think that others might like to use the programs, they put them on the FTP servers.

Some of this software is **shareware**. Shareware is software that you can try out before deciding that you want to buy it. It's not free, however. Shareware usually contains a license agreement (including pricing) from the developer and information on how to register it. The developer often provides upgrades and bug fixes to registered users. If you use shareware on a regular basis without registering and paying for it, you are likely committing a criminal offense. The cost of shareware is usually nominal, and the quality often rivals commercial products, so please make sure to pay for it.

Freeware, on the other hand, is distributed by the author for use by anyone at no cost. The developer retains rights to the software, however, and usually prohibits it from being distributed as part of a commercial product.

Public domain software is software that the developer has released all rights to and has made available for anyone to use in any manner. This often means that the developer makes the source code available for others to modify and distribute.

When you get the software for your FTP program, you'll probably get a .zip file that contains the actual executable program, any necessary configuration files, and some documentation. The documentation should include installation instructions, information about software features, and possibly online help.

First, unzip the file into the directory where you want to keep the software. Then make an icon for the FTP program in one of the program groups in your Program Manager.

◐ (Tip)

> The easiest way to make an icon for your FTP program is to drag the executable file from the File Manager into a program group. Make sure that the program group is on your desktop and that the File Manager is open to the directory where you keep the FTP program. Then drag the .exe file into the program group.

✱ {Note}

> After you've installed a shareware or freeware program on your disk, check to see if there are any README files, or any documentation files (.doc, .txt, or .wri files). Read these before using the program to find out about the program's features and to learn about any configuration instructions. Many developers also build a help feature into their software that gives you online help while you use the software.

WS_FTP

WS_FTP is a popular Windows FTP program. The author allows noncommercial, government, or educational users to use it free. To get the program, you must already have an FTP application installed on your computer. (You probably got one with the Internet communications software your Internet provider gave you.)

WS_FTP is available from a number of FTP sites on the Internet (the current version is ws_ftp.zip). For the most recent version, look on the FTP server **ftp.usma.edu** in the directory /pub/msdos/winsock.files. You should also be able to find the file at the large CICA (Center for Innovative Computer Applications) software library. It's on the FTP server **ftp.cica.indiana.edu** in the directory /pub/pc/win3/winsock. If you can't connect to either of those sites, a number of servers keep copies (mirrors) of the files that are on CICA. Some of the mirror servers are:

wuarchive.wustl.edu	**ftp.monash.edu.au**
ftp.cdrom.com	**ftp.uni-stuttgart.de**
polecat.law.indiana.edu	**nic.switch.ch**

❗(Tip)

When you're looking for something at a mirror site, start by looking for a directory that has the name of the site that's being mirrored (cica, for example). This directory may be found under a /pub directory. Or, the mirror site may skip having a directory that has the name of the mirrored server. It may instead just have the same directory structure as the mirrored server. You'll probably need to poke around a little to find the file you're looking for at a mirror site. Mirror sites are often much easier to connect to than the mirrored server.

Connecting to FTP servers is as simple as clicking a few buttons. WS_FTP comes with a preconfigured list of many popular FTP servers and lets you add servers to the list. In addition, it's easy to customize WS_FTP's looks and behavior to your preferences.

The WS_FTP window (see fig 3.1) lets you easily select the current directory on your computer and on the FTP server. The push-button interface lets you transfer files with a few clicks.

Fig. 3.1

The WS_FTP window lets you transfer files between your computer and an FTP server, and also lets you examine and operate on local and remote files and directories.

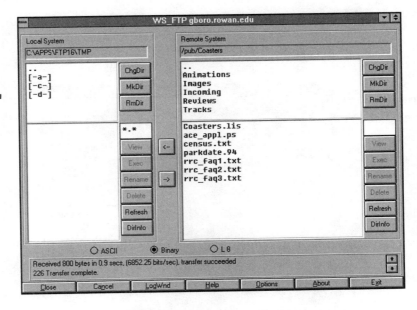

In addition to letting you transfer files, WS_FTP lets you do a number of other things to files and directories on your machine (or on the remote server, if you have privileges to do those operations from the account you've logged in to). Chapters 5–9 cover WS_FTP in detail.

WinFTP

WinFTP is a freeware variation of WS_FTP. Its looks and behavior are very similar to WS_FTP, with some new features added. The design of the window is a little nicer. It has a menu bar to give you access to some of the features instead of a lot of buttons in the window. And it lets you do some things that WS_FTP doesn't—like enter FTP commands directly, and sort the files you are viewing.

To get this program, you must already have some FTP application installed on your computer. (You probably got one with the Internet communications software your Internet provider gave you.)

WinFTP is available from **ftp.cica.indiana.edu** in the directory /pub/pc/ win3/winsock (the file is winftp.zip). As suggested in the previous section "WS_FTP," if you can't connect CICA, there are a number of servers that keep copies (mirrors) of the files that are on CICA.

Figure 3.2 shows the WinFTP window. It's very similar to the WS_FTP window. Like WS_FTP, WinFTP lets you connect to preconfigured FTP servers with a few clicks and add more servers to the preconfigured list.

Fig. 3.2
The WinFTP window lets you transfer files between your computer and an FTP server, and also lets you examine and operate on local and remote files and directories.

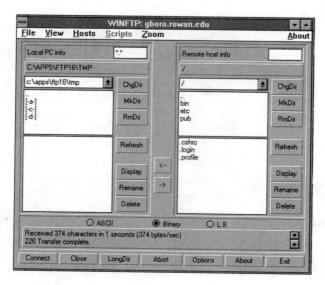

The buttons along the bottom of the window are similar to those in the WS_FTP window—they let you connect and disconnect from FTP servers, cancel your file transfers, and set up your preferences. In WinFTP, though, you have the option to access these features through the menu bar. The menus also let you sort the server file list, **ping** a **host**, or use FTP commands directly.

 Plain English, please!

> **Ping** is a program you can use to see if an Internet host is up. Ping informs you if the host you tried to contact responded or not, and how long the response took.
>
> A **host** is any computer connected to the Internet.

Unlike WS_FTP, WinFTP doesn't have online help. To find out more about the features of this program, you need to read the winftp.doc file (actually a text file, not a Word document) that is included in the ZIP file.

Macintosh software

In keeping with the easy-to-use reputation of the Macintosh, it's no surprise that FTP software for the Mac is equally user-friendly. Mac FTP programs offer a point-and-click interface and require very little keyboard input from you. In addition, most Macintosh FTP clients decode and decompress files on-the-fly—saving you extra time and effort.

Another excellent feature of Macintosh FTP clients are **bookmarks**. These are preset pointers to FTP sites that carry popular software and files for your Macintosh. These come in very handy when you know what you need but don't know where to look.

The two FTP clients that we discuss in this book, Fetch and Anarchie, can be found at all the "usual" FTP sites. The following are just a few FTP sites that have these two FTP clients:

- **cadadmin.cadlab.vt.edu/peterlewis/Anarchie-140.sit**
- **boombox.micro.umn.edu/pub/gopher/Macintosh-TurboGopher/ helper-applications/Anarchie-140.sit.hqx**
- **ftp.luth.se/pub/mac/comm/FTP/fetch2.12.sit.hqx**
- **ftp.switch.ch/mirror/umich-mac/util/comm/fetch2.12.sit.hqx**

This section gives you a look at both Fetch and Anarchie. Anarchie is also covered in great detail in Chapters 10–13.

Anarchie

Anarchie is probably the best FTP client for Macintosh. It's really two applications in one. In addition to being an excellent FTP program, it's also an Archie client. (Archie was introduced in Chapter 2 and is discussed more in Chapter 4.) This allows you to both search and retrieve files with the same application. Anarchie even provides you with a list of Archie servers on the Internet so you don't have to search for one.

Anarchie uses a multiwindow, multitasking interface for maximum useful-ness. Every site, directory, download, and Archie search you're working with has its own window. Also, several sessions can run at the same time. You can conduct an Archie search for one file at the same time you're downloading an application from an FTP site (see fig 3.3).

Fig. 3.3
Anarchie shows off its multitasking capabilities by downloading a file in one window while conducting an Archie search in another one.

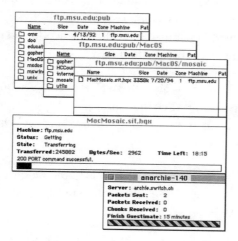

Configuring Anarchie is also simple, as all settings are contained in one window—you don't have to worry about multiple menus and hundreds of settings. Archie has an online guide for those who have System 7.5. This guide lets you go step by step through certain procedures and offers definitions and instructions for various special tasks. The overall documentation for Anarchie is excellent and this software comes from Peter Lewis, one of the most trusted names in Macintosh software.

Fetch

Fetch was one of the original FTP clients for Macintosh and is still in widespread use today. It's fast and easy to use, offers bookmarks of popular FTP sites for quick access, and lets you customize often-used sites for click-and-retrieve FTP sessions.

Unlike Anarchie, Fetch doesn't offer Archie search capabilities, which is a drawback. However, it can be an excellent utility once you're familiar with FTP and have identified common sites.

One advantage that Fetch does have over Anarchie is its **post-processing** capabilities. Fetch can make use of a number of decoding and decompressing utilities to allow you to download Macintosh, Windows, even UNIX files on-the-fly. As encoding and compressing techniques change, you will need multiple utilities to decompress and decode different types of files. Fetch's ability to use different decoding and decompression utilities can be an invaluable asset. Fetch also allows you to automatically view graphics immediately on download.

66 *Plain English, please!*

Post-processing refers to any operation done on a file after the original application's job is done. For instance, if a compressed application is downloaded, another application normally needs to decompress the file after it has been downloaded. A program like Fetch with a post-processing capability completes the original function and then carries out the subsequent operation. 99

Another main difference between Fetch and Anarchie is Fetch's single-window interface. Fetch uses a window much like a Finder dialog box to conduct FTP sessions. One window displays one directory at a time, but you can still easily move between directories (see fig 3.4). Fetch allows for limited multitasking, such as downloading multiple files at once. Some people prefer this simpler interface and find it somewhat less confusing than Anarchie.

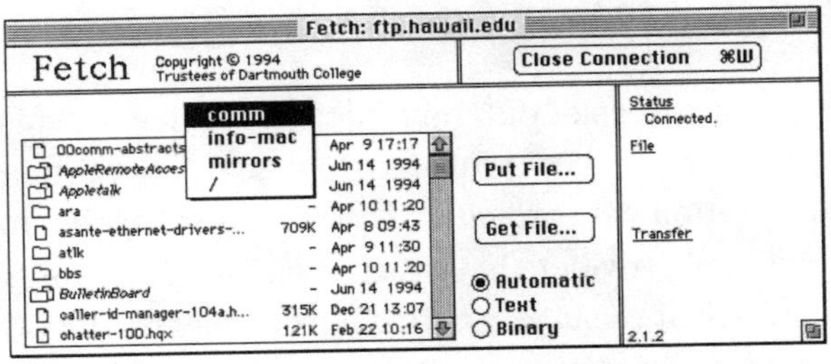

Fig. 3.4
Fetch only displays one directory at a time, although you can easily change directories with a click.

Even if you decide to use Anarchie almost exclusively, Fetch is still a good FTP client to have around. It's simple, fast, and very useful for fast downloads.

FTP with special service providers

If your eyes start to glaze over when you hear terms like SLIP, PPP, and Winsock, you may want to look into a "canned," or prepackaged, Internet interface that is available from many service providers. There are two basic types of canned interfaces—those that provide only Internet services, and those that are part of more general online service providers such as America Online and CompuServe. The canned interfaces have the following things going for them:

- The interfaces are usually easy to install and include all the software you need to run them.

- The service providers usually have free technical support if you're having trouble installing or using the interface.

- The interfaces often have online and printed help available.

The major drawback to the canned interfaces is that if you don't like the interface, you can't change it. Some of the interfaces don't implement all of the features for a particular Internet service. Or sometimes, the interface makes using the Internet service awkward. But, if you like the convenience of not having to find and set up all the different programs you need to use all the Internet services, one of the following providers may be right for you.

NETCOM's FTP interface

There are hundreds of different Internet service providers all over the country. Some are local providers that give you a command-line account and some are nationwide providers that have local access numbers. Many of these national providers have their own interfaces for the various Internet services. One of the bigger national providers is NETCOM, which has its own custom interface software.

NETCOM has a canned Internet interface called **NetCruiser** that provides custom interfaces for all of the Internet services. The NetCruiser FTP interface is very simple and easy to use (although a little limited compared to WS_FTP).

 **{Note}** The latest version of NetCruiser allows you to install and use other programs such as WS_FTP with it. If you find the NetCruiser FTP interface too limited, you may want to try WS_FTP in conjunction with it.

To access NetCruiser's FTP interface from the main NetCruiser window, you just choose the button that looks like several telephone poles with wires going between them (see fig. 3.5). A window containing a map of the United States appears (see fig. 3.6).

Fig. 3.5
NetCruiser lets you
start FTP with the press
of a button.

If you know the machine you want to connect to, enter its name in the Site text box at the top of the window and press OK. If you don't have any particular site in mind, you can use this map to explore the servers available in different areas of the country:

1 As you pass your cursor over the map, the name of the state you're over appears in the text box in the lower right corner. Click a state to find out about some of the FTP servers in that state.

Fig. 3.6
Put your cursor over a
state and click it to get
a list of FTP servers in
that state.

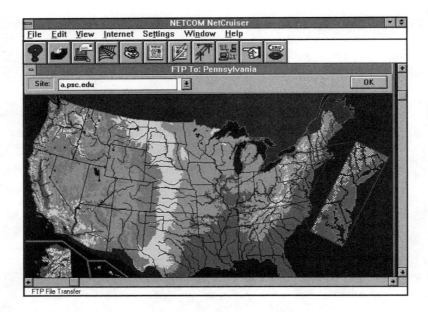

2 You can now click the arrow to the right of the Site text box to get a
drop-down list showing some of the FTP servers available in that state.

To get a list of international FTP servers, click the red area.

3 Select the server you want to connect to.

4 If you want to clear the drop-down list, click the water.

Once you've entered the name of the host you want to connect to, click OK.
You get a dialog box that lets you log in to an anonymous account using your
e-mail address as the password. If you want to log in to a personal account,
however, follow these steps:

1 Deselect the anonymous check box.

2 Enter the user ID of your personal account.

3 Enter the password you for your personal account on the FTP server.

After you enter your login information, click OK and NetCruiser tries to
connect to the FTP server. If it connects successfully, you get the FTP
window shown in figure 3.7 and an FTP menu item is added to your menu
bar.

You find out all about terms like **anonymous login** and learn about general FTP concepts in Chapter 4, "FTP Concepts and Culture."

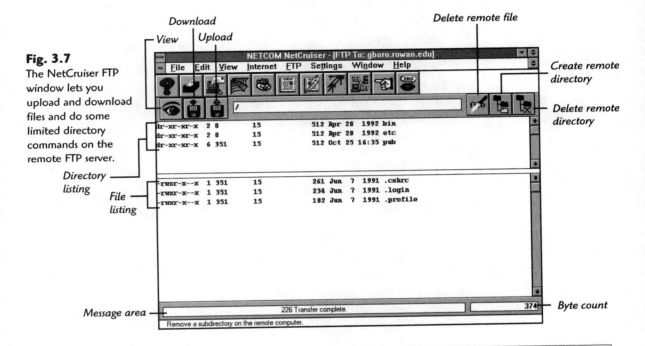

Fig. 3.7
The NetCruiser FTP window lets you upload and download files and do some limited directory commands on the remote FTP server.

(Tip)

If there's a welcome message from the FTP server, you get that in a separate window. This message often contains important information about the FTP server. After you're done reading it, close (or minimize) the window.

The FTP interface is easy to use. Double-click a directory to move to that directory. Or, if you know what directory you want to look at, enter the path name in the text box at the top of the window and press Enter.

To upload a file, click the Upload button. You get a dialog box that lets you navigate your local file system to find the file you want to send to the host.

If you find a file that you think you might be interested in, you can download it to your computer. Or you can download it temporarily and view it before you decide if you want to save it to your computer.

- To download a file, select the file and click the Download button (or double-click the file). First, you get a dialog box asking if you want the file transferred in ASCII or binary mode. Then you get a dialog box that lets you navigate your local file system to specify where to store the file. As the transfer is taking place, FTP commands appear in the message bar at the bottom of the screen, as do the number of bytes transferred.

- If you want to download a file and open it to read, click the View button. You get a dialog box letting you navigate your local file system to specify where you want the file stored. After NetCruiser transfers the file to your local disk, it displays the file in a window for you to view. (You can minimize or close the window when you're done.)

The FTP window also has buttons that let you create a subdirectory on the remote server, or delete files or subdirectories on the remote server. You can use these buttons only if you have permission to do these kinds of things on the remote server.

Once you're finished using the FTP server, you can disconnect from it by opening the FTP menu item and selecting Done, or by closing the FTP window.

CompuServe

CompuServe, the oldest of the online services, has been slow to introduce Internet access. At first, e-mail was the only access to the Internet. However, you can now use FTP, among other Internet services, from CompuServe.

Getting to FTP in CompuServe

If you are using WinCIM or MacCIM (the Windows and Macintosh interfaces for CompuServe), your main CompuServe window has several buttons for accessing popular features. One of these buttons is for the Internet, which includes CompuServe's FTP service. To get to this, follow these steps:

1 Click the Internet button in the Services window (see fig. 3.8). A window appears with the list of available Internet services.

Fig. 3.8
CompuServe makes accessing Internet services as easy as pressing a button.

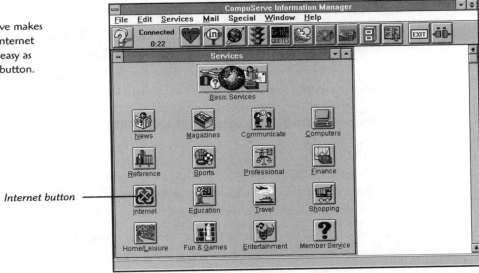

Internet button ——

2 Select File Transfer Protocol (FTP)+, and then choose Select to use FTP (this costs extra!); or double-click the FTP item.

3 The File Transfer Protocol+ window that appears lets you read some informational documents about FTP, connect to one of a list of suggested sites, or connect to a specific site (see fig. 3.9). You can also get a description of many available FTP sites.

Fig. 3.9
Do a quick connect to some of the most popular FTP servers, or connect to a specific server at the touch of a button.

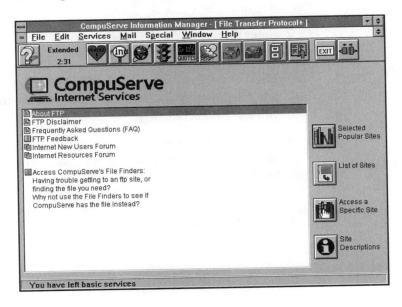

Connecting to FTP sites

The Selected Popular Sites button gives you a window with about eight popular FTP sites, such as Microsoft and UUNET Technologies. Click the button for that site to bring up the Access a Specific Site dialog box with the connection information for that site filled in. Click OK to connect.

If you want a slightly larger selection of preconfigured sites to pick from, do the following:

1 Click List of Sites to bring up a window containing a list of about a dozen popular FTP sites, including Walnut Creek and Wiretap (see Chapters 17 and 18 for descriptions of these sites).

2 Select the site you want to connect to and choose Select (or double-click the site) to bring up the Access a Specific Site dialog box with the connection information for that site filled in.

3 Click OK to connect. The Site Descriptions button lets you get a short description of the sites in the list when you click them.

If you know the name of the FTP server you want to connect to, you can directly enter that information. To do so:

1 Click Access a Specific Site button to bring up the Access a Specific Site dialog box (see fig. 3.10).

2 Enter the name of the FTP server you want to connect to in the Site Name text box.

3 If you want to start in a particular directory on the server, you can enter it in the directory text box. (You'll start at the top level of the server if you leave it blank.)

4 If you want to connect to a personal account on the FTP server, you need to enter the user name and password information for that account. The information for an anonymous FTP connection is filled in automatically.

5 Click OK to connect.

Fig. 3.10
The Access a Specific
Site dialog box lets you
enter the information
you need to connect
to an FTP server.

FTP server

Starting directory

Account name

Password

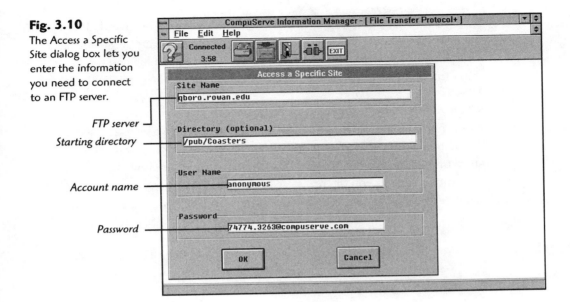

What to do once you're connected

If you successfully connect to the FTP server, you get a message dialog box
showing you the login information and greeting from the server. Once the
login process is complete, you see the FTP window shown in figure 3.11.

Fig. 3.11
The CompuServe FTP
window lets you up-
load, download, and
view files.

Current directory

List of directories

List of files

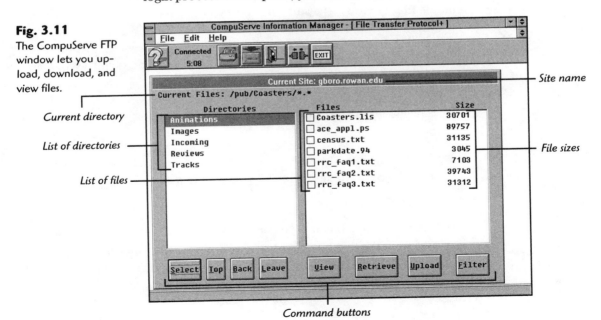

Site name

File sizes

Command buttons

To move to a directory in the list, select it and choose <u>S</u>elect (or double-click the directory). To move to the directory above the current one, select <u>B</u>ack. There is no way to directly go to a directory—you must navigate the directory structure. To go to the very top-level directory of the server, select <u>T</u>op.

When you're ready to download a file, select that file from the list. (The check book next to it will have an x in it). Then click <u>R</u>etrieve. You get a dialog box that lets you navigate your local file system to specify where to store the file. As the file is being transferred, you get a dialog box that has a bar graph showing you the progress of the transfer, the size of the file, the number of bytes transferred, and the estimated time remaining to do the file transfer.

✸ *{Note}* — You can transfer multiple files at one time by selecting all the files you want to transfer (just click the check box next to each file you want to transfer), and then choosing <u>R</u>etrieve.

If you just want to view a text file and don't want to store it on your local computer, select a file from the list and choose <u>V</u>iew. This brings up a dialog box that shows you the contents of the file. You can scroll through and read the file, and then choose OK to dismiss the dialog box. You can select multiple files to view—they are shown to you sequentially.

You can also upload files to some FTP servers that allow anyone to submit programs and other files to their collections. If you want to send a file to an FTP server, follow these steps:

1 Navigate to the directory on the FTP server where you want to store the file.

2 Choose <u>U</u>pload. This gives you a dialog box warning you that you must have the rights to anything that you send to a site.

3 Click <u>O</u>K to continue.

4 The next dialog box lets you enter the path to the file on your local file system in the text box next to the File button. Or, you can choose <u>F</u>ile and get a dialog box that lets you navigate your local directories to find the file you want to upload.

5 Select the type of the file you are transferring (binary, text, GIF, or JPEG) from the File Type drop-down list.

6 Choose OK.

If you're looking for certain file types at an FTP site, you can limit what you see in the file list by using the Filter button. When you select Filter, you get a dialog box asking you what type of files you want to display (both DOS and UNIX wildcards can be entered in the text box). Enter the mask (such as *.gif), and choose OK. The file list shows only files that match the mask you entered.

Once you're finished using an FTP server, choose Leave. This returns you to the FTP window where you can select another FTP server to connect to, use another Internet service, or use any of CompuServe's other services.

America Online

From the beginning, America Online was determined to provide an easy-to-use Internet interface. FTP was one of the earlier Internet services that AOL provided.

Getting to FTP in AOL

To use any of the America Online Internet interfaces, first select the Internet Connection button from the Main Menu window (see fig. 3.12).

The Internet Connection window lets you choose from the available Internet services with the press of a button (see fig. 3.13).

You also can read some information files, or go to one of the Internet-related forums. To use FTP, select the FTP button. The window that appears lets you read some documents that describe America Online's FTP interface, search for FTP sites, or use FTP (see fig. 3.14).

Fig. 3.12
America Online makes accessing Internet services as easy as pressing a button.

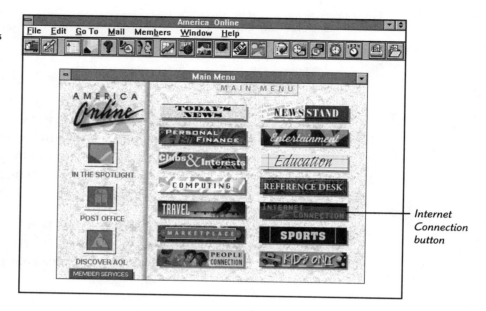

Internet Connection button

Fig. 3.13
The Internet Connection window gives you access to all of America Online's Internet services.

FTP button

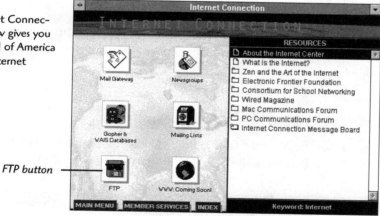

Fig. 3.14
The FTP window lets you search for FTP sites or connect to FTP sites that interest you.

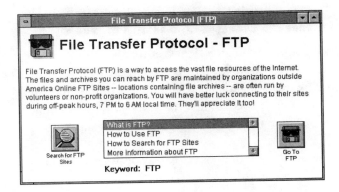

Searching for an FTP site

One of the nice features of America Online's FTP interface is the ability to search for an FTP site that contains information of interest to you. To do a search, follow these steps:

1 Click Search for FTP Sites in the FTP window.

2 The FTP Search dialog box lets you enter a word or part of a word that describes the information you want to look for (see fig. 3.15). Enter the words you want to search for.

You can narrow your search by entering multiple words separated by **and**, **or**, **not** (for example, *food or drink*).

3 Click Search. A list of FTP servers that have information on that topic appears in the bottom of the window.

4 Make note of the server names, and then close the window.

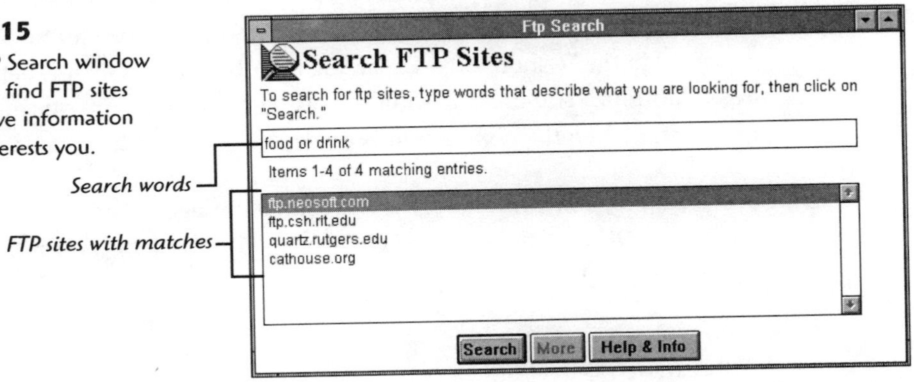

Fig. 3.15
The FTP Search window lets you find FTP sites that have information that interests you.

Search words ─

FTP sites with matches ─

Connecting to an FTP site

Once you've found an FTP server that looks interesting, you can connect to it by choosing the Go To FTP button in the FTP window. The Anonymous FTP window that appears has a list of a few of the more well-known FTP sites on the Internet. If you can find the site you want to connect to in the list, select it and choose Connect (or double-click the site).

If you don't want to connect to any of the servers in the Favorite Sites list, follow these steps:

1 Choose Other Site. This brings up the Other Site dialog box shown in figure 3.16.

Fig. 3.16
The Other Site dialog box lets you connect to any FTP server on the Internet.

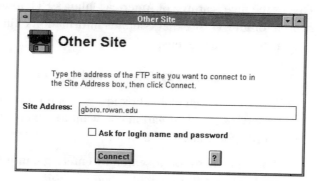

2 Enter the name of the site you want to connect to in the text box.

3 If you're using an anonymous login, just choose Connect.

If you're connecting to a personal account, select Ask for Login Name and Password, and then choose Connect. Enter your account name and password in the Remote Sign-On dialog box that appears, and then press Continue. You are logged in to your personal account on the remote site when the connection is made.

A Connected dialog box containing the welcome message of the server appears. Choose OK to dismiss the dialog box. A window for that server appears (see fig. 3.17).

Fig. 3.17
Once you've con-
nected to a server
you'll see the contents
of the top-level
directory for that
server. Directories are
shown as folders.

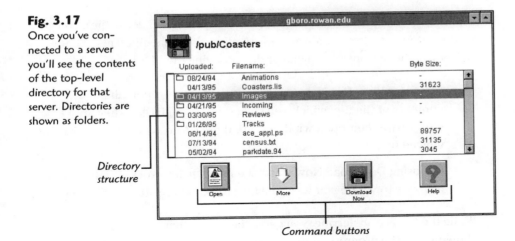

Directory
structure

Command buttons

⊛ *{Note}* ____ | America Online keeps local copies (mirrors) of the files on some of the more
popular Internet FTP sites. When you try to connect to a site and the connection is refused, you're connected to America Online's mirror of the site if there
is one.

What to do once you're connected

Whether you log in to an anonymous or a personal account, you are put at the
top-level directory for the account.

To move to a directory, select it and choose Open (or double-click the
directory). The listing for that directory appears in a new window. There's no
way to directly go to a directory—you have to navigate the directory structure. When you find a file you want to download, select it and choose Download Now. This brings up a dialog box that lets you navigate your local file
system to specify where to store the file.

⊛ *{Note}* ____ | At this time, you cannot upload files to FTP sites using America Online's FTP
interface.

If you select a file and choose Open (or if you double-click the file), you get a new window that gives you some information about the file. This window offers you the options of viewing or downloading the file:

- Choosing View File Now brings up a new window containing the contents of the file, which you can scroll through (gee, they aren't stingy with their open windows, are they?). Choose OK to dismiss the viewed file.

- Choosing Download Now starts the file transfer process (letting you navigate to where you want the file stored before starting the transfer).

While the file is transferring, you get a dialog box that has a bar graph showing you the progress of the transfer and a rough estimate of the amount of time until the transfer is finished. If your computer is set up for playing sounds, a voice announces "File's done!" when the file has been transferred. You also get a dialog box telling you that the file has been transferred (click OK to dismiss the dialog box).

!(Tip)

If you're doing a transfer that takes a while, you can select the Sign Off After Transfer check box in the Transfer dialog box. This disconnects you from the FTP server after you're done transferring the file.

!(Tip)

Every time you look at a directory or file, a new window opens. Things can get confusing quickly. Close the windows of directories that you won't be using to keep the clutter down.

When you're finished using an FTP server, you must close all of the windows associated with it to disconnect from the server. Once you've disconnected, you can connect to a new FTP server, close all of the FTP-related windows and use another Internet service, or close all Internet-related windows and use any of America Online's other services.

Prodigy

Prodigy is another of the older online services that was slow in adding Internet access. Although they still haven't added interfaces for many of the Internet services, what they've done is just as good. They've added a tool that lets you interface to many Internet services—and that tool is Prodigy's World Wide Web browser.

To get to Prodigy's Web browser (Jump:**web**), follow these steps:

1 Click the Communications button on Prodigy's highlight screen.

2 Click the Internet Forum button.

3 Click the World Wide Web button. You now see the main World Wide Web screen.

You're probably tempted to click the FTP/Gopher button to launch the browser, but this only gives you some introductory information about FTP and Gopher. Instead, click Browse the Web to launch the browser.

Chapter 16 covers basic Web browsing. You might need to read that chapter first for this section to make much sense. But, if you're adventurous, read on and we'll show you how to use the browser for FTP.

Using the browser for FTP is as simple as typing in the proper URL. When you want to go to an FTP site, you have to start the URL with **ftp://**, followed by the address of the site.

> **❝ Plain English, please!**
>
> **URL** stands for **Uniform Resource Locator**, an address that tells your Web browser exactly where on the Internet to find a Web document. **❞**

For example, let's say you want to go to Microsoft's FTP site. Its address is **ftp.microsoft.com**, so you enter the following URL in the Document URL field:

    ftp://ftp.microsoft.com

When you press Enter, the browser automatically goes to this site and loads the first level of the FTP directory.

Let's say you're looking for a document with the file name DRIVERS.ZIP, located in the /Services/TechNet subdirectory. From the top-level directory, you need to first click the Services directory, and when the contents of that directory are displayed, click the TechNet directory.

❶(Tip)

> You can avoid all this clicking to move from directory to directory by simply typing the entire directory path as part of the URL. For this example, you'd enter **ftp://ftp.microsoft.com/Services/TechNet/**.

When the contents of that directory are displayed, click the DRIVERS.ZIP file. You get a message that says `There is no viewer available for this item. Do you want to retrieve it anyway?` Answer Yes, and you see another message—this one stating `No viewer is available for this object type. Do you want to save this object to disk?` Answer Yes again, and you are prompted for a file name and directory (on your hard disk) for this file. Give the file a name and a directory, click OK, and the file is downloaded to your computer.

Some types of files—like text files—automatically display when you click them in the browser. If this happens, just click the browser's Save button to save the file to your hard disk.

4 FTP Concepts and Culture

FTP has its own culture and language, but they're easy to learn—and very useful to know!

You walk into a small Texas cafe to wash the trail dust down your throat. A waitress comes up to you and asks you what you want.

"I'll have a Coke," you say.

"What kind?" she asks, without batting an eye.

"A Dr. Pepper." She nods, moves off, and brings your ice-cold drink a moment later.

Some of you who've never been to the Southwest might be scratching your head. How can somebody order a Coke and a Dr. Pepper at the same time and be understood? In Texas, it's no problem—cold drinks in general are referred to as *cokes*, just as they're commonly referred to as pops, soda pops, and sodas elsewhere in the nation.

If you happened to be from New York and were moving down South, this is one of those aspects of the culture that you would find out about sooner or later, one way or another. If you were going to move there, do you think it would be helpful to find out some of these things before you moved? Could it save you some time? Embarrassment?

Just as different parts of the country have different ways of speaking, acting, and living, so too do the various parts of the Internet. Gopher works differently from e-mail, the Web isn't the same as Telnet. And on and on it goes.

FTP has its own little language and culture that is somewhat unique to how it works. We show you some of the ins and outs of that unique culture and protocol. Think of this chapter as a guide that will help you place your order correctly from your electronic server.

What's in a name?

Ninety-nine percent of the time you spend using FTP will be retrieving files. Text files, data files, applications, utilities, patches, and a hundred other types of files will present themselves. But how will you make sense of them all? How will you know a Macintosh file from a DOS file from a UNIX file? How should you download them?

Words and more words—text files

There are really two main types of files that you'll encounter when using FTP. The first (and probably the most recognizable) type of file is called an **ASCII file**—sometimes referred to as a **text file**. An ASCII file is made up of any or all of the standard characters that can be produced on a keyboard.

⚹ {Note}

Just because a character can be produced on a standard keyboard doesn't mean that it's an ASCII character. For instance, on a Macintosh computer, using the Courier New font, you can produce the characters ™, £, ¢, and ∞ while holding down the Option key and pressing the 2, 3, 4, and 5 keys, respectively. These are not ASCII characters because they can't be reproduced on any keyboard, on any computer, using any font as you can with characters such as 2, x, and #.

Quite often, these files appear on FTP sites as a name with no extension. For instance, a file called **readme** is probably a text file that goes along with another application. When a text or ASCII file has an extension, the two most common are **.doc** (e.g. compfile.doc) and **.txt** (e.g. readme.txt).

⊛ {Note}

> One other common extension you'll run into is **.ps**. This represents a PostScript file, which is a unique type of word processing document that can be sent directly to a PostScript printer. The benefit of this type of file is that it contains entire page descriptions so that no formatting is lost.

⊗ <Caution>

> No matter how many examples or different types of files we show you here, there will always be more. No listing or explanation can be exhaustive. Beware: when using FTP you must have a spirit of exploration and a willingness to probe the unfamiliar.

Zeros and ones—binary files

The other file type is the **binary file**. All of the code your computer uses to run is at some point translated into 0s and 1s—otherwise known as a **binary counting system** because there are only two possible values for any element. If you try to view a binary file with a text reader, what you see on your screen will probably send you searching frantically for the Cancel command. That's because the instructions expressed by binary code can't be easily transferred into recognizable characters.

This type of code is required of all the applications we use, whether they're word processors, 3D renderers, System utilities, or any other application—they are all stored and transferred in their binary forms.

⓵ (Tip)

> In addition to the file name, looking at the directory path can also give you clues to the types of files you might find in a given place. If a file appears in the /pub/utils/documentation/ directory, you might expect to find text files. Files in the /pub/utils/ directory are probably binaries.

Binaries comprise by far the biggest chunk of information available on FTP. Much of what you eventually retrieve from FTP sites will come in the form of executable applications that your personal computer can run.

⊛ {Note}

It is very rare on FTP sites to see a binary file that doesn't have an extension (such as .exe).

There are a couple of problems with binaries, though. First, they tend to be big, some of them *very big*. Second, unlike generic text files, binary files tend to be **platform-specific**. Applications written for a Macintosh rarely work on an IBM or a NeXT computer.

❝ Plain English, please!

A **platform** refers to any given computer and its operating system. DOS and Windows platforms run on IBM PCs and compatibles, MacOS is the Macintosh platform, and UNIX is the platform that computers such as NeXT, Sun, and SGI use. **❞**

Less than meets the eye—compression and encoding

FTP sites use **compression** and **encoding** for a variety of reasons. To try to solve the dilemma of file size, FTP sites use compression. Compression makes a binary file smaller so it can be stored and retrieved more efficiently. A compressed file can't be executed—it must be decompressed first.

Encoding is a way of translating binary files so they can be transmitted through ASCII-based media, such as e-mail. Files are usually encoded after they have been compressed. Although there is no need to encode a binary file for FTP transfer, many times they are encoded anyway.

⊛ {Note}

Don't confuse encoding with encryption. Encoding is not "secret." Anyone with a standard encoding utility can decode and read an encoded file. Encryption, on the other hand, is often used for private or secure information. Encrypted files usually require certain keys or privileges in order to be used.

The following three tables explain some of the different compression and encoding extensions for different platforms.

Table 4.1   DOS/Windows extensions

Extension	File information
.arc	This is one of the original DOS compression techniques and stands for ARChive. There aren't very many .arc files anymore, but you can still find them. The applications UNARC or PKUNARC will usually decompress an .arc file.
.zip	The most common DOS compression. Most DOS and Windows applications are "zipped." Use PKUNZIP or WinZip to decompress a .zip file.
.lzh	Lempel-Ziv compression with Huffman encoding. This is probably not as frequently used as other methods, but is very effective nonetheless. There are no commercial restrictions on its use for creating self-extracting files.
.exe	This extension usually represents an executable file. However, this extension also is used to represent a self-extracting .zip file. Executing this file decompresses the compressed files that make it up and put them in a readable form.

The .zip file is by far the most common for Windows and DOS. Be careful, though. If you get an old copy of PKUNZIP from a friend (or even from an FTP site), it may not work on some of the newer .zip files, so make sure you are using version 2.04g or later.

①(Tip)

> We highly recommend that you get a copy of WinZip (preferably version 5.6). It handles both .zip files and various other formats commonly used on the Internet. Among other places, you can get the current version at CICA at **ftp.cica.indiana.edu** in the /pub/pc/win3/util/ directory or at any of the sites that mirror this directory. Several mirrors are listed in Chapter 17.

Table 4.2   Macintosh extensions

Extension	File information
.sea	This stands for Self-Extracting Archive (SEA). These files are usually created with one of the StuffIt utilities and are designed to extract themselves when double-clicked.
.sit	This is a standard StuffIt archive and probably the most common form of compression for Macintosh. There are two common versions in use—the 1.5 and 3.x formats.

continues

Table 4.2 Continued

Extension	File information
.cpt	This is a ComPacT Pro archive. .cpt files have become less common over the years, but there are still a lot of them out there. The StuffIt utilities, as well as Compact Pro, will decompress these files.
.hqx	This is an encoding scheme referred to as BinHex. Many Macintosh files are stored both compressed and encoded, so you might see a file called foo.sit.hqx. Some Macintosh FTP software automatically de-binhexes a file for you, although StuffIt will also de-binhex a file.

As you can see, there are various compression and encoding techniques for Macintosh. Anarchie and Fetch, the two main FTP programs for Macintosh, automatically recognize, decode, and decompress these file types.

Table 4.3 Other extensions

Extension	File information
.gz	This is a UNIX compression called Gnu Zip. Most .gz files can't be used by DOS or Macintosh.
.tar	.tar is another type of UNIX compression and stands for Tape ARchive. As with .gz files, a .tar file can rarely ever be used by a PC or Macintosh.
.Z	This is a UNIX compression scheme and is usually added to a .tar file, so it's common to see a UNIX file called foo.tar.Z. Again, this extension indicates an application for use on a UNIX-based computer.
.uue	UUEncode was originally a UNIX encoding scheme. However, both Windows and Macintosh now use UUEncoding. A majority of .uue applications are UNIX, but some may be usable on a Macintosh or PC.

The Internet began with UNIX, so it's no surprise that there are a lot of UNIX files out there. Since FTP sites are still used mostly by programmers and other high-end users, UNIX files continue to make up a large portion of all that's available via FTP.

Also, a lot of Internet documentation is compressed and encoded in some of the popular UNIX formats, so it's good to be able to handle those types of files, as well. For Windows users, WinZip now handles most UNIX compression formats. DropStuff with Expander Enhancer is an add-in program for StuffIt Expander that handles some UNIX file formats for Mac users.

Where am I?

Two common phrases that you'll hear both on the Internet and in this book are **local** and **remote**. Although it would be easy to explain these terms in geographical terms, such an explanation might be confusing. It's better to think of these terms relationally.

The local machine is the one on your desktop. It is the computer that you happen to be using at the moment. If you're typing notes into a computer while reading this, you're using your local machine. When accessing an FTP site, your goal is to download files to this local machine.

The term **client** is also often used to refer to the local machine. In a way, your computer is seen as a customer (client) of the FTP site computer that you're using.

⊗<Caution> The term client can have different meanings depending on *when* and *where* it's used. For instance, the actual piece of software that is used to access an FTP site is often referred to as an FTP client or client software. Also, the actual computer you are working on can be considered a client.

A remote machine, on the other hand, is any other machine that is not on your desktop. A remote computer can be as close as the next room in your house or as far away as Tokyo, Japan. A remote computer that you connect to is also called a **server**, since it "serves" the client.

It's for this reason that it can be confusing to think of remote and local machines in geographic terms. If, for instance, you lived in Sacramento and you accessed an FTP site in Sacramento, you might be tempted to think of the FTP site as local as opposed to remote. In this case, it is better that you think of the relationship between the two machines as opposed to their actual locations.

Who am I?

Most of the time you're a nobody! That is, most of your dealings with FTP will be with **anonymous FTP**. Simply, this means that you can use FTP anonymously, without having to establish IDs, passwords, or authorizations on the machine you want to get files from. Although various characteristics and uses of anonymous FTP are discussed later in this book (see Chapters 7 and 12), there are some basics that we can talk about here.

⊗<Caution> Don't let the word "anonymous" fool you. Most FTP servers can generally determine the address that you're logging in from. In order to protect themselves from illegal activities, most FTP sites log this information on their server.

First, all anonymous FTP sites ask for two pieces of information—a **login ID** and a **password**. For most of these sites, you enter **anonymous** at the login prompt. Then, if you observe good **netiquette**, you type in your e-mail address as your password. A few anonymous FTP sites ask users to log in as **guest** or **ftp**. These sites are not real common, however, and you are given a message saying that you need to log in with the different ID.

❝ Plain English, please!

Netiquette is a combination of InterNET etIQUETTE. Netiquette refers to the unwritten rules that generally govern use on the Internet. **❞**

Usually, an anonymous FTP site also serves specific users in addition to anonymous users. This means that there are certain directories and files that you are told you can't access.

Those particular directories and files are reserved for specific users. Don't hang your head and think that you're not worthy or that you did something wrong—you didn't, these files just aren't available for use by the general public.

Another consequence of anonymous FTP comes in the ability to upload files. A few anonymous FTP sites don't allow anonymous users to upload files at all. Most others allow uploads on a limited basis.

On these sites, users generally have to upload files to a specified directory. They are notified if their uploads are accepted. (This is another good reason to provide your e-mail address as the password.)

There are too many anonymous FTP sites to list here—literally thousands of them. As you read this book, you'll discover some of the more common and useful ones, as well as sites where you can find specific software and files that will be of particular use to you. For listings of some excellent FTP sites, refer to Chapter 17, "The Best Sources of Software and Computing Information," and Chapter 18, "FTP Sites Just for Fun."

It's like a tree

There are three vital pieces of information that you need to be able to recognize when using FTP—the name of the FTP site, the directory a file is found in, and the file name itself. We looked at how to recognize different file names in a previous section. This section looks at the other two elements.

The first element is the **name** of the FTP site. If you've had very much exposure to the Internet, you'll probably recognize the familiar *xxx.xxx.xxx.xxx* domain name structure. Most anonymous FTP sites have such a name. There are **wuarchive.wustl.edu**, **nic.switch.ch**, **mac.archive.umich.edu**, and thousands more—each with its own unique name. The site name is what your FTP software uses to locate and log in to the site.

The second element we'll deal with is the **directory path**. The path is what you need to follow to get to a particular file on an FTP site. A directory path might look something like /pub/util/graphics/. Each slash represents a subdirectory of the previous directory.

Much like the branches of a tree, each directory "branches" off from a previous one. If you were to climb a tree, you would start at the trunk, climb off on a branch, then move out on a limb (if you were really light!), and so on.

FTP sites are the same. You start at the trunk, called the **root directory**, and then choose branch directories from the root directory. In the

/pub/util/graphics/ example, you take the /pub branch from the main trunk, go to the /util limb, and then jump to the /graphics twig. Presumably, the file you want is on that last twig.

✱ {Note} Depending on what software you use, you may never see the dreaded paths divided by slashes (/'s). They might appear as folders in Windows or on a Macintosh. They are usually apparent when conducting an Archie search—which we discuss in the next section.

Some directory entries aren't what they seem

As we've explained, UNIX directories are like the branches of a tree, where you have to follow along a particular branch to get to one of the twigs. Well, that's what it's like most of the time. Sometimes, you go to move to a branch or twig and find yourself transported to another part of the tree entirely.

As you move through a UNIX directory, you will occasionally find a directory or file that is linked to another directory or file. A linked directory or file points to a completely different directory or file (these links are similar to Macintosh aliases).

When you move to a linked directory, you are actually moving off of your current directory branch to a completely different branch. Similarly, a linked file is not actually in the directory it appears to be in.

Normally, you will not even notice if you move to a linked directory or retrieve a linked file. You will have a problem, however, if you move to the directory you originally came from. Links are one way. Once you've gone to a linked directory, you need to work your way to the root directory, and from there go to the original directory.

Who is Archie and why does he care about FTP?

Well, first off, **Archie** isn't a *who*, it's a *what*. Imagine walking into a huge, four-story mall with a thousand stores. Now imagine each one of those stores had a sign on the front that simply said *Store #3* or *Store #5*—no description, no nothing.

What would you do? "That's easy," you say, "I'd just go to one of those little directories they have at the malls and find out which stores carried what I wanted." Good for you—you've just used a very rudimentary form of Archie.

The number of stores in a four-story mall is nothing compared to the number of directories and files in the thousands of FTP sites out there. Even if you *could* get a directory of every "store," it would take you forever to find what you need. To solve this problem, it was necessary to find an **interactive** directory. Enter Archie.

Archie allows you to search FTP sites for directories or files that you want to find. As you'll see a little later, you can search for general information which you can then browse, or you can pinpoint the location of a particular file (see fig. 4.1).

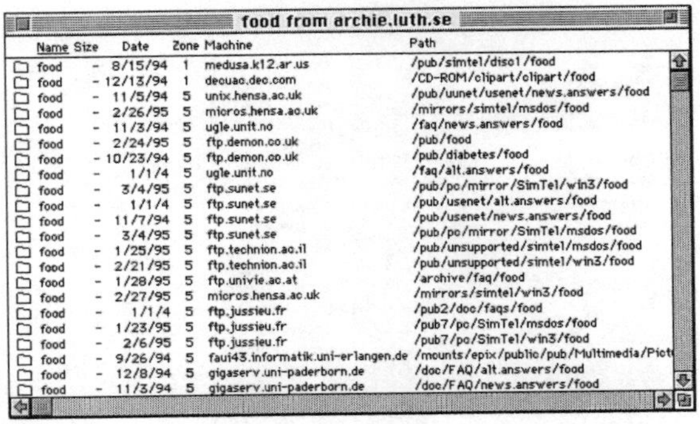

Fig. 4.1
If you were looking for recipes, you might conduct an Archie search for "food." This search gives you the results by listing the directory or file name, site name, and directory path.

Where does Archie live?

There are Archie servers everywhere—Japan, Nebraska, New Zealand—you name it. Each Archie server is basically the same. It has a database of files and directories on a particular set of FTP sites which it searches upon request.

Are all Archies created equal?

The answer is "No." There are dozens of Archie servers out there. However, don't be fooled—they don't all search every existing FTP site. In fact, none of them do. On the other hand, some of them search more sites than others.

The primary determinant in where an Archie server looks is geography. In this regard, there's a significant difference between North America and Europe (see the figure). Notice that there are Archie servers from all over the world—Italy (**archie.unipi.it**), Finland (**archie.funet.fi**) and North America (**archie.unl.edu**), among others.

As a general rule, European Archie servers tend to search FTP sites in Europe, U.S. Archie servers tend to search North American sites, and Canadian and Australian Archie servers also tend to search North American FTP sites. *This is not a hard and fast rule!* It's a general tendency.

There's one other thing to note. The European Archie servers and FTP sites are usually less busy than North American ones. Even though they may not be as big, they will often have the files and software that you want or need.

This is a list of some of the different Archie servers that are available throughout the world.

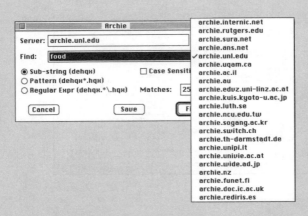

The main North American Archie Servers are at **archie.unl.edu** and **archie.rutgers.edu**. However, these servers are often busy. Good alternatives are **archie.sura.net** and **archie.uqam.ca**. Some good (and generally available) European servers can be located at **archie.funet.fi** and **archie.switch.ch**.

⓵ (Tip)

> When you begin using Archie, experiment with different sites. Depending on what time of day you use Archie, along with other factors, you might find a different site of greater use to you than the ones recommended.

Simple Archie searches

Ninety percent or more of the time you use Archie, you will search for a word or file name. If you are looking for an application that will play sounds on your computer, for example, you might do an Archie search for *sound*. If you are looking for the application SoundApp, you would search for *soundapp*. These are often called **substring searches**.

Another type of simple search that is really an extension of the substring search is an **exact search**. This allows you to search for a program or directory if you know exactly what it's called. All of the software covered in this book allows for exact searching.

✳ {Note}

> Archie is case-insensitive. Don't bother using capital and small letters since it won't make a difference. A search for *Graphic* yields the same results as a search for *graphic*. Some programs allow you to conduct a case-sensitive search, but it often isn't necessary.

Keep in mind a few things when conducting Archie searches:

- **The Inverse Ratio Rule**. In essence, this is quite simple. The more general the search term, the more results the search yields. For instance, a search for *food* produces more hits than a search for *chili*. On the other hand, a very narrow search term yields fewer hits than a more general one.

- **The Relevance Rule**. Although a more general search yields more results, it also produces more irrelevant hits. In other words, if you are searching for recipes, a search for *food* may produce a lot of hits. But a smaller portion of those hits actually have something to do with recipes than they would if you search for *recipe*. As with the Inverse Ratio Rule, the opposite is also true here.

- **The Term+ Rule**. Always remember that, with a simple search, Archie returns hits that match your search term plus anything else. For instance, a search for *food* might produce a hit like food_recipes-10.hqx, because the hit contains the original phrase *food*.

- **The No-Space Rule**. FTP files and directories *never* have spaces in them, so never use one in a search. If you want to search for something that has two words, use some of the standard characters where a space would normally be. For instance, try searching for *chili_recipes* or *chili-recipes*.

Make it a point to always know what "level" you're searching at. If you know that you really only have a general idea of what you're looking for, then make your search broad. If you have a better idea, get more specific. If you know the exact name of the file, search for that.

You can also use a little common sense. There are standard directory names for certain types of files (see Chapter 10, "Connecting to FTP Sites with Anarchie"). If you know what category the file you're searching for is in, try that. For instance, if you're looking for a utility that renders pictures, trying a search for *graphicutils* or *graphics* makes sense.

Advanced Archie searches

There will still be times when you want to be a little more specific with your search than regular search terms allow. Fortunately, Archie allows you to search in more advanced ways.

The most common type of advanced search is called a **pattern search**. This type of search allows you to search for a particular pattern by using **wildcards** in your search phrase. This offers several advantages over standard Archie searches.

Plain English, please!

Wildcards are symbols that are used to represent unknown quantities. Much like the term *x* is used in the equation *x*+3=5 to represent something unknown, wildcards allow you to let Archie help you solve search equations.

There are two basic types of wildcards you can use: the **star** or **asterisk** (*), and the **question mark** (?). A * allows for an infinite number of unknowns. The ? allows for one unknown. An example might help clarify this. A search for *sword** yields both *swords* and *swordplay* as hits. However, a search for *sword?* produces only the *swords* hit.

You may want to use a pattern search for a number of reasons. Perhaps your simple search produced too many hits and you want to narrow it down some. Maybe you know part of a file name and want to be able to use that information in your search.

X<Caution> Pattern searches generally take longer than a simple search, so take this into consideration when using Archie. Weigh the benefits of a more efficient search against the loss of time it will cost you.

Whatever the reason for using them, pattern searches can be very handy. Let's say that a friend of yours tells you about a great new Macintosh application called WebMap that allows you to produce an index map for your Web page.

You might not want to conduct a search for *webmap* because there might be all sorts of hits out there. Not only that, you're a smart person, so why would you want to search for more than you really need? Since you know that this is Macintosh software, you know that whatever it's really called, it likely ends with .hqx.

So, you formulate your search and tell Archie to look for *webmap*.hqx*. Using the * wildcard means that you don't need to include a specific version number or other variables that might affect the hits you get, and you are quite likely to see only results that are exactly what you're looking for (see fig. 4.2).

Fig. 4.2
This pattern search yielded only relevant hits and excluded unneeded results.

Name	Size	Date	Zone	Machine	Pat
webmap-10.hqx	171k	2/8/95	5	ftp.technion.ac.il	
webmap-10.hqx	171k	2/8/95	5	ftp.luth.se	
webmap-10.hqx	171k	2/8/95	5	unix.hensa.ac.uk	
webmap-10.hqx.gz	130k	2/8/95	5	src.doc.ic.ac.uk	
WebMap.1.0.sea.hqx	1k	11/18/94	5	chalmers.se	
WebMap.1.0.sea.hqx	1k	11/18/94	5	chalmers.se	
webmap1.0.opt.hqx	171k	10/1/94	5	faui43.informatik.uni-erlangen.de	
webmap1.0.opt.hqx	171k	10/1/94	5	nic.switch.ch	
webmap1.0.opt.hqx	171k	2/25/95	5	ftp.luth.se	
webmap1.0.opt.hqx.gz	130k	10/1/94	5	gigaserv.uni-paderborn.de	

What is a regex?

Sooner or later, you will hear about a **regex search**. Regex (pronounced *reg-eks*, not *rej-eks*) is the UNIX term for **REGular EXpression**, and it's a very sophisticated type of search. So sophisticated, in fact, that we won't cover it in great detail in this book. A regex search can be helpful on occasion, but isn't used to the extent that other types of searches are.

Any explanation of regex would take a whole chapter by itself (the UNIX manual takes over 10 pages), and the average Internet user usually just doesn't need to do this kind of search. Rest assured, you really aren't missing out on a lot.

A regular expression search allows you to define a range or possible values for a search. For instance, if you wanted to search for a file that you knew had a name (say, *foo*) and a digit and was zipped, you could search for *foo[0-9]\.zip*. The *[0-9]* tells Archie to look for any single digit and the \ tells Archie to begin looking for regular characters again. For more information on a regex search, see Chapter 8.

Each software-specific section tells you exactly how to conduct these different types of searches. When you get there, just keep these principles and tips in mind.

Part II:

Transferring Files with Windows

5

Connecting to FTP Sites with WS_FTP

In this chapter:

- Get WS_FTP installed on your computer
- How do I connect to an FTP server?
- I want to move between directories
- Get me outta here! How do I disconnect from a server?
- The ways to know where you've been and what you've done

Connecting to an FTP server anywhere on the Internet is as easy as clicking a few buttons.

Before graphical FTP interfaces were developed, you had to enter cryptic commands to view local and remote directories and to transfer files. WS_FTP is an easy-to-use freeware graphical interface that lets you transfer files and view directories simply by clicking buttons.

How to install WS_FTP

Installing WS_FTP is very simple. The only restriction on running this application is that you must be running Windows 3.1 or higher. To install WS_FTP, you just need to copy the WS_FTP ZIP file to your hard disk and unpack it.

⊛ {Note} _____ | WS_FTP is available from a number of FTP sites on the Internet (the current version is ws_ftp.zip). For the most recent version, look on the FTP server **ftp.usma.edu** in the directory /pub/msdos/winsock.files. You should also be able to find the file at **ftp.cica.indiana.edu** in the directory /pub/pc/win3 /winsock. If you can't connect to either of those sites, a number of servers keep copies (mirrors) of the files that are on CICA. Some of the mirror servers are:

wuarchive.wustl.edu	**ftp.monash.edu.au**
ftp.cdrom.com	**ftp.uni-stuttgart.de**
polecat.law.indiana.edu	**nic.switch.ch**

1 Copy the file ws_ftp.zip to a directory on your computer where you want to keep it.

2 Use an unzip utility such as PKUNZIP or WinZip to uncompress the files. After they're unpacked, you should have the following files:

File	Description
ws_ftp.exe	The WS_FTP executable file
ws_ftp.hlp	The files containing the online help screens
ws_ftp.ini	The WS_FTP configuration file
ws_ftp.ext	A list of file extensions that WS_FTP will automatically transfer as ASCII (text) instead of binary
ws_ftp.txt	Information about the program, including licensing information, bug fixes, and so on

Be sure to keep the .ini file in the working directory for WS_FTP.

3 Create a new program group if you don't want to put the icon in one of your current groups.

4 Add the icon for WS_FTP to the program group of your choice by dragging the .exe file from the WS_FTP directory into the open program group. Your icon should look like the one in figure 5.1.

Fig. 5.1
Putting the WS_FTP
icon in a program
group lets you start up
WS_FTP quickly from
the Program Manager.

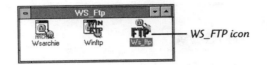

— WS_FTP icon

Connecting to an FTP site in the Profile Name list

You can't upload or download files until you've connected to a server, so let's see how to do that first. WS_FTP has a **Session Profile dialog box** that lets you specify what host you want to connect to. You can predefine the login information for any number of FTP servers.

WS_FTP also comes with built-in connection information for some of the most popular hosts on the Internet. Some of the connection profiles are named for the software you can find there (such as Mosaic or Trumpet Winsock DLL), and others have the name of the site (such as Microsoft).

32-bit or not 32-bit

The version of WS_FTP that is discussed in this book is the 16-bit version that was designed to run under Windows 3.1. There is also a 32-bit version of WS_FTP that was primarily designed for use with Windows NT and the Windows 95 operating system. You can find this version in the same places as the 16-bit version in the file ws_ftp32.zip. Installing this application is similar to the 16-bit version (copy it into a directory and unzip it), although many more supporting files come with it. The application itself is very similar to the 16-bit version, with only a few minor

differences in the appearance of the main window.

To use the 32-bit version with Windows 3.1, you need to have the Win32s libraries loaded on your PC. However, don't use the 32-bit version with Windows 3.1. Getting it to work can be difficult, and there's no advantage to running it. If you want to use WS_FTP to automatically retrieve files found with WSArchie, note that the 32-bit version of WS_FTP may not work correctly with WSArchie.

The WS_FTP window

The WS_FTP window shows you the local and remote file systems, and lets you manipulate files and directories on both systems.

Use this button to change directories on your local computer.

These are the directories (top) and files (bottom) under the current directory on the FTP server.

This is the current directory on your local computer.

This is the current directory on the remote computer.

These are the directories (top) and files (bottom) under the current directory on your local computer.

Use this button to change directories on the FTP server.

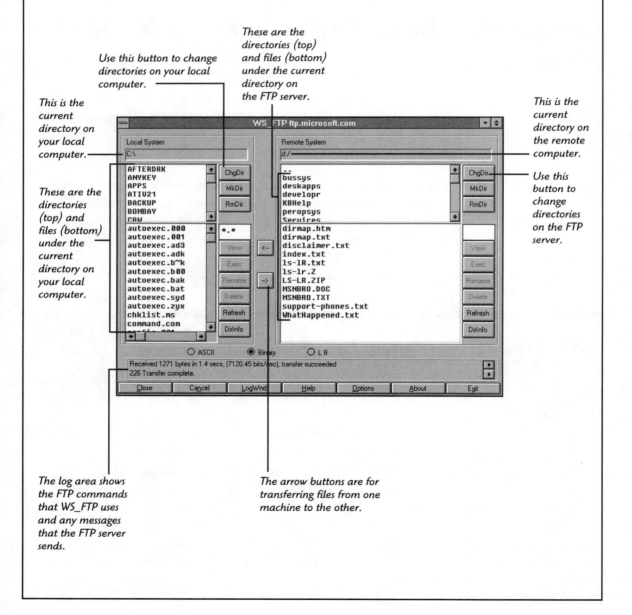

The log area shows the FTP commands that WS_FTP uses and any messages that the FTP server sends.

The arrow buttons are for transferring files from one machine to the other.

When you want to use WS_FTP to retrieve or send a file, the first thing you have to do is connect to the Internet (if your computer isn't permanently connected to the Internet). After you're connected to the Net, follow these steps:

1 Start WS_FTP by double-clicking its program group icon. By default, the Session Profile dialog box opens when you start WS_FTP (see fig. 5.3).

Fig. 5.2
The WS_FTP Session Profile dialog box lets you connect to any FTP server on the Internet.

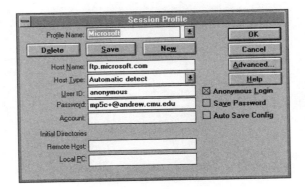

Changing the way the window is arranged

If you're a horizontally oriented person rather than vertically oriented, you can rearrange the buttons and viewing areas in your WS_FTP window to be more to your liking. To change the layout of the window, follow these steps:

1 Click Options.

2 In the Options dialog box that appears, click Program Options to open the Program Options window.

3 Select the Alternate Screen Layout check box to reformat the WS_FTP window so that the local directory is shown in the top half of the window, and the remote

directory is shown in the bottom half of the window. For each directory, the directory list is on the left, and the file list is on the right. This places your directory and file operation buttons along the bottom of each directory area.

4 Select the Show Buttons at Top of Screen check box to move the row of command buttons from the bottom of the window to the top of the window.

5 Click Save to make your changes take effect. (Click Cancel to abort the changes.) Then click Exit in the Options dialog box.

2 If you need to open the Session Profile dialog box after WS_FTP is started (if, for example, you've disconnected from one FTP server and want to connect to another one), click <u>C</u>onnect.

3 To connect to a predefined host, click the down arrow to the right of the Profile Name text box. WS_FTP comes with preconfigured profiles for a number of the most popular anonymous FTP sites (see fig. 5.3).

Fig. 5.3
The Profile Name drop-down list contains a number of hosts with predefined login information.

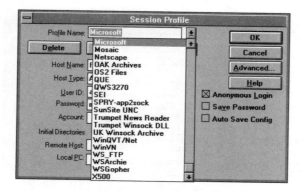

To connect to an FTP server that's not in the list, see Chapter 7, "Adding Sites to WS_FTP's List," for information about how to fill in the Session Profile dialog box.

4 Scroll through the list until you find a host that you want to connect to. When you select the host from the list, the list disappears, and the text boxes and check boxes in the Session Profile dialog box are filled in with the information for that host.

5 Enter your full Internet e-mail address in the Passwo<u>r</u>d text box.

If you have already set up your e-mail address in WS_FTP, that address is entered automatically as your password. (See the "Setting up your e-mail address in WS_FTP" sidebar following these steps for an explanation of setting up your e-mail address in WS_FTP.)

6 Choose OK to make the connection.

The Session Profile dialog box disappears, and WS_FTP attempts to connect to the server that you specified. You see the actual FTP commands in the log area at the bottom of the WS_FTP window. As long as everything is going well, you don't have to worry about these messages. If a problem occurs, you are notified.

Setting up your e-mail address in WS_FTP

To log in to an anonymous account, you should enter your full Internet e-mail address in the Password field. If you set up WS_FTP to know your e-mail address, it's automatically entered in the Password field of any session profiles that have the Anonymous Login box selected. (If you don't configure your e-mail address, WS_FTP will default the password to "guest," which is not allowed by many anonymous FTP servers.) These are the steps for configuring your e-mail address:

1 Click Options in the WS_FTP window.

2 Click Program Options in the Options dialog box.

3 Enter your full Internet e-mail address in the E-Mail Address text box.

4 Click Save in the Program Options dialog box, and then click Exit in the Options dialog box.

Some anonymous FTP servers allow you to use any password to log in. Others, however, check to see that you've entered a valid e-mail address. Although the servers can't verify your specific account, they can verify that the host name in your e-mail address is in the same domain as the machine you're FTPing from. So, enter your actual e-mail address. If your e-mail address is in a different domain than the account you're FTPing from, most servers let you connect, but warn you.

Q&A — **Why can't I connect to the FTP server I've picked?**

When you try to connect to a predefined FTP server, you may get one of several different error messages in the log area of the WS_FTP window. If you get an error saying that the host was not found, this may mean that the machine no longer exists or that its name has changed.

Another message you may get is that your connection is refused. This usually occurs when a machine is already at its maximum capacity for FTP connections (many servers only allow a limited number of anonymous FTP connections). Try to connect at a later time, or try another machine that has the same information. A number of sites, called **mirrors**, have copies of the files that are on popular servers. Many popular servers show you a list of mirror sites if they refuse your connection.

Do you want the Session Profile dialog box to open when you start WS_FTP?

Because you're going to need to connect to a remote server in order to do anything useful with WS_FTP, it starts with the Session Profile dialog box open by default. If you don't like this and you only want to see the dialog box when you choose Connect, you can change the default:

1 Choose Options.

2 In the Options dialog box that appears, click Program Options to open the Program Options window.

3 Deselect the Show Connect Dialog on Startup check box. The Session Profile dialog box will not open when you start WS_FTP.

4 Click Save in the Program Options dialog box. (Click Cancel to abort the changes.) Then click Exit in the Options dialog box.

Navigating directories

If you successfully connect to the FTP server you picked, your WS_FTP window shows the name of the remote machine in the title bar, and the Connect button changes to Close. If you haven't changed the layout of the window, the left side of the window is labeled Local System, and the right side is Remote System.

Both sides contain a split viewing area. The top half of the viewing area shows the directories under the current directory, and the bottom half shows the files in the current directory. From here, you can navigate through the directories of the remote server and of your local computer.

Moving up and down the directory list

After you establish your FTP connection, the WS_FTP window shows the current directory on your local computer on the left side of the window and the current directory on the remote server on the right side of the window. You can easily move between directories on your computer and on the remote server.

If there are more subdirectories than can be shown in the directory list area, scrollbars appear to the right of the directory list. Use the scrollbars to find the directory you want to move to. Select the directory and click ChgDir to move to that directory.

(Tip)

You also can double-click a directory to move to that directory.

Notice that at the top of your directory list, there's an entry containing only two dots (..). Selecting this entry moves you to the directory above the current one. (When you are at the top-level directory, there isn't a two-dot entry because you can't go up any further.)

Jumping to any directory

If you know the path to the directory you want to go to, you can go there directly rather than navigate through each intermediate directory. If you click ChgDir without selecting a directory, you get the Input dialog box shown in figure 5.4.

Fig. 5.4
When you click ChgDir, the Input dialog box asks for the name of the directory you want to go to.

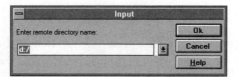

The current directory is highlighted as your starting point. To go to a directory below the current one, click at the end of the directory name in the text box and finish entering the path information. For example, say you're in the /pub directory on the FTP server, and you want to go to the /Images directory two levels below. You add /Coasters/Images to the end of /pub.

To go to a completely new directory, simply begin entering the path when the dialog box appears. The highlighted text is replaced with what you type. Once you've entered the directory information, click OK to go to that directory. You can go directly to directories on your local computer or on the remote server.

? Q&A

> **I'm looking for a particular directory, but it's shown as a file and I can't get to it. What can I do?**
>
> FTP servers (particularly UNIX-based servers) occasionally have directories that are actually links to other directories, and files that are links to other files. The linked directories don't have any files in them, but they point to directories that do contain the files. By the same token, linked files do not have anything in them, but they point to the actual files.
>
> Unfortunately, you have to choose whether WS_FTP interprets links as links to files or links to directories. If you tell WS_FTP to interpret links as files, it doesn't understand what the linked directories are and shows them as files. Then when you try to examine the linked directory, you get the error Not a plain file. If you tell WS_FTP to interpret links as directories, it shows linked

files as directories, and you get the error No such file or directory when you double-click one.

If you have WS_FTP set to show links as directories, you can still download a linked file. To do so, make sure no files are selected (click Refresh to clear any previously selected files). Click the left transfer arrow, and enter the name of the file in the input box that appears. Click OK, and WS_FTP will begin downloading the file.

If you have WS_FTP set to show links as files, and you know that a directory is linked, or if you get the error that indicates a linked directory, you can still get to the directory. All you need to do is click the remote server's Refresh button to clear any previously selected directory. Then click the ChgDir button, and enter the path to the linked directory in the Input dialog box. You don't need to know what the directory is linked to.

For example, if under /pub you know there's a linked directory named /documents, you can just enter **/pub/documents** in the ChgDir Input dialog box and click OK. This takes you to the directory that actually contains the file, which in this case is the directory /public/documents. The name of the real directory is shown at the top of the Remote System directory listing. If you try to use the two-dot entry to go up to the next directory level, you go to the directory above the real one (/public, in this example), not the linked one (which would be /pub).

To choose how WS_FTP shows links, follow these steps:

1   Click Options in the WS_FTP window.

2   In the Options dialog box, click Session Options.

3   In the View Links area of the Session Options dialog box, click either the As Directories or the As Files radio button. (The default is As Directories.)

4   Click Save in the Session Options dialog box to save this setting for the current session. To save it as the default for all future sessions, click Save as Default before clicking Save. (Click Cancel to abort the changes.)

5   Then click Exit in the Options dialog box.

Additional things you can do in local directories

In addition to the ChgDir button, there are two other buttons to the right of the local and remote directory areas that let you manipulate your directories (see the "Adding and removing directories at remote sites" sidebar below).

If you want to make a new directory under the current directory on your local computer, click MkDir. The Input dialog box appears, asking for the name of the directory you want to create. Enter the name of the new directory in the text box and click OK to create it. (Click Cancel to close the dialog box without making the new directory.) The directory listing is refreshed and the new directory appears there.

You can also remove a directory from your computer's local file system. Select the directory you want to remove and click RmDir. You see the Verify Deletion dialog box asking if you're sure that you want to delete the directory (see fig. 5.5). Click Yes if you want to delete the directory, or No if you've changed your mind. (You can also Cancel this dialog.) The directory listing is refreshed, and the directory disappears from the list.

Fig. 5.5
WS_FTP prompts you for confirmation before deleting a directory.

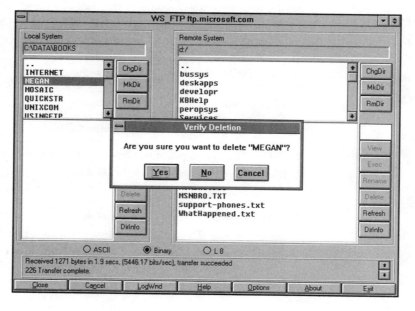

How to get more information about a directory

WS_FTP's directory and file listings don't give you any information other than the name of the files and directories. If you want to see more information about the contents of the current directory (on either your local computer or the remote server), click DirInfo. Notepad starts and shows a long directory listing of the current directory (see fig. 5.6). You can save this information as you can any Notepad file.

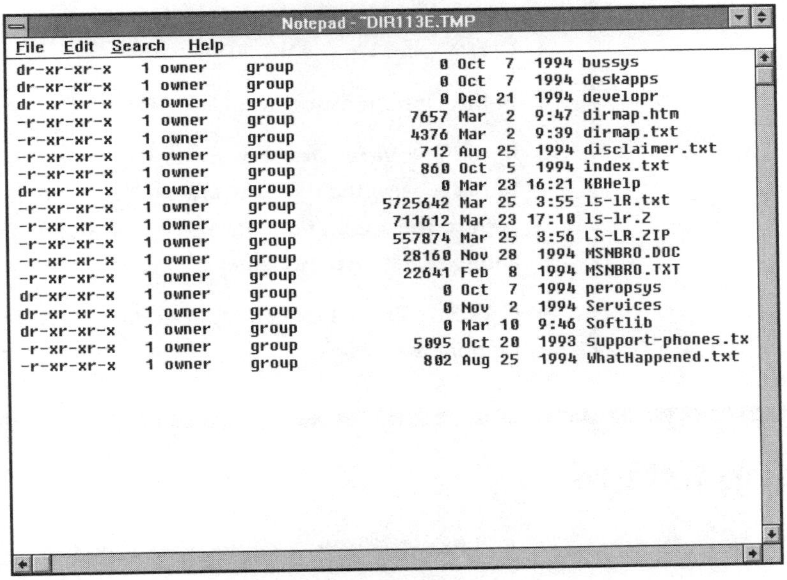

Fig. 5.6
Clicking DirInfo brings up Notepad with a file list showing the modification dates and sizes of the files in the current directory.

```
                           Notepad - ~DIR113E.TMP
 File   Edit   Search   Help
 dr-xr-xr-x   1 owner      group            0 Oct  7  1994 bussys
 dr-xr-xr-x   1 owner      group            0 Oct  7  1994 deskapps
 dr-xr-xr-x   1 owner      group            0 Dec 21  1994 developr
 -r-xr-xr-x   1 owner      group         7657 Mar  2  9:47 dirmap.htm
 -r-xr-xr-x   1 owner      group         4376 Mar  2  9:39 dirmap.txt
 -r-xr-xr-x   1 owner      group          712 Aug 25  1994 disclaimer.txt
 -r-xr-xr-x   1 owner      group          860 Oct  5  1994 index.txt
 dr-xr-xr-x   1 owner      group            0 Mar 23 16:21 KBHelp
 -r-xr-xr-x   1 owner      group      5725642 Mar 25  3:55 ls-1R.txt
 -r-xr-xr-x   1 owner      group       711612 Mar 23 17:10 ls-1r.Z
 -r-xr-xr-x   1 owner      group       557874 Mar 25  3:56 LS-LR.ZIP
 -r-xr-xr-x   1 owner      group        28160 Nov 28  1994 MSNBRO.DOC
 -r-xr-xr-x   1 owner      group        22641 Feb  8  1994 MSNBRO.TXT
 dr-xr-xr-x   1 owner      group            0 Oct  7  1994 peropsys
 dr-xr-xr-x   1 owner      group            0 Nov  2  1994 Services
 dr-xr-xr-x   1 owner      group            0 Mar 10  9:46 Softlib
 -r-xr-xr-x   1 owner      group         5095 Oct 20  1993 support-phones.tx
 -r-xr-xr-x   1 owner      group          802 Aug 25  1994 WhatHappened.txt
```

Adding and removing directories at remote sites

There are MkDir and RmDir buttons for the remote directory list as well as the local one. You can only use them, however, if you have permission to write to the remote directory. Usually, you don't have this permission if you're connecting to an anonymous FTP server (you have permission only to read directories). If you use WS_FTP to connect to a personal account, you can use the MkDir and RmDir buttons for your remote directories just as you do for your local directories.

The directory information is in the format normally used by the operating system of the computer where the directory lives. For example, when you're looking at a directory on your local computer, you get a DOS-formatted listing of the directory. If you're looking at a directory on a remote UNIX server, however, you get a UNIX-formatted listing of the directory. So you may see different file information (file size, protection, modification date, etc.) in the long directory listing depending on the type of computer the files are on.

❋ **{Note}** — Some directory listings may be too large to be edited with Notepad. To set a different editor as your default:

1 Click Options in the WS_FTP window.

2 In the Options dialog box, click Program Options.

3 In the Text Viewer text box, enter the name of the application you want to use to view the directory listings. You need to enter the complete path to the application if the directory where it lives is not in your autoexec.bat PATH statement.

4 Click Save in the Program Options dialog box. Then click Exit in the Options dialog box.

Sorting listboxes

When WS_FTP shows the files on the FTP server, it does not necessarily show them in alphabetical order. It shows them in whatever order the server sends them. If you want to be sure that the files are shown alphabetically, you need to tell WS_FTP to sort the remote file listbox. Here's how to do it:

1 Choose Options.

2 In the Options dialog box that appears, click Session Options to open the Session Options dialog box.

3 Select the Sorted Listboxes check box if you want the remote file list to be sorted alphabetically (otherwise, the files are shown in the order they are sent from the remote host).

4 Click Save in the Session Options dialog box to save these values for the current session. To save them as defaults for all future sessions, click Save as Default before clicking Save. (Click Cancel to abort the changes.)

5 Then click Exit in the Options dialog box.

When do you need to refresh a window?

If the contents of the current directory (either on your local computer or on the remote server) are changed outside of WS_FTP, WS_FTP doesn't show you the changes unless you rescan the directory. Click Refresh to get the most recent directory listing.

Disconnecting from a site

When you have a connection open to an FTP server, you're taking up one of a fixed number of slots available for people who want to use that server. As soon as you're finished looking through directories and transferring files, disconnect from the server so that someone else can use the slot.

To disconnect, click Close. At this point, you can make another FTP connection by clicking Connect. If you're finished using WS_FTP, choose Exit.

?Q&A

Why can't I do anything with the remote directories or files?

If you try to do directory or file operations on the server and WS_FTP seems to be busy for a long time without doing anything, or if you see send:error 10009 in the log area, your connection to the FTP server may have timed out. Most servers disconnect you after a period of inactivity (if you stop changing directories or transferring files) in order to free up the connections for others to use. WS_FTP doesn't seem to recognize that the server has disconnected, and still indicates that it's connected. You must click Close in order to reset WS_FTP so that you can make a new connection. (You may have to click Cancel before Close if you've tried to start a file transfer.)

The Message Log window shows you where you've been

You can see the actual FTP commands executed for any remote operation in the log area at the bottom of the WS_FTP window. If you double-click the log area, or if you choose LogWnd, you get the Message Log window which shows a complete history of all the FTP commands WS_FTP has executed in this session (see fig 5.7).

Fig. 5.7

The Message Log window shows you all the FTP commands that have been executed by WS_FTP in this session. CWD commands show the directories you've examined; /bin/ls commands show when directory listings were done.

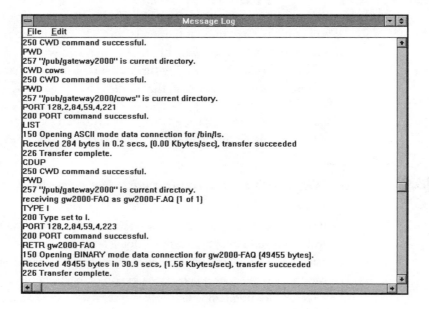

You can get some interesting information from this Message Log window, such as how long it takes files to transfer and the average transfer rate. You can also see all the directories you've visited and the files you've transferred.

You might want to save the log of a session if you want to remember which directories were most useful to you on a particular server. To save the contents of your Message Log window, follow these steps:

1 Open the File menu and choose Save As. This opens the Input dialog box.

2 In the text box, enter the path to the file on your local computer where you want to store the log information.

3 Click OK to store it.

When you no longer want to see the Message Log window, open the File menu and choose Exit.

What if you just want to keep track of the files you've transferred, instead of keeping all the information that's in the Message Log window? WS_FTP lets you designate a log file for saving file transfer information. You can tell WS_FTP to keep information about file transfers by following these steps:

1 Click Options.

2 In the Options dialog box, click Program Options.

3 In the Program Options dialog, select Enable Logging and enter the path to your log file in the Log Filename text box. If you omit the full path and just enter the log file name, the log file will be stored in the WS_FTP working directory.

4 Click Save, and then click Exit in the Options dialog box.

Now when you transfer a file, WS_FTP writes information in the log file about where the file was copied from and where it was stored.

Getting help from the remote site

What should you do if you can't find something that you're sure should exist at a particular site, or if you're having a lot of problems (getting connected to the site, being disconnected frequently, and so on)? Well, if you've looked through all the informational files that exist at the site (for example, files with names like INDEX or README) and can't find any help, there are a couple of things you can do.

If you know who runs that site, send them e-mail and ask about the problems. If you don't know a particular person at the site, you can always send e-mail to the **postmaster**. This is a person who serves as a point of contact for the site. You may need to strip the machine name from the FTP server address in order to send mail to postmaster. For example, if you are connected to the server **ftp.sei.cmu.edu**, send questions to **postmaster@sei.cmu.edu**.

Another address that you might be able get a response from is info. Many sites now have an info address that lets you ask for information about the site. Like when you're sending mail to postmaster, you may have to strip the machine name from the site in order to address the mail correctly (for example, change **ftp.product.com** to **info@product.com**).

6

Getting and Sending Files

How do you get all those files? Where do you put them? For the answers to these questions and more, read on.

After all your reading and preparation, it's time for action. You've waited to start downloading all that neat stuff you've heard about, and now it's time. You might be a little anxious that downloading will be hard. Don't worry! WS_FTP makes transferring files easy.

You'll spend most of your time with FTP downloading, as well as possibly doing an occasional upload. As you're already aware, there is a lot of very useful stuff available on FTP and it's finally time to take advantage of it.

How to download files

First, you must decide on a file to download and connect to that FTP site. After you've located the file you want to download (as explained in Chapter 5), you're ready go. Simply double-click the file you want to retrieve. (Or click the file to select it, and then click the left arrow in the middle of the screen.) WS_FTP will begin transferring the file to your default directory (see fig. 6.1).

(Tip)

There are three choices for downloading using WS_FTP: ASCII, Binary, and L8. You can always use **Binary**, the default setting, for downloading, even for text files. Because some documents might already possess some formatting, you might want to always download using the Binary setting. If you are certain that a file is all text, you may use the **ASCII** option. The **L8** option is used for transferring nontext files from a VMS mainframe. Since most FTP sites do not run VMS, you should rarely, if ever, have to use this option.

Fig. 6.1
After double-clicking the file you want to download, WS_FTP notifies you of its progress as it transfers the file to your default directory.

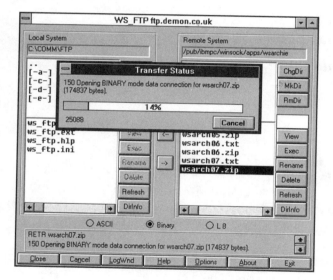

Where does the file go?

By default, the file goes to the directory path that is displayed in the local system directory (for the example in figure 6.1, the default directory is c:\comm\ftp). It's fine to download files to this directory. However, you might want to consider another option.

Many users create a directory just for downloads. There are two popular places to put this directory:

- Under the root directory (c:\download)

- As a WS_FTP subdirectory (c:\comm\ftp\download)

Choosing to save files this way gives you one central location for all your downloads. For files you wish to keep in other locations, they can easily be moved to other directories at a later time.

Setting your double-click options

One of the functions that WS_FTP allows you to set to your tastes is the double-click setting. Normally, double-clicking something in Windows selects it for execution. However, you might want to change this convention when using WS_FTP, although doing so won't change what a double-click does in Windows.

To select your double-clicking options, click the Options button from the main window and then click the Program Options button. The new dialog box will display a Double-Click area (see the figure).

If you leave this setting at the default, Transfer, double-clicking a file in the FTP window will automatically begin a download of that file. If you choose the View setting, WS_FTP will attempt to display the file in Notepad, or the text editor you've assigned, when you double-click it. Choosing the Nothing option will disable all double-clicking options while in WS_FTP.

Most people will view and transfer files most often, so you might want to leave this setting at the default.

The Program Options window lets you choose how you want WS_FTP to handle a double-click.

Program Options

- Alternate Screen Layout
- Buttons on Top
- Show Directory Information
- Auto Save Host Config
- ☒ Verify Deletions
- ☒ Auto Connect
- Debug Messages

Text Viewer: notepad
E-Mail Address: noele@msu.edu

Listbox Font
- ○ System Variable
- ● System Fixed
- ○ ANSI Variable
- ○ ANSI Fixed
- ○ Custom Font
- □ Scale Fonts

Double Click
- ● Transfer
- ○ View
- ○ Nothing

Recv Bytes 4096
Send Bytes 512

Save
Cancel
Help

It's easy to create such a directory. First, click the MkDir button, which is next to the Local System window in WS_FTP. You'll then be asked for the name of the new directory. Type in the desired path and directory name, and click OK. WS_FTP creates the new directory (see fig. 6.2).

Fig. 6.2
WS_FTP allows you to
create new directories
for easier file access.

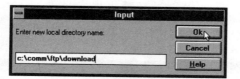

After you have created the new directory, you can use the directory navigation techniques you learned in Chapter 5 to go to the new directory. Remember, the same methods you use to navigate the directories at a remote FTP site work for navigating your local directories. An alternative way is to click the ChgDir button and type in the path of your new directory. After you've changed to the new directory, you're ready to download files to it.

❓Q&A

Whenever I try to create or change a directory, nothing happens. Is there something wrong?

Probably not. Some computers simply don't work correctly with WS_FTP to allow you to create and change directories. If this function doesn't work on your system, you will have to go to the File Manager to create the appropriate directory.

Telling files where to go

There may be times when you might want to download files to a number of different directories that have already been created during a single session. For example, let's say that you've found an FTP site that contains a lot of files that you want to save in different places under different file names (for instance, graphics, utilities, text files with nonstandard names). You can always use the directory navigation techniques previously covered, but if you plan on going to many directories in different paths and renaming a lot of files, this may not be the best way. How do you do it?

To direct WS_FTP to the proper directory with each download, you must enable the appropriate session option:

1 First, click the Options button.

2 Next, choose to view the session options by clicking the Session Options button.

3 When the Session Options dialog box appears, select the Prompt for Destination check box (see fig. 6.3).

4 Once you have completed this, click the Save button in the Session Options dialog box; then click the Exit button in the Options dialog box, and you're done. Although it's unlikely that you'd want to, you can make your change permanent by clicking the Save as Default button instead of the Save button.

Fig. 6.3
Select the Prompt for Destination check box so that WS_FTP will ask you where you want to save files when you download.

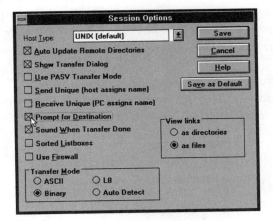

The next time you download a message after setting this option, you will be prompted for the file name you want to use for the download. If, for instance, you want to save the file wsarchie07.zip in the directory c:\comm\ftp\download, you might type **c:\comm\ftp\download\wsarchie.zip** when prompted. You couldn't call the file "wsarchie07.zip" because that would exceed the number of characters (eight plus an extension) allowed by DOS.

⊛ {Note}

Remember that if you save this setting as the default but decide to have files once again automatically download to the default directory, you will need to repeat the above steps and deselect the Prompt for Destination check box.

If you want to look first

Text files are among the different types of files available on FTP. These can describe another file you want to download (often called a README file) or be an actual stand-alone document (such as a file that contains song lyrics).

It's possible that you might want to open one of these in a simple word processor, either because you want to see what's in the file before downloading it or because you know you don't want to actually download the file.

Viewing a file without downloading it can often save you some time. When you choose only to view a file, WS_FTP automatically deletes that file once you close it. This saves you the time of having to manually delete a file every time you read it. Of course, if you do decide to save it, you can do so from within Notepad (or the application you choose to view files in).

Viewing a file without saving it is easy with WS_FTP. First, click the file you want to view. Next, click the View button. WS_FTP will open the file in Notepad as a temporary document (see fig. 6.4).

Fig. 6.4
WS_FTP opens a temporary document in Notepad when you choose to view a text file.

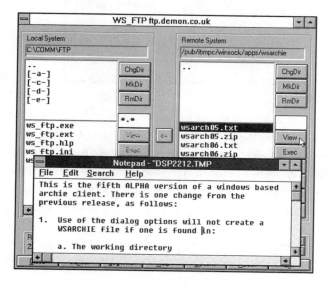

You don't have to use Notepad as your viewer; you can use any word processor that you like. To change the viewer you use:

1 Click the Options button.

2 Then click the Program Options button.

3 Next, type in the path and application name you want to use as your viewer in the Text Viewer dialog box. For example, if you want to use the Windows Write program, you'd type **c:\windows\write.exe** (see fig. 6.5).

4 Click the Save and Exit buttons, and you are done. The next time you view a file, it will be in the viewer you selected.

 **<Caution>** Don't attempt to view a binary file. It definitely won't be readable and can cause problems for your viewer. Only view files that you know contain text.

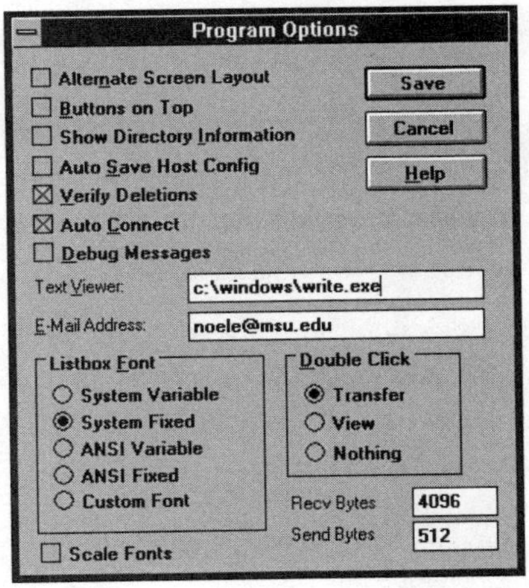

Fig. 6.5
You can decide what viewer you want to use to view files when using WS_FTP.

 (Tip) It is recommended that you keep Notepad as your default. It is fast and easy. Only choose a more time-consuming and memory-intensive word processor, such as WordPerfect or Word, if you know it will always be running in the background or if you plan on viewing very large files.

Saving viewed files

There will be many occasions when you'll want to permanently save a file you are viewing. Doing this is very easy. Just choose the Save option in your viewer, give the file a permanent name, and you're done.

For example, if you want to save a file in Notepad, choose the Save <u>A</u>s option from the <u>F</u>ile menu. If you use the <u>S</u>ave option instead, the file will be saved under the temporary name. Finally, give the file an appropriate name and save by clicking the OK button.

Executing downloaded files

What if you want to see what a program does as soon as it's downloaded to your machine? Can you do it? Yes, you can. WS_FTP allows you to immediately execute a file as soon as it's downloaded, as long as it has a recognizable file association. (See the "Files of a feather flock together" sidebar below.)

Select the program file you want to execute by clicking it, and then click the Exec button. WS_FTP will begin downloading the file and attempt to execute it as soon as it's successfully transferred to your machine.

(Tip)

> Remember that you can also perform functions, such as executing a file, on your local directories, as well. This can come in handy if you want to execute a program on your machine without going to the File Manager.

You can also create file associations from within WS_FTP.

1 From the main window, click the <u>O</u>ptions button.

2 Next, click the <u>A</u>ssociations button.

3 Type the extension in the <u>F</u>iles with Extension text box—**gif** in this example.

4 Next, type in the path and application name in the <u>A</u>ssociate With text box. For our example, LView 3.1 is being used to display .gif files (see fig. 6.6).

If you don't know the exact name or directory of the application you want to associate with, click the Browse button to find it. The Browse dialog box that opens lets you navigate through your directories until you find the correction application.

5 Once you've included this information, click the OK button and your association will be saved for future use (see fig. 6.6).

Fig. 6.6
You can create file associations by telling WS_FTP the extension and program you want to link together.

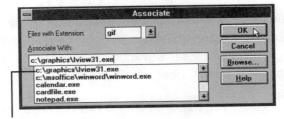

LView 3.1 has been added to the Associate With list.

Files of a feather flock together

If you've been using Windows long, you're probably familiar with what a **file association** is. Briefly, Windows "knows" that certain files extensions should execute a certain way. For example, a file named do-it.exe will run as an executable program, and a file with the .wri extension will be opened using the Windows Write word processor.

When executing a file on download, it's important to know something about file associations. For example, if you execute a .exe, .pif, .com, or .bat file, Windows will know what to do with it and should execute it properly. Windows will also

know what to do with files that have created associations (for example, Microsoft Word creates a file association for .doc file extensions during its installation).

However, if you download a file with an extension that Windows can't automatically associate, such as do-it.gz, it won't execute. WS_FTP will ask you to associate the downloaded file if it is not recognizable, though. Afterwards, Windows will remember the association for you. Pay close attention to the file extensions on the files you wish to execute.

⊛ *{Note}*_____

In the Associate window that appears, you'll see that a lot of associations have already been created for you. These associations are created from the [Extensions] section of the win.ini file.

When a name is too long

So you've finally found a picture of that '65 Mustang that you've wanted to use as your desktop wallpaper. The only problem is that the file is called 1965_Ford_Mustang.gif. You know that your PC can only handle files in an 8.3 character format. How will WS_FTP transfer the file to your hard drive?

Not to worry! WS_FTP automatically forces the file name to fit into DOS format for you. It does this by truncating the file name based on the original file name. For example, the file discussed in the preceding paragraph would be saved as 1965_For.gif. Some standard types of truncation are listed in this table.

This remote file name	Becomes this DOS file name
1000-tapes-new.tar.Z	1000-tap.tar
README.index	README.ind
.readme	readme.
1965_Ford_Mustang.gif	1965_For.gif

⊛ *{Note}*_____

When you get a file name that is truncated, you will probably want to change the file name to something containing an extension that Windows can associate. As an example, if WS_FTP truncates README.index to README.ind, you might want to change it to README.wri so it will be associated to a Windows word processor.

What's in a name?

On occasion, you will download two files with the same file names. For example, let's assume that you're downloading the help.txt files from a number of different applications. There's only one problem—they're all called help.txt! As you know, DOS can't handle more than one file with the same name in a single directory.

By default, WS_FTP automatically overwrites a duplicate file. In other words, if the file help.txt already exists in your download directory and you download another file with the same name, WS_FTP deletes the first one and replaces it with the second one.

Fortunately, however, WS_FTP allows you to solve this thorny problem. You can change the default to actually create new files. To make this change, first click the Options button and then the Session Options button. Next, select the Receive Unique (PC assigns name) check box (see fig. 6.7).

Fig. 6.7
By selecting the correct option, you can have WS_FTP automatically save and rename multiple files with the same name.

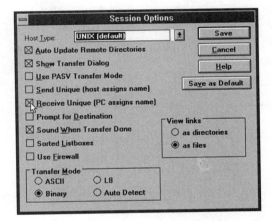

After you have saved this setting, WS_FTP will rename duplicate files without overwriting the original. To stay with the original example, if you download a second help.txt file, WS_FTP will rename it help000, the next one help001, and so on.

Three's a crowd

You've found it—an FTP site with tons of files that you want. You've only been on the site a few minutes and you've already found a dozen files you want to download.

But there's a problem: if you try to download them all one at a time, it would take you forever. It'd be nice if you could just tell WS_FTP to download all of them and go do something else instead of baby-sitting the computer for hours just so you can send a new download command every 30 minutes.

Downloading multiple files is not only possible, it's also convenient—with WS_FTP. First, simply Shift+click or Ctrl+click the files you want to download. When you've selected all the files you want, just double-click one of the selected files (or click the Download button) and WS_FTP will begin downloading them, one at a time (see fig. 6.8). WS_FTP downloads multiple files in succession, so as soon as the first one is transferred, the second one begins, and so on, until they've all been downloaded.

Fig. 6.8
Selecting multiple files at once will allow you to download them all with one command so you can do something else while they're being transferred.

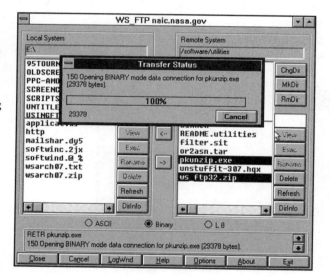

Uploading files

Suppose you found a great file on some FTP site in Timbuktu that's almost impossible to get to, and now you want to make that file available on a local or more accessible FTP site? Or, maybe you just finished compiling all of the Star Trek Captain's logs and want to share them with the world? Can you do it, and if so, how?

Well, the answers are "it depends" and "easily." Many FTP sites severely limit who can upload and what can be uploaded to their systems. Still others don't allow uploads at all. However, many do allow anonymous users to upload files to their FTP sites. As with downloading, uploading files with WS_FTP is very easy.

> As you read the rest of the section on uploading, you'll realize that there's a little more to completing a successful upload to FTP than you might at first think. It's recommended that you open the Session Log window while doing uploads, as the messages captured in that window can prove to be very useful to you.

There are a couple of ways you can upload a file. The first way uses the same process as downloading a file. Simply navigate your local directories until you find the file you want to upload and double-click the file, or select the file and click the Upload button (just make sure you're connected to an FTP site!). If you have authorization, the file will begin to transfer to the remote machine. If you do not have authorization, you should contact the system's administrator to find out how.

Drag-and-drop uploads

With WS_FTP, you can upload files using the drag-and-drop method:

1 Make sure you've selected the correct remote directory that you want to transfer the file to.

2 Next, open the File Manager and locate the file that you want to upload.

3 Finally, drag the file to the WS_FTP window, and the upload will begin.

If the site accepts the upload, the transfer should proceed successfully. If not, it won't. There are some hints and instructions on how to get your uploads accepted in the "Who do I notify about uploads?" section later in the chapter.

Multiple uploads

Just as you can download multiple files at once, you can also upload multiple files at once. There are two different ways to do this. First, using the Shift+click or Ctrl+click methods, simply select all the files you want to upload from the Local Machine window and double-click one of them to begin the upload.

You can also upload multiple files from the File Manager. After selecting the proper remote directory, open the File Manager and locate the files you want to upload. After they're selected, simply drag and drop them on the WS_FTP window and they will be transferred to the FTP site, one file at a time.

Where do you put files?

You might be thinking that an FTP site administrator would have a tough time keeping up with all the new files if just anybody could upload files to any of the site's directories, which might number in the hundreds. If you are, you're right. Keeping track of uploads to an FTP site proves to be a logistical nightmare on even a modest-sized FTP site.

As you also might have guessed, site administrators have a way around this little dilemma. Most of them set up a special directory to receive uploaded files. The most common name given to this directory is /incoming. Most FTP sites that allow uploads of any type have an /incoming directory in the root directory. Always upload to this directory if it's available.

What happens to the files?

You've just completed your upload, and you log back in to the FTP site to see your newly uploaded file. You go to the /incoming directory and... Hey! Waitaminit! It isn't there! What happened? Well, it's still there—you just can't see it.

Most FTP sites that accept uploads don't instantly put the file online. The site checks the file for viruses, determines what directory it belongs to, possibly informs you of the site's plans, and ***then*** actually puts the file on the site. While this whole process is occurring, the file stays hidden to anonymous users.

Who do I notify about uploads?

It's quite likely that you'll need to talk to someone at the FTP site regarding your upload. Many FTP sites require that you e-mail the site administrator with information on your upload before they even consider putting it up permanently (see fig. 6.9).

Fig. 6.9
This FTP site requires you to contact the site administrator before the upload is accepted.

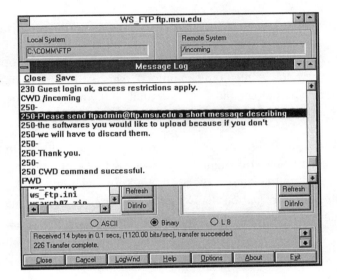

Most FTP sites ask you to contact them for one reason or another regarding your upload. In any event, it's just good etiquette to let them know what you're up to. You don't need to do anything fancy, just a simple note telling the administrator the name of the file you uploaded, where it was uploaded to, and a short description of the file should suffice.

There are other reasons you might want to contact the site administrator. What if they don't have an /incoming directory and you'd like to find out whether they'll accept an upload? What if you uploaded a file two weeks ago and it still isn't on the site? For these or any of a number of other reasons, you'll probably need to contact someone in charge of the FTP site.

To do this, you'll generally need to use e-mail. Unfortunately, not all sites operate the same way. A couple of common e-mail addresses for FTP site administrators are listed below:

admin@*site.host.name*	Ex: admin@ftp.mcp.com
ftpadmin@*site.host.name*	Ex: ftpadmin@ftp.msu.edu
sysadmin@*site.host.name*	Ex: sysadmin@ftp.msu.edu

Remember when we told you it might be a good idea to open the Message Log window while doing an upload? This is the perfect reason why. When you do an upload, many sites actually tell you who you need to contact regarding your upload (refer to fig. 6.9).

Although it might be a while before you actually do any uploading on a regular basis, you might want to review this section occasionally to remain familiar with exactly how it's done. Knowing how to upload is yet another piece of information that will make you more knowledgeable about FTP and the Internet.

7 Adding Sites to WS_FTP's List

In this chapter:

- How do I set up a session for a new site?

- How to add a new site to WS_FTP's site list

- Tell me about advanced connection features

- I want to give my site lists to a co-worker

WS_FTP lets you speed dial the FTP servers that are most interesting to you.

If you have dozens of friends or business contacts that you call occasionally, you know how hard it is to memorize all those phone numbers. That's why manufacturers have come out with those phones that you can program a hundred numbers into. Trying to remember the addresses and directories of all those FTP sites you like to connect to is a problem similar to remembering the phone numbers of all your acquaintances. Well, WS_FTP has a programmable feature, too. You can create a list of FTP server profiles that lets you enter all of the pertinent information about a server once, and then connect with the click of your mouse anytime you want to visit that server.

Why add more sites?

You're sure to find servers that you want to visit on a regular basis that aren't in WS_FTP's preconfigured list of session profiles. You can pick up a lot of great stuff from these preconfigured sites: PC software, Internet software, games, and more. Literally thousands of FTP servers are on the Internet, and there's no doubt you'll want to visit some sites that aren't already configured.

When you open the Session Profile dialog box, you can enter the information for any server on the Net and connect to it. Add that server information to the list of preconfigured servers, and you don't have to enter it each time you want to connect to the server. All you have to do is select the server from the Profile Name list box and the other information is filled in automatically.

All the information WS_FTP needs

To add an FTP server to the preconfigured list, click Connect, fill in the Session Profile dialog box, and click Save (see fig 7.1). To connect to most servers, you can just fill in the first five text boxes. The following sections describe these boxes:

- Profile Name

- Host Name

- Host Type

- User ID

- Password

Fig. 7.1
Connect to any FTP server on the Internet through the Session Profile dialog box.

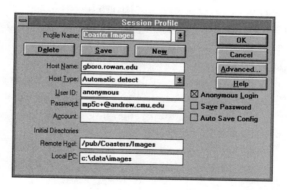

Profile Name

Notice the Profile Name text box at the top of the Session Profile dialog box. Click the down arrow and select a preconfigured server from the list. To enter a new profile, click New to clear the text fields and then type the name for this session in the Profile Name text box.

(!) (Tip)

Give each server a meaningful profile name. For example, if you want to have a profile for the server **gboro.rowan.edu** (where you can find a lot of roller coaster information), name the profile something like *Coasters*, not something similar to the server name.

You can have more than one profile entry for a particular FTP server. Because you can specify the starting directory on the FTP server in a profile, you can have different profiles that connect to the same FTP server but start in different directories (see "Local and remote directories" later in this chapter). In the roller coaster example, you can have one profile called *Coaster Images* starting in a directory that contains pictures, and one profile called *Coaster Reviews* starting in a directory that contains reviews of amusement parks and their coasters. Both profiles connect to the same server, **gboro.rowan.edu**.

Host Name

Enter the name of the FTP server you want to connect to (for example, **gboro.rowan.edu**) in the Host <u>N</u>ame text box.

(!) (Tip)

If you know that an Internet site has an FTP server, but you don't know the name of the server, add "ftp." to the front of the domain name to get the server name. For example, if you know that Microsoft has a site called **microsoft.com**, try to connect to the server **ftp.microsoft.com**.

Of course, if it's a really large site, you may have to add "ftp." to a subdomain name to find the server you want. For example, the Software Engineering Institute at Carnegie-Mellon University has the subdomain **sei.cmu.edu**, and their FTP server is **ftp.sei.cmu.edu**.

(*) {Note}

Instead of entering the name of the FTP server you are connecting to, you can enter the actual Internet address (called the **IP address**) of the server. IP addresses are explained in more detail in the "Host names and IP addresses" sidebar in Chapter 14. It is very rare that you would need to enter the IP address—it's better in almost all cases to use the name of the FTP server.

Host Type

Unless there's a problem reading the directories on the remote host, leave the Host Type set to **Automatic detect**. If you know the type of host you're connecting to, select it from the list box.

?Q&A

Why can't I see any remote directories after I've connected?

If you connect to your FTP server okay, but no directories or files are shown for the server, it may be that WS_FTP doesn't know how to handle the directory information that the server's returning. Try changing the WS_FTP host type from Automatic detect to the particular operating system or FTP server that's running on the machine you are connecting to. For example, if you know that you are connecting to a Macintosh running an NCSA FTP server, choose MAC NCSA from the list. If you know that you're connecting to a machine running the Sun Solaris operating system, choose that entry from the list.

If the directory that you've connected to is a directory where you can upload files, you might not be able to see any files listed in the directory. Be sure that you can't see *any* files or directories on the FTP server before you conclude that you need to specify the host type.

Anonymous login

Most of the time, you'll log in to **anonymous FTP** accounts on the FTP servers. Select the Anonymous Login check box, and the User ID is automatically set to *anonymous*.

User ID

Although the main focus of this book is using WS_FTP to log in to anonymous accounts on FTP servers, you can also use FTP to connect to any of your **personal accounts** on the Internet (if the sites where those accounts are permit external connections). You can transfer files from one of your Internet accounts to another. If you're going to log in to a personal account on the remote machine, type your user ID in the User ID text box.

(Tip) _____ When you're logging in to a personal account from FTP, make sure that you deselect the Anonymous Login check box.

Password

To log in to an anonymous account, you need to enter your full Internet e-mail address in the Password field. If you configure WS_FTP to know your e-mail address, it's automatically entered in the Password field when you select the Anonymous Login check box. (If you don't configure your e-mail address, WS_FTP will default the password to "guest," which is not allowed by many anonymous FTP servers.) To configure your e-mail address:

1 Click Options in the WS_FTP window.

2 Click Program Options in the Options dialog box.

Using the SYST command

If you are having a problem seeing the files and directories on an FTP server, you may need to set the specific host type of the server. What if you don't know what type of host you are connecting to?

WS_FTP lets you ask the FTP server what type of host it is. Click the right mouse button inside the WS_FTP window and you see a menu that gives you access to some of WS_FTP's features. This menu also allows you to send some FTP commands directly to the remote server. Click FTP Commands and then select SYST. This command asks the remote server what type of host it's running on.

Look at the log area of the window or choose LogWnd to open the Message Log window. There you see the SYST command that you sent and the

server's reply. Normally, the server tells you the type of host the server is running on. The server may return an error message saying that it didn't understand the SYST command, however.

You can also find the host type in the connection log because WS_FTP usually sends a SYST command when it connects. Just scroll back through the connection information in the Message Log window or Log area of the WS_FTP window. You'll find the SYST command and the server's reply.

When you know the host type, select it from the Host Type list. Not all host types will be in the list—the WS_FTP author has been adding new hosts to the list on a regular basis, however. Now you should see the directory and file information on the server.

3 Enter your full Internet e-mail address in the <u>E</u>-Mail Address text box.

4 Click Save in the Program Options dialog box, and then click E<u>x</u>it in the Options dialog box.

✱ {Note}

Some anonymous FTP servers allow you to use any password to log in. Others, however, check to see that you've entered a valid e-mail address. Although the servers can't verify your specific account, they can verify that the host name in your e-mail address is in the same domain as the machine you're FTPing from. So, enter your actual e-mail address. If your e-mail address is in a different domain than the account you're FTPing from, most servers let you connect, but warn you.

If you're logging in to a personal account, type your password for that account in the Passw<u>o</u>rd text box.

Saving and autosaving

After you've entered all the profile information, you could just choose OK to connect to the FTP server. However, if you're going to be using this server more than once, you need to tell WS_FTP to save it in the list of session profiles. You can save the profile information in two ways. One way is to choose <u>S</u>ave in the Session Profile dialog box. This writes out the profile information to your ws_ftp.ini file and adds it to the list of session profiles. The Session Profile dialog box remains open, and you can:

• Connect to the server you just entered in the list

Should you save your password?

It's not really a good idea to save your password with the session information if you are connecting to a personal account. Someone could find your password stored on the hard disk and decrypt it, or simply use the stored password to connect to your personal account and access your files. To save the profile without the password, make sure the Sa<u>v</u>e Password check box isn't selected.

- Select another server from the Profile Name list and connect to it

- Click New and enter the information for another server's profile

A second way to save the profile information is to tell WS_FTP to save it automatically. To do this, select the Auto Save Config check box. Now, each time you connect to a server, the information for that server is saved (or updated if you saved it previously).

(Tip)

You can make the Auto Save Config check box always be selected. Set this up from the Options dialog box.

1 Click Options in the WS_FTP window.

2 In the Options dialog box, click Program Options.

3 Select the Auto Save Host Config check box.

4 Click Save in the Program Options dialog box. Then click Exit in the Options dialog box.

Other information you can add

To connect to most FTP servers, all you need is the information in the first five text boxes in the Session Profile dialog box. You can add more information if you want to or if it's needed. For example, some FTP servers require you to log in to an account, as well as provide a user ID. Also, for each server, you can specify the starting directories on your local computer and on the remote server. Read on to find out about some of the optional and advanced profile information.

Account name

If you're connecting to a machine that needs an account name as well as a user ID, click in the Account box and enter the account name. It is rare for you to have to do this—you may never encounter a machine that requires it.

{Note}

If you are connecting to a personal account on an IBM VM/CMS machine, the Account field is used for the password of your default directory (and you are prompted for a password each time you change directories).

Local and remote directories

With some servers, you always want to start in the same directory. You can add that directory information in the Remote Host text box. The same is true for the starting directory on your own computer. You can set it in the Local PC text box.

If you want to set initial directories for the server or your computer, follow these steps:

1 Click Connect to open the Session Profile dialog box.

2 Select the profile you want to set directories for.

3 Enter the directory information for the server, your computer, or both:

- For the server, click the Remote Host box under Initial Directories and enter the path of the directory. If you leave this blank, you'll see the top-level directory for the server when you connect to it.

- For your computer, click the Local PC box under Initial Directories and enter the path to the initial directory on your local file system.

Saving the current directories when you are at a site

Once you've connected to a server and found a directory you like, there's an easy way to tell WS_FTP to use that directory as the initial directory for the current session profile. At the same time, you can set a directory on your local computer as the initial local directory.

Navigate your local and remote directories so that the current directories are the ones you want as default starting directories. Choose Option to open the Options dialog box, and then choose Save Dir Name.

Retrying if you don't get connected

Sometimes you can't connect to a server even if you've entered the correct address. For example, the host may be slow to respond, it may be down, or there may be network problems. If the host or network is busy, you may be able to connect by trying again immediately. You can set WS_FTP to automatically retry the connection a number of times before giving up entirely.

Click Advanced in the Session Profile dialog box and you'll see the dialog box shown in figure 7.2. Type the number of retries you want in the Retry text box.

Fig. 7.2
Set up advanced connection features for your profiles in the Advanced Profile Parameters dialog box.

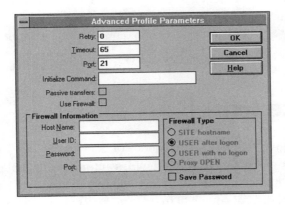

Timeout

A busy FTP server can be slow to respond to WS_FTP. You can specify how long WS_FTP waits for a response before it assumes that there's a problem with the server.

Click Advanced in the Session Profile dialog box and you'll see the Advanced Profile Parameters dialog box. In the Timeout text box, enter the amount of time (in seconds) that WS_FTP should wait for a response before giving up. (Your initial connection timeout is set by your WinSock DLL.)

Port

When you connect to any Internet host, you connect to a particular *port* on the host, depending on what service you are requesting from the host. FTP normally connects to port 21, but you may need to set it to something else if you're going through a firewall (ask your Internet system administrator).

To set the port to something other than 21, click <u>A</u>dvanced in the Session Profile dialog box. Then enter the port you want WS_FTP to connect to in the P<u>o</u>rt text box (refer to fig. 7.2).

Get rid of the profiles you don't use

WS_FTP comes with a number of predefined session profiles that allow you to get to Internet hosts containing popular programs. You probably won't use most of these servers on a regular basis. You can delete unused profiles to keep your list clutter-free. Just select a profile you don't want and then click D<u>e</u>lete. WS_FTP deletes the profile immediately, without a confirmation warning.

Share your site list

Want to give your site list to friends or colleagues? WS_FTP doesn't have a button or menu item to share the files automatically, but doing it yourself isn't that hard. Go to the directory where you keep WS_FTP and find the ws_ftp.ini file. All you need to do is make a copy of the ws_ftp.ini file, and then use Notepad or another editor to edit the copy and extract the profile list from it.

Each profile begins with a line containing the Profile Name in brackets, and ends with a blank line (see fig. 7.3). Delete everything except the profiles that you want to share, and then save the file. Be sure to save the file as text only if you are using an editor like Word.

 **<Caution>** Be sure to edit a copy of the ws_ftp.ini file. If you edit the original ws_ftp.ini file and then accidentally save it, you will have destroyed WS_FTP's configuration information.

Fig. 7.3
WS_FTP stores the
profile configurations
you've added at the
end of the ws_ftp.ini
file.

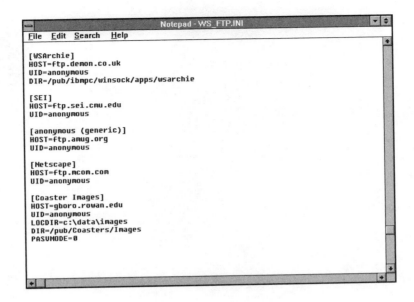

```
                              Notepad - WS_FTP.INI
 File  Edit  Search  Help

 [WSArchie]
 HOST=ftp.demon.co.uk
 UID=anonymous
 DIR=/pub/ibmpc/winsock/apps/wsarchie

 [SEI]
 HOST=ftp.sei.cmu.edu
 UID=anonymous

 [anonymous (generic)]
 HOST=ftp.amug.org
 UID=anonymous

 [Netscape]
 HOST=ftp.mcom.com
 UID=anonymous

 [Coaster Images]
 HOST=gboro.rowan.edu
 UID=anonymous
 LOCDIR=c:\data\images
 DIR=/pub/Coasters/Images
 PASUMODE=0
```

Whoever gets your list just needs to copy it into the end of their ws_ftp.ini file. Don't worry about arranging the profiles alphabetically; WS_FTP takes care of that when it displays the profiles in the Profile Name list box.

 **{Note}**

If any of the profiles you are sharing have passwords saved in them, you should delete the password line. (WS_FTP shouldn't save the password unless it is something other than your e-mail address.) If the login for the profile is anonymous, WS_FTP will use the e-mail address of the person you are sharing with if you delete yours. If the login is not anonymous, you should not share the profile. Most sites prohibit anyone but the owner of a personal account from logging in to it.

Finding Files with WSArchie

In this chapter:

- Where can I get WSArchie and how do I install it?
- How do I use WSArchie to perform searches?
- What WSArchie search results mean
- Once WSArchie finds a file, how do I retrieve the file?
- Advanced WSArchie searches

The Archie databases are like big online catalogs that you can search through to find files at FTP libraries.

Imagine that you went into your local public library and found the books were in piles all over the floor. Instead of having a central card catalog, there were notes on some of the piles describing what people had found in that pile. This scenario is how the Internet has been for most of its existence; many resources are available, but there is no easy way to locate them. Archie databases help order these resources and make them easier to find.

You can find an anonymous FTP server for almost any kind of information you might want—network statistics, computer games, pictures of roller coasters, recipes—the list is endless. Archie can find anonymous FTP servers that have the files and programs that you're looking for. WSArchie is an easy-to-use Windows application that lets you do Archie searches.

Getting WSArchie

WSArchie is readily available from many FTP servers on the Internet. You can use WS_FTP to get the most recent version of the WSArchie .zip file (currently wsarch07.zip) from **ftp.demon.co.uk** in the directory /pub/ibmpc /winsock/apps/wsarchie. See Chapter 5, "Connecting to FTP Sites with WS_FTP," and Chapter 6, "Getting and Sending Files," if you need help connecting to the FTP server and transferring the file.

⊛{Note}

You can usually find WSArchie at some of the FTP servers that have big software libraries, too. For example, **ftp.cica.indiana.edu** usually has the WSArchie file in the directory /pub/pc/win3/winsock (although, as of the writing of this book, CICA still had version 6 of WSArchie instead of version 7).

The CICA FTP server is often very busy. But if CICA has a current copy, you can also get the file from any of the CICA mirror sites. When you can't connect to CICA because there are already too many anonymous users, you get a big list of alternative FTP sites, including these CICA mirrors:

wuarchive.wustl.edu	**ftp.monash.edu.au**
ftp.cdrom.com	**ftp.uni-stuttgart.de**
polecat.law.indiana.edu	**nic.switch.ch**

❝ Plain English, please!

Mirror sites are FTP servers that keep exact copies of the files on other FTP servers. ❞

⊛{Note}

Shareware programs such as WSArchie are often improved, and you may find a new version when you look for it on an FTP server.

Installing WS_ARCHIE

⊛{Note}

To use WSArchie, you must have some form of Winsock libraries installed on your system. The Winsock libraries provide an interface to the Internet communications protocol. You almost undoubtedly have these libraries installed if your computer is connected to the Internet (they are usually provided with the software that you use to connect to your Internet account). You also must be running Windows 3.1 or better.

After you've retrieved the WSArchie .zip file from an FTP server, it's a simple matter to install it. A few short steps and you're ready to find those files you just have to have. Follow these steps and WSArchie will be ready to run:

1 Put the .zip file in a directory on your computer where you want to keep WSArchie. You will probably want to create a separate directory just for WSArchie.

2 Use PKUNZIP, WinZip, or some other ZIP utility to uncompress the .zip file. After you unpack the file, you will have the wsarchie.exe program file in the directory, plus a few others: a Windows help file, an .ini file that defines WSArchie defaults, and a text file that gives you some information about the development and use of WSArchie.

(Tip)

Put the WSArchie icon in the same program group as WS_FTP.

3 Create an icon for WSArchie in the program group of your choice. When you do this, you see the icon pictured in figure 8.1.

Fig. 8.1
Put the WSArchie icon into a program group that is convenient for you.

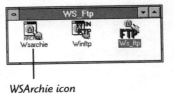

WSArchie icon

(Tip)

The easiest way to do this is to drag the wsarchie.exe file from the File Manager into a program group. Make sure that the program group is on your desktop, and that the File Manager is open to the directory where you keep the WSArchie .exe file. Drag the .exe file into the program directory to create an icon.

4 Delete the WSArchie .zip file to save space on your disk. You're now ready to run WSArchie.

A simple Archie search with WSArchie

Now that you've installed WSArchie, how do you use it? WSArchie is a Windows-based Archie client that allows you to search for file names on registered anonymous FTP sites by filling out a simple form. After you submit the form containing the information you want to search for, Archie returns the host names and directory paths of the matching files it found.

Filling out the form

To use WSArchie, you first need to connect to the Internet. Then, simply start WSArchie and fill out the form.

1 Double-click the WSArchie icon from the Program Manager to open the WinSock Archie Client window (see fig. 8.2).

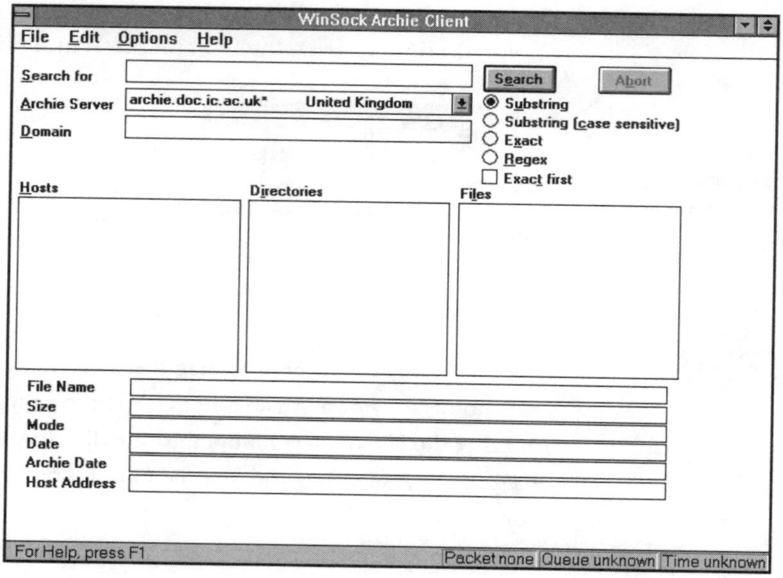

Fig. 8.2
The WinSock Archie Client window allows you to choose your Archie server, enter your search string, and specify the search type.

2 Click the radio button next to the type of search you want to do. Substring usually returns the most matches. We explain what the different search types mean later in this chapter in the section "Search types in WSArchie."

3 Click the Search For text box and enter the name of the file (or part of the name) that you want to search for.

4 If you want to use a different server, choose one from the Archie Server list (see fig. 8.3). You might want to scroll through the list and pick one geographically close to you.

Fig. 8.3
You can use a number of different Archie servers to do your search.

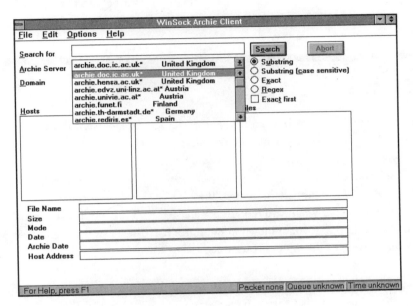

During peak hours (generally from 9:00 a.m. through 6:00 p.m.), it may be better to pick a site overseas where it is the middle of the night. Sites such as these may have less traffic than local sites and may respond faster.

Of course, overseas Archie servers have their problems, too. They will probably default to European FTP sites (you can usually set the *domain* on the Archie server so that it will search US sites, too). But their server may not have any US listings for the file you're looking for, and transferring files from overseas may be slow. A little bit faster here, slower there, it may all even out.

5 Leave the Domain text box blank.

6 Click Search.

WSArchie starts your search by connecting to the Archie server you've specified. Your title bar shows the server you selected and the timeout period for connection attempts. The timeout period specifies how long WSArchie waits for the server to respond before it decides that the request failed. WSArchie tries to connect to the Archie server three or four times before it gives up. When WSArchie connects to the Archie server, you're assigned a place in the server's queue after other searches are requested.

Status messages

In the status bar at the bottom of the window, WSArchie gives you information about the progress of your request. Archie servers process the search requests one-at-a-time as they receive them. As new searches are requested, they are put into a queue. When you request a search, your place in the queue is shown in the status bar at the bottom of the WSArchie window.

In addition to the queue position, you see the number of seconds that the Archie server expects to elapse before your search is completed (this information isn't updated after you're placed in the queue). This is not always an accurate estimate, but it can give you some idea of how long you have to wait (10 minutes versus an hour, for example). If your queue position is much over 10, or the estimated time over 10 minutes, you might want to cancel the search and try it again later.

When your search is completed, WSArchie increments the **packet** count (the number of transmitted data units) in the status bar as it receives the results from the Archie server.

You may see timeout errors in the status bar as the information from the search is returned to WSArchie. This is usually okay because the communications protocol tries again if the transmission fails occasionally. As long as your packet count is increasing in the status bar, your connection is okay. If the connection is for some reason broken (the Archie server goes down, or serious noise develops on the communications line), you get an alert box informing you of a timeout failure.

 Plain English, please!

Packets are the chunks of information that get sent from one computer to another on the Internet. Packets are limited in size, so it may take dozens of packets to transmit the Archie search results to your computer.

②Q&A

> **Why can't I connect to the Archie server I've picked?**
> If you try to do an Archie search and get a message saying that you can't connect to the server you've chosen, the server may be down or may no longer exist. Or, that server may just have reached its limit for the number of people allowed to do searches at one time. Try selecting a different server and doing the search again.

Understanding the search results

If the Archie search is successful, WSArchie gives you information about all the files that matched. In the Hosts area of the window, you see a list of hosts that had files that matched your search string. (See the figure in "The WSArchie search results" sidebar on the following page.) The Directories area shows you the directory paths to the files, and the Files area shows you the names of the files that matched in the selected directory.

①(Tip)

> After WSArchie receives the results of the Archie search, you can disconnect your Internet connection if you need to and still examine the results of the search.

You can get detailed information about all of the files in the results. To examine the information about the files that were found, follow these steps:

1 Click the host you want to look at. The Directories area shows you the directories on that host that contain matching files.

2 Click the directory you want to examine. The files that match your search are listed in the Files area.

3 When you click a file, WSArchie shows you information about that file, including:

- The name of the file
- The size of the file, in bytes
- The protection of the file (Mode)

The WSArchie search results

The WinSock Archie Client window shows you the FTP server and directory location of the files that matched your search parameters.

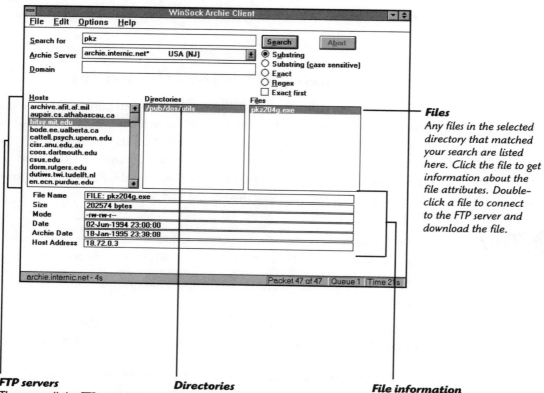

Files
Any files in the selected directory that matched your search are listed here. Click the file to get information about the file attributes. Double-click a file to connect to the FTP server and download the file.

FTP servers
These are all the FTP servers that WSArchie knows about that have the file that you were searching for. Click an FTP server to get a listing of directories that contain matching files.

Directories
The directories on the selected server that contain the file you were looking for are listed here. Click a directory to get a list of matching files. Double-click a directory to get a complete listing of the directory.

File information
The attributes of the selected file are shown here. This includes the name of the file, the size of the file in bytes, the file protection (Mode), the date the file was last modified, the date that Archie last checked the file, and the IP address of the FTP server where the last file was found.

- The date the file was last modified
- The date the Archie server last checked the file's existence
- The IP address of the host where the file resides

⊛ {Note}

You really don't need to know anything about the file protection (Mode) field. The file protection normally limits who can read, write to, and execute a file. All you're concerned about is whether you can read the file or not, and files that are placed on anonymous FTP servers should be protected so that anyone can read them. That is, after all, the purpose of an anonymous FTP server.

If any of the results shown in the Files area are directories, you can retrieve the contents of those directories. Click the item, open the File menu, and select Retrieve (or just double-click the directory name in the Files area). All of the files in that directory are shown in the Files area.

❶ (Tip)

If you want to see the entire contents of any of the directories that contain matching files, select the directory in the Directories area, open the File menu, and choose Expand. Or double-click the directory.

Canceling a search

What if you decide you want to cancel the search after you've started it? Maybe the search time in the status bar (discussed in the "Status Messages" sidebar earlier in this chapter) indicates that your search will take a very long time to finish. Or maybe you've thought of a better search to do. After the search begins, you can abort it by clicking Abort in the WinSock Archie Client window. Once you abort a query, you can submit another one.

Retrieving files that WSArchie finds

Now that you have the results of your WSArchie search, you can retrieve any files that interest you. To do this, you can always write down the name of the host and the directory path of the file that interests you, and then use any

FTP program to connect to the host's anonymous FTP server and retrieve the file. If you have WS_FTP, however, retrieving the file is a much simpler process.

Setting up WSArchie to work with WS_FTP

If you have WS_FTP installed on your system, you can retrieve files directly from WSArchie. First, you must tell WSArchie where to find the WS_FTP program and what parameters it should use when it tries to connect to an FTP server. Follow these steps:

1 Start the WSArchie application. Open the Options menu and choose FTP setup. You see the FTP Setup dialog box shown in figure 8.4.

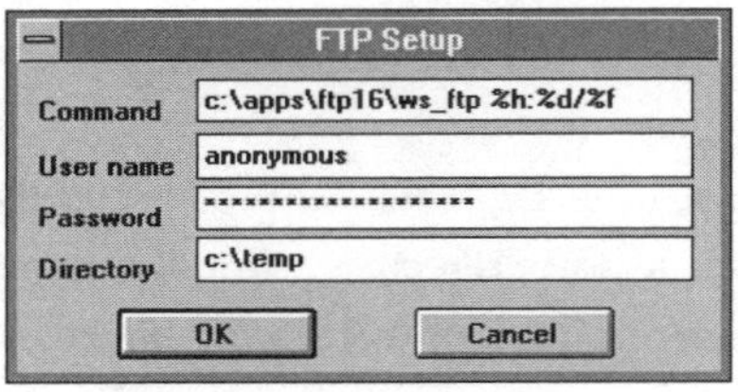

Fig. 8.4
The FTP Setup dialog box allows you to set up WSArchie to automatically use WS_FTP to retrieve files found in the Archie search.

FTP Setup

Command c:\apps\ftp16\ws_ftp %h:%d/%f
User name anonymous
Password ·····················
Directory c:\temp

OK   Cancel

2 Click the Command text box and enter the complete path to the WS_FTP file on your hard disk. Do not delete the "ws_ftp %h:%d/%f"; simply add the path information to the front of it.

3 The User Name text box defaults to "anonymous." Don't change it.

4 Click the Password text box and enter the password you'll use to log in to the account. Many anonymous FTP servers allow you to log in with any password; however, others ask that you use your e-mail address, and some require it, so enter your Internet e-mail address here. (Your password will appear as asterisks.)

5 Click the Directory text box and enter the path to the directory on your computer where you want to put the retrieved file.

●(Tip)

Set up a default temporary directory to initially store the files that you retrieve. Transferring the files to a temporary directory avoids accidentally overwriting other files on your disk that have the same name as the files you are transferring.

❓Q&A

Where did the file go?

If the directory name that you entered in the FTP Setup dialog box doesn't exist, WS_FTP doesn't give you any type of error message and simply exits without completing the transfer. Make sure that you enter a valid directory. The default value is "." (period), which stands for the current directory (the working directory for WSArchie).

6 Choose OK to complete the setup.

Retrieving a file from WSArchie

After you set up your WS_FTP information, you can automatically retrieve a file from the list of matching files that WSArchie returns to you.

1 Select the file that you want to retrieve in the Files area of the WinSock Archie Client window.

2 Open the File menu and choose Retrieve (or double-click the file you want to retrieve).

3 You'll get a dialog box showing the WS_FTP command that is being used to transfer the file (see fig. 8.5). Choose OK to retrieve the file, or choose Cancel if you don't want to transfer the file.

Fig. 8.5
A confirmation dialog box showing the location of the file you are retrieving appears when you request a file transfer.

```
                    FTP Command
c:\apps\wsftp\ws_ftp bitsy.mit.edu:/pub/dos/utils/pkz204g.exe
              OK              Cancel
```

❋ {Note} _____

If you decide to download one of the files you've found, check the size of the file in the file statistics section of the WinSock Archie Client window. Make sure that your computer has enough space to store the file; you may have to remove some files on your disk to successfully complete the download.

❓ Q&A _____

Why didn't WSArchie get the file?

When you try to download a matching file, you may get a "file not found" error from WS_FTP. Remember that the Archie servers only update their information every so often—and things are constantly changing on the Internet. The file may have been deleted from the server, or it may have been moved to another directory. It's also possible that the file has a new name.

If this happens to you, try to download another one of the files in the results list. Pick one that has a recent Archie Date. Or, you can use WS_FTP to connect to the server you originally tried to load the file from, and look around the server to see if you can find the file in a new location.

WSArchie starts WS_FTP minimized. When WS_FTP successfully connects to the FTP server and finds the file, it starts the transfer process. A Transfer Status dialog box opens behind all of your other windows (see fig. 8.6). If you want to see how far along the transfer is, you can minimize your other windows, or switch to WS_FTP to see the Transfer dialog box. When the transfer is complete, the WS_FTP icon disappears. You can check the incoming directory you specified to see if the file transferred successfully.

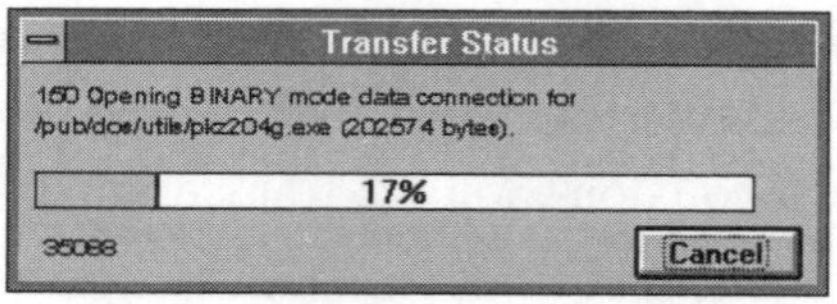

Fig. 8.6
The Transfer Status dialog box tells you the type of FTP transfer you're doing, the location of the file you're transferring, and the percentage complete. It also lets you cancel the transfer.

⊗\<Caution\> WS_FTP doesn't check to see if you already have a file in the incoming directory with the same name as the one you're transferring (unless you activated the Receive Unique feature in the Session Options dialog box). If you transfer a file with the same name as one already in the directory, the one in the directory is overwritten.

❓Q&A *Why does the program or picture I've retrieved seem to be corrupted?*

If the file you want to download is a **binary file**, your FTP program may not be set to properly transfer it. A binary file is one that contains characters that can't be printed or displayed. Generally, executable programs, compressed files (files made smaller with a program such as PKZIP or the UNIX compress program), and picture or sound files are binary data. Most FTP programs have a binary command that lets you properly transfer binary files. If you aren't sure whether the file is binary, set your FTP program so that binary is the default transfer mode; in most cases (unless the remote computer and yours specify end-of-line differently), you can transfer nonbinary files in binary mode without problems.

More sophisticated Archie searches with WSArchie

Archie lets you narrow your search so that the matching files are as close to what you're looking for as possible. For example, if the file name that you're looking for has upper- and lowercase letters, you can tell WSArchie to match the case of the file name exactly when it does the search. You can also limit the types of servers you want Archie to search if you have an idea of where the file is.

Limiting the search to a domain with WSArchie

You can limit your search to a specific domain (such as "edu" for educational hosts), or site (such as "umn.edu"), or even a specific server (**ftp.umn.edu**). You might want to do this if you know the server where a file is located, but can't remember the directory it's in. Or, you may know that the file is likely to be found on an educational server, or a server in a particular country. Click the Domain text box and enter the domain information for the servers you want to search.

Search types in WSArchie

If you know the exact (or almost exact) name of the file you want to search for, you can tell Archie to narrow the search. You can search for files that match your search string exactly (including the case of the letters), or you can specify partial matching.

Search limitations

The main limitation of Archie is that you must know at least something about the name of the file to search for it. If you don't have any idea what the file is called (for example, you want a program that searches for viruses on your machine and don't know that it is called *scanv*), you may have to try several searches using different strings before you find something that looks useful.

Because Archie servers can only search for names of the files, you must know at least part of the file name you are looking for. For example, if you're looking for a program that compresses files (makes them smaller), you can search for *com-press*. Archie returns the location of all the files named "compress," or that have "compress" as

part of their name, depending on whether you specified an exact match or substring search. However, doing this particular search doesn't find any of the compression utilities whose file names are based on the term "zip."

Another limitation of Archie is that not all sites on the Internet that have anonymous FTP participate in the Archie database. Somewhere on the Net there may be a file that matches your search, but if it's at a site that's not registered in the Archie database, you can't find that file with Archie.

Even given these limitations, Archie is a very useful tool for locating files.

There are four radio buttons and a check box under the Search button that let you pick the type of search you want WSArchie to do. Click the radio button next to the type of search that you think will return the best results for you. The table below describes the different types of searches. If you select the Exact first check box, WSArchie tries to perform an Exact search first. If it doesn't find a match, it does the search over again, using the search type specified by the radio button.

Search type	Description
Substring	WSArchie returns any files it finds whose names contain the search string (upper- and lowercase letters are ignored).
Substring [case sensitive]	WSArchie returns any files it finds whose names contain the search string with the case of the letters matching exactly.
Exact	WSArchie returns any files it finds whose names exactly match the search string that was entered (including case).
Regex	WSArchie returns any files it finds that match the regular expression specified.

⊛ {Note}

A **regular expression** is a way of specifying the possible values for a search string without specifying the exact letters. When you enter the search string, enter the character pattern that you want Archie to search for. You can use individual characters, ranges of letters and numbers, and special characters to build your search string. The following table lists the most common regular expression elements you can use.

⊛ *{Note}*

Element	Definition
.	Matches any single character
*	Matches zero or more occurrences of the preceding character
[ ]	Lets you specify a range or set of characters
^	Matches anything but the character following it
\	Lets you tell Archie to include the special character following it (like ^) in the file name instead of interpreting it as a special character.

This is not a search type that you'll need to use very often. But you might find it useful for doing something like searching for the most recent version of a file. For a more detailed discussion of regular expressions (including some examples), see the "Regular expression" section in Chapter 16.

Copying Archie search results

If you get a lot of matching files from your Archie search, you might want to keep a copy of the results so that you can explore the matching servers at your leisure. Or, you might want to copy pieces of the results and paste them into another application. WSArchie lets you save the results of a search to a text file, or you can copy any of the file, directory, or host information to the Clipboard.

Copying the whole thing

There are two ways you can save the entire search results. One way is to save the results directly to a text file. To do this, open the File menu and choose Save. Use the file browser in the Save As window to specify the file where you want to write the results. The results are saved as a list of hosts. Each directory that contains matching files is listed under its host name, with the names of the matching files shown under each directory.

If you don't want to save the results directly to a file, you can copy the results to the Clipboard, open the Edit menu, and choose Copy Result. The results are formatted the same way they are when you save them to a file. You can now paste the results into another application as you would any Clipboard contents.

Copying a site, directory, or file name

Rather than copying the entire results from your search, you may just want to keep the information about a few of the matching files. WSArchie lets you copy individual pieces of the results to the Clipboard. Select the host, file, or directory that you're interested in and open the Edit menu. If you want to keep the file name, choose Copy File. If you want to keep the directory information, choose Copy Directory. If you want to keep the host name, choose Copy Host. The individual piece that you've copied will be on the Clipboard, and you can paste it into an editor or any other application as you would any Clipboard contents.

Setting your default search parameters

You can set default values for the search parameters so that every time you start WSArchie, these values are set to the ones most useful to you.

1 Open the Options menu and select User Preferences. The User Preferences dialog box appears (see fig. 8.7).

Fig. 8.7
The User Preferences dialog box lets you set the default values for your WinSock Archie search window.

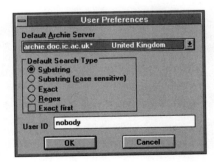

2 Select your default Archie server from the Default Archie Server drop-down list.

3 Select the radio button that corresponds to the type of search you do most frequently (Substring, Substring [case sensitive], Exact, or Regex).

4 If you want to try exact matches first, select the Exact first check box.

It's not necessary to change the User ID field.

Exiting WS_ARCHIE

When you complete all your Archie searches, open the File menu and choose Exit to close WSArchie.

Security and Other Advanced Features

In this chapter:

- What is a firewall and why do I need to know about it?
- Can I still use FTP if I'm behind a firewall?
- Can I transfer a file automatically?
- What if I need to send a special command to an FTP server?

The Internet's getting to be like a big city neighborhood—you have to lock your doors if you don't want people nosing around.

At one time, the Internet was a small community. All of the people who used it worked for a university or the government. People who developed Internet software in this environment weren't really worried about security. Internet citizens trusted each other, and if anyone violated that trust, they were severely chastised.

Things are different now. Anyone can get an Internet account. Some of the original Internet services and common Internet operating systems had security holes. Creative vandals drove the proverbial trucks through the holes (and loaded those trucks up with goodies from the violated sites). Seriously, if you don't take some precautions, putting sensitive data on your Internet site can be like leaving the door to your house open and inviting people to steal your jewelry.

Although you want your site to be secure, certain security measures can make it difficult to use many of the basic Internet services. One of the most common types of security measures at Internet sites is the **firewall**. Certain types of firewalls can make it difficult to transfer files to and from a site. WS_FTP can be configured to let you transfer files through common firewalls, which can be very convenient if your site has a firewall.

> 66 *Plain English, please!*
>
> A **firewall** is a piece of communications hardware that is placed between your organization's network and the rest of the Internet. Its purpose is to keep unauthorized communications from entering (and sometimes leaving) your organization's site. 99

How to control site access

One of the best ways your system administrator can prevent unauthorized access to an Internet site is to keep track of what's sent to and from your network. This can be done several different ways. One way is with a simple piece of communications hardware that all sites need to connect to the Internet: a **router**. A router normally sorts out where to send communications going to and from your network. Your system administrators can set up a router so that it automatically refuses certain types of communications and directs other communications to a specific machine at your site.

Some sites have more elaborate firewalls where all external communications must be handled by a specific host. A firewall can let you:

- Prevent outside hosts from using any ports on hosts connected to your network

- Restrict the use of various Internet services

- Limit what external hosts can connect to your site

> 66 *Plain English, please!*
>
> **Ports** are addresses on a host that outside computers can request a connection to. Usually, these addresses run a program. This is how most Internet services are provided (for example, most hosts use port 21 for FTP services). 99

However, keeping others from getting into your site can also make it hard for users to get out of your site to use Internet services. Often you're required to connect to the firewall host and do all of your transfers from that host. WS_FTP lets you configure the firewall host information so that WS_FTP can connect to remote hosts and do file transfers without you having to deal explicitly with the firewall.

What are passive transfers?

When you transfer a file between two hosts, the hosts talk to each other to set up the transfer. When you connect to an FTP server, the server makes a request to your host to open a communications channel that it can use to send the data that you want to transfer. Most router-based firewalls prohibit an outside host from opening a communications channel. To get around this, you can request that an FTP server use **passive transfer mode**.

When you connect to an FTP server using passive transfer mode (PASV), the FTP server sends a message telling you what communications channel it wants to use. It then lets your FTP program open the channel from behind the firewall (rather than the remote server opening the channel). This is usually not a problem, since most firewalls allow internal hosts to open outgoing connections.

Although many FTP servers are starting to use PASV mode by default, you may find that you need to specifically ask the FTP server to use it if you are behind a firewall. If you're using WS_FTP, you can configure it to always request PASV transfers.

1 Choose Options. The Options dialog box appears (see fig. 9.1).

2 Click Session Options. The Session Options dialog box appears (see fig. 9.2).

3 Select Use PASV Transfer Mode, Save as Default, and then click Save. The Sessions Options dialog box closes and you see the Options dialog box.

4 Click Exit.

Fig. 9.1
The Options dialog
box lets you configure
the look and behavior
of WS_FTP.

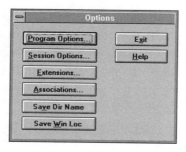

Fig. 9.2
The Session Options
dialog box lets you
configure how WS_FTP
behaves while
connected to an FTP
server.

*Select this check box
for PASV transfer
mode*

*Select this check box if
you are behind a firewall*

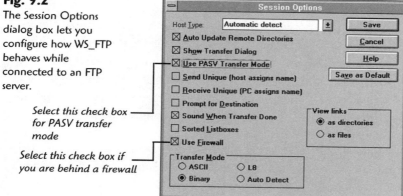

⊛ {Note}

A few FTP servers don't support PASV transfer mode (which is in violation of
the Internet standards). If you're behind a firewall and need to use PASV mode
for your transfers, you can't connect to FTP servers that don't support PASV.

To learn more about FTP passive transfers (and FTP in general), read the
Internet RFC documents 959, 1123, and 1579. You can find these RFCs at a
number of FTP sites that have collections of Internet-related information. See
Chapter 17, "The Best Sources of Software and Computing Information."

Setting firewall options

All of your external communications will need to go through your site's
firewall. You can configure the name of the firewall and the account
information that WS_FTP needs in order to use the firewall for file transfers.

If WS_FTP is configured properly, it can go through the firewall automatically, without your having to see the commands that connect to the firewall.

To tell WS_FTP that you're behind a firewall:

1 Click Options. The Options dialog box appears.

2 Click Session Options. The Session Options dialog box appears.

3 Select Use Firewall and Save as Default.

4 Click Save. The Sessions Options dialog box closes and you see the Options dialog box.

5 Click Exit.

(Tip)

> If you just click the Save button in the Session Options dialog box, your changes are in effect during the current FTP session only. If you want WS_FTP to use the new settings all the time (which you probably do if your system is behind a firewall), select Save as Default before clicking Save.

Once you've told WS_FTP that you're behind a firewall, you need to enter the firewall information in your session profiles. The Session Profile dialog box that appears when you choose Connect from the WS_FTP command buttons has an Advanced button that lets you get to the firewall definition section (see fig. 9.3). The various parts of the Firewall Information box are described in the following sections.

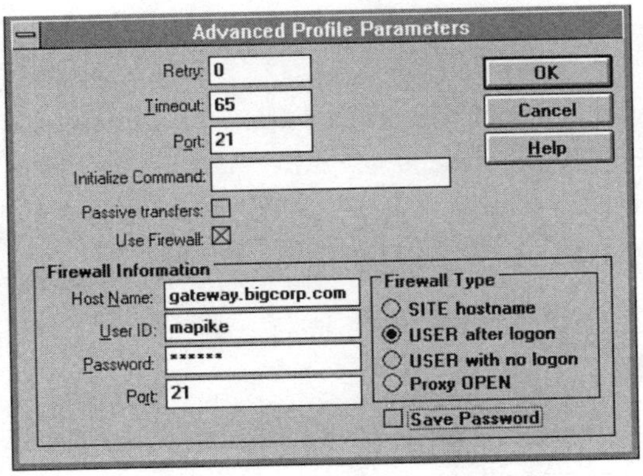

Fig. 9.3
The Advanced Profile Parameters dialog box lets you configure your firewall information and save it so that you don't need to enter it every time you connect to an FTP server.

* *{Note}*___ If your site uses some type of firewall, your system administrator may have already provided you with a WS_FTP configuration file that has the firewall information set up so that you don't have to do it yourself. If you have any questions about the firewall configuration for your site, talk to your system administrator. They're paid to understand that kind of stuff.

Hostname

If you're behind a **gateway** type of firewall (where all external communications are handled by one host on your network), you need to let WS_FTP know the name of the gateway machine. Enter the gateway's Internet host name (for example, gateway.bigcorp.com) in the Host Name text box.

User ID

If your gateway requires that you actually log in to do file transfers, you need to enter your user ID on the gateway machine in the User ID text box.

Password

If your gateway requires that you actually log in to do file transfers, you need to enter your account password on the gateway machine in the Password text box.

Port

Normally, you connect to port 21 to do FTP transfers, but your gateway may require WS_FTP to connect to a different port. Get this information from your system administrator. If WS_FTP needs to connect to a port other than 21, enter the port number in the Port text box.

Firewall Type

WS_FTP understands how to do file transfers through four different types of firewall gateways. Ask your system administrator which type of gateway your site uses, and then click the radio button that corresponds to your gateway type. WS_FTP understands the four types of firewalls described in the following table.

Firewall type	Description
SITE hostname	This type of firewall requires you to log on to the firewall with an account name and password. WS_FTP sends the name of the FTP server you want to connect to the gateway machine.
USER after logon	This type of firewall requires you to log on to the firewall with an account name and password. WS_FTP passes the login information for the FTP server to the gateway machine so that it can do the login for you.
USER with no logon	This type of firewall doesn't require that you log on. WS_FTP passes the login information for the FTP server to the gateway machine so that it can do the login for you.
Proxy OPEN	This type of firewall doesn't require that you log on. The firewall accepts a command from WS_FTP to connect to the FTP server. This allows the gateway to open the connection to the FTP server instead of your doing it from your machine.

Should you save your password?

When you set up the firewall information for your FTP sessions, you have the option of saving the firewall password (if it's required) so that you don't have to enter it each time. WS_FTP saves the password (in an encrypted format) in its configuration file. This means that someone who gets hold of your WS_FTP configuration file can't tell what your password is by looking at your file.

However, if someone copies the firewall information out of your configuration file and puts it in their own WS_FTP configuration file, this lets them use the firewall when they probably aren't authorized to do so (why else did they copy your firewall information?). The idea of having a firewall that requires logons is that not everybody at a site is allowed to do external communications. You might not want to save your password if there's any chance that someone else might have access to your files.

?Q&A

> ### Do I always need to use my site's firewall?
>
> You will need to use your firewall any time that you want to communicate with hosts outside of your network. If you only use WS_FTP to connect to outside hosts, you can set it up so that all of your session profiles will use the firewall information.
>
> If you select Use Firewall in the Session Options dialog box, WS_FTP by default checks the Use Firewall box in the Advanced Profile Parameters dialog box and fills in the firewall information for each of your session profiles. However, you might not always need to use the firewall for your FTP connections.
>
> For example, if you're at a large site and often FTP to other machines on your network, you shouldn't need to use the firewall to get to those machines. In this case, you might not want to select the Use Firewall check box in the Session Options dialog box. Instead, you can just select the Use Firewall check box in the Advanced Profile Parameters dialog box of the session profiles for any external FTP servers you connect to (remember to save the profiles after you configure the firewall information). This way, WS_FTP does not try to use the firewall when it connects to internal FTP servers.

Auto transferring files with command-line options

What if you regularly connect to an FTP server and retrieve the same file in order to get the latest version (or, send the same file to a server to update it)? Wouldn't it be nice to automatically transfer the file by clicking an icon instead of having to open up WS_FTP, connect to the server, and retrieve or send the file? Well, you can do this using WS_FTP's command-line options. To create an icon that starts WS_FTP and transfers a file automatically:

1 Create a new program group if you want to. To do this, open the File menu in the Program Manager and select New. Click the Program Group radio button and then click OK. Enter the name of the program group in the Description text box, and then click OK.

If you don't want to create a new program group, open the program group that you want the icon to appear in.

2 Now create a new program item. To do this, open the File menu in the Program Manager and select New. Click the Program Item radio button and then click OK.

3 Enter the name of the program item in the Description text box.

4 If you want WS_FTP to retrieve a file, set the Command Line to:

```
ws_ftp hostname:full_path_to_file
[local:full_path_to_destination] [-ascii]
```

If you want WS_FTP to send a file, set the Command Line to:

```
ws_ftp local:full_path_to_file
hostname:full_path_to_file [-ascii]
```

The parameters in the command line are as follows:

Parameter	Description
hostname	Either the name of a session profile or the name of the FTP server that you want to connect to
full_path_to_file	The directory path to the file you want to send or receive (you also need to use this to specify where you want to store a file on the remote server when you're sending a file)
full_path_to_destination	Optionally lets you specify where to store the retrieved file on your local file system (if you have the Working Directory set in the program item, you don't need to use this option)
-ascii	Tells WS_FTP to use ASCII mode to transfer the file (it defaults to binary)

Here are some examples of commands you might use to retrieve files using an icon. The first example uses the "gw2000" session profile as the hostname. The second example shows the full path to the WS_FTP executable and uses an actual host name.

```
ws_ftp gw2000:/pub/gateway2000/README
local:c:\temp\gwreadme.txt

c:\slip\ftp\ws_ftp.exe ftp.microsoft.com:
➥/peropsys/Win_News/Newsltr/v2n2.txt
```

Here are some examples of commands you might use to send files using an icon. The first example uses the "que" session profile as the hostname. The second example shows the full path to the WS_FTP executable and uses an actual host name.

```
ws_ftp local:c:\book\areview.zip que:/incoming/
map_ar.zip

c:\slip\ftp\ws_ftp.exe local:c:\data\images\tboltmp.gif
gboro.rowan.edu:/pub/Coasters/Images/tboltmp.gif
```

 *{Note}*

If you enter the directory where WS_FTP lives as the working directory, you don't need to give the path to WS_FTP in the command. If your working directory is different, however, you need to put the full path to your WS_FTP executable in the command.

5 Set the <u>W</u>orking Directory to the directory where you want to store a retrieved file. If you specified the full path to the WS_FTP executable in the command line, the working directory is set to the WS_FTP directory by default.

6 Click OK to create the program item.

Now, all you need to do to transfer the file is click the icon. WS_FTP logs in to the remote host using the information in the session profile, if one exists. (If you specify a host name rather than a profile name, WS_FTP does an anonymous login to that host.) If you need to enter a password for the session profile you used, you're prompted for one. Once the connection is made to the host, the file transfers automatically. If there are any problems connecting to the host or transferring the file, you should get a dialog box indicating the problem.

Sending quoted commands

Occasionally, you may want to send an FTP command directly to an FTP server. For example, if you log in to a personal account on the FTP server, and you want to change to a different personal account (or to the anonymous account on that server), you can use the USER FTP command to change your current account on the server. WS_FTP lets you send FTP commands directly:

1 Right-click anywhere in the WS_FTP window to display the menu shown in figure 9.4.

Fig. 9.4
The FTP menu lets you get at WS_FTP's commands from a menu instead of from the command buttons in the window.

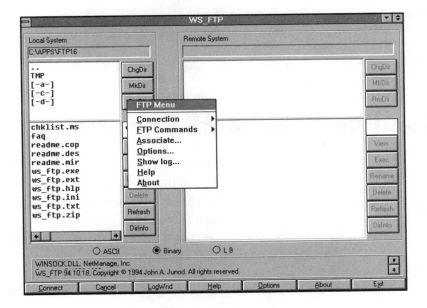

2 From the pop-up menu, select FTP Commands to get a list of FTP commands you can send directly to a server (see fig. 9.5).

3 Select QUOTE from the list of commands. The Input dialog box appears (see fig. 9.6). Enter the FTP command followed by any parameters it needs in the text box. For example, if you want to change your current account from your personal account to the anonymous account on the server, enter **USER anonymous** in the text box.

Fig. 9.5
The FTP Commands list
lets you send FTP
commands directly to
the remote server.

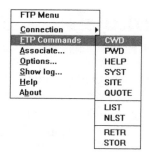

Fig. 9.6
The Input dialog box
lets you enter the
information that you
want to send directly
to the remote FTP
server.

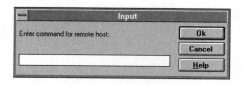

4 Choose OK to send the command to the remote FTP server.

Sending commands specific to a site

Occasionally, you may find that you need to send a command to an FTP
server that isn't one of the standard FTP commands. For example, if certain
files on an FTP server can only be accessed by a particular group of people,
the FTP server may have a GROUP command that lets you tell the server that
you belong to that group. WS_FTP lets you send site specific commands
using the following procedure:

1 Click the right mouse button in the gray background of the WS_FTP
window. This brings up the pop-up menu shown in figure 9.4.

2 From the pop-up menu, select FTP Commands to get a list of FTP
commands you can send directly to a server (see fig. 9.5).

3 When you select SITE from the list of commands, you get the Input
dialog box shown in figure 9.6. Enter the parameters for the SITE
command in the text box. For example, if you want to send the command SITE GROUP eteam, enter **GROUP eteam** in the text box
(WS_FTP automatically sends the SITE part of the command).

4 Choose OK to send the command to the remote FTP server.

Part III:

FTP for Macintosh

10

Connecting to FTP Sites with Anarchie

In this chapter:

- How do I install, register, and customize Anarchie?
- Anarchie Bookmarks give you easy FTP access
- Getting around FTP sites
- How you can find what you want
- How do I quit?
- You can keep track of what you've done

You use a Mac and you want to be able to fully utilize the capabilities of FTP. Anarchie is the tool for you.

Anarchie (pronounced *an-ar-kee*), which comes from the active mind of Macintosh Internet guru Peter Lewis, is probably the best FTP client available today. Not only does Anarchie allow you to perform any FTP function you'll ever need, it also lets you conduct Archie searches from the same application. Its interface also lets you go from Find to Transfer in one easy step.

Anarchie version 1.4 is the most current and can be found at **ftp.mcp.com/ pub/que/macnet-cd/Anarchie-140.sea**. If you get your copy of Anarchie from FTP, we suggest that you use the Macmillan Computer Publishing's site, since this self-extracting version is the easiest to install.

If you located and acquired your copy from a different source, you may have a slightly different version. Version 1.4 comes with updated Bookmarks, documentation, registration information, and Help files (see fig. 10.1).

Fig. 10.1
The current version of Anarchie has extensive documentation, Help files, updated Book-marks, and more.

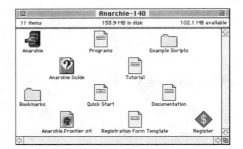

Installing Anarchie

Installing Anarchie is easy. Depending on how you got your copy, there are several different things that you may have to do. If your copy already has all of the separate files decompressed, installing is merely a matter of dragging the folder to the location of your choice. Anarchie contains no files that need to be placed in Control Panels, Extensions, or other special folders.

If you have a copy that is compressed, how you extract the various files depends on the compression method used. Anarchie is generally compressed in one of three ways: as a self-extracting archive (.sea), as a StuffIt archive (.sit), or as a BinHex archive (.hqx).

- **.sea.** If your version is a self-extracting archive (indicated by a file name like anarchie-14.sea), then simply double-clicking the file's icon successfully decompresses it. Once it has extracted the appropriate files, you can then proceed with the installation. If you got your copy from **ftp.mcp.com**, this is the procedure you will use.

- **.sit.** If your version is a StuffIt archive (indicated by a file name like anarchie-14.sit), you need to use a program such as StuffIt Lite or StuffIt Expander. To expand this type of file, drag and drop the compressed Anarchie icon onto the Unstuffing program's icon and follow the prompts to decompress it. You can find both StuffIt Lite and StuffIt Expander at **ftp.switch.ch** in the /mirror/info-mac/Compress-Translate/ directory. For Anarchie, we suggest you use StuffIt Expander.

- **.hqx**. If your file has a name like anarchie-14.hqx or anarchie-14.sit.hqx, you need to use a utility such as StuffIt Lite. StuffIt Lite both de-binhexes and unstuffs a file if you simply drag and drop the file's icon onto StuffIt Lite's icon.

Where do I put it?

If you are like many Internet users, you will have more than just one program to access the Internet. For simplicity, ease-of-use, and accessibility, we recommend that you create a folder where you can put all your communications software. We also recommend that you keep all the files in the Anarchie-140 folder together in one place. You can then throw away any icons as they become unnecessary.

One possibility is to create a folder and call it Communications. Then, you can drag the Anarchie folder into this folder, along with your e-mail client, your Gopher client, and whatever other Internet clients you may have.

How do I get to it?

You can, of course, simply open the folder and double-click the Anarchie icon anytime you want to use it. However, you may not want to go through the trouble of opening several folders every time you want to use it. In a few easy steps you can make Anarchie instantly accessible.

1 Single-click the Anarchie icon.

2 In the Finder, open the File menu and choose Make Alias.

3 A new icon called **Anarchie Alias** appears. Rename this icon if you want to. Simply drag this icon to the Apple Menu Items folder located in the System folder. From now on, simply open the Apple menu and choose Anarchie and you'll be ready to go.

Registering Anarchie

If you try out Anarchie and decide to continue using it, you are asked to pay the shareware fee of 10 dollars. Considering all that Anarchie gives you, 10 dollars is a bargain. The registration process for Anarchie is quick and easy.

⊛ *{Note}*

Only a small percentage of users who use shareware actually pay for it. We encourage you to be one of the minority. Paying for shareware is not only ethical, but also provides the money necessary for software authors to continue writing useful, inexpensive software.

First, double-click the Register icon located in the Anarchie-140 folder. You are asked to provide your name, e-mail address, payment method, and registration information (see fig. 10.2). Fill out the registration form and print it. Then mail it along with your payment (made out to Kagi Shareware) to:

Kagi Shareware
1442-A Walnut Street #392-PL
Berkeley, CA 94709-1405

If you choose to pay with Visa or MasterCard, you can e-mail the registration form to **shareware@kagi.com**, or fax a copy to 1-510-652-6589.

Fig. 10.2
After filling out the appropriate information, simply print out the registration form and mail it in with your payment. This example shows that the user chose to pay with a check.

After registering your copy, you can eliminate the annoying registration notice that appears every time you use Anarchie. Not only that, but, as Anarchie tells you, you can brag to all your friends that you register all your shareware.

⑪(Tip)

The Help Guide recommends that you pay for Anarchie using a check or cash. We highly recommend that you pay by check as opposed to either cash or credit card. This is not only the preferred method of payment, but offers the most protection to you, as well.

Customizing Anarchie

Anarchie is one of those few programs that comes practically preconfigured. It doesn't take long to give Anarchie the information it needs for you to use it to its fullest potential (see fig. 10.3). Even though you configure Anarchie as soon as you install it, you should feel free to experiment and reconfigure it as your needs and wants change. This section gives a brief overview of Anarchie configurations. Subsequent sections give more complete coverage of some of the configuration options.

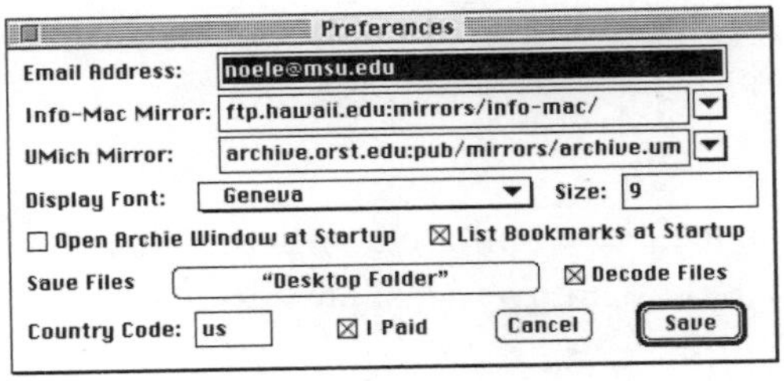

Fig. 10.3
Anarchie requires very little information for anyone to use it effectively. This is just one way in which Anarchie can be configured.

To configure your copy of Anarchie:

1 Open Anarchie by double-clicking its icon, or open it from the Apple menu.

2 Open the Edit menu and choose Preferences. The Preferences window asks you to provide several pieces of information to customize your copy of Anarchie.

3 The first piece of information you need to supply is your e-mail address. This allows Anarchie to supply your e-mail address to the FTP sites you access.

4 Next, choose your default Info-Mac and UMich mirrors. Info-Mac and UMich are both FTP sites that carry *lots* of Macintosh software. If you remember from Chapter 1, **mirrors** are FTP sites that keep copies of information available on FTP sites that are usually both popular and busy. Since Info-Mac and UMich are the most popular, Anarchie gives you a way to quickly access them. Initially, you might want to try using the default mirrors that Anarchie supplies and then experiment with them later if they don't work out for you.

 (Tip)

> As Internet usage continues to increase, it's becoming harder and harder to find FTP and Archie sites that aren't constantly busy. Mirror sites in different time zones, such as Hawaii and Europe, can often help you get through when others won't.

5 Next, you need to tell Anarchie whether you want the **Bookmark list** or the **Archie window** to display at startup:

- The Bookmark list contains addresses of sites that you or Anarchie saved for future use (see Chapter 11 for more information on Bookmarks).

- The Archie window allows you to immediately search for information.

You can also choose what font size and type you want Anarchie to display.

6 Finally, you are asked where and how to download files. Where you choose to have your files downloaded is up to you. You can choose where to save files at this time or wait until later. Chapter 11, "Getting and Sending Files," offers some tips on how to set this configuration.

You will also want Anarchie to automatically decode files. To save space and make file transfer easier, many files that are stored at FTP sites are both encoded and compressed.

Anarchie, along with StuffIt Expander, is able to decode and uncompress most of the files you'll download. So,

7 To have Anarchie do this automatically, install a copy of StuffIt Expander on your Macintosh and click the Decode Files option in the Preferences window. Since Anarchie does not decode automatically if you have a utility other than StuffIt Expander, such as Compact-Pro or StuffIt Lite, you'll want to make sure you have it.

After you have customized Anarchie according to your preferences, click the Save button and you are ready to begin!

Where to begin?

One of the first decisions you need to make when using Anarchie is where to start. Do you want a list of Bookmarks to appear when you first start Anarchie, or do you prefer to begin an Anarchie session by conducting an Archie search?

The answer to this question is largely determined by you. The answer may be different depending on whether you just like to browse, or you prefer to always look for a specific item. Expertise is also another factor. Once you are familiar with the locations of your favorite files and directories, you may find yourself conducting fewer Archie searches. On the other hand, a list of Bookmarks is often confusing to a new user because they are often unfamiliar or unknown.

You might want to try using the Bookmark list. If you find you're looking up a lot of files, you can always start Anarchie with an Archie window. Feel free to experiment according to your needs and wants.

Using Bookmarks to connect to FTP sites

Connecting to any particular FTP site using the Bookmarks list is as easy as pointing and clicking. Anarchie Bookmarks are listed by topic or other keyword. For instance, if you wanted to find a directory of National Center for Supercomputing Applications information, you would look for the NCSA Bookmark. If you wanted to access an Info-Mac mirror, you'd look for an Info-Mac Bookmark.

 **{Note}**

Anarchie allows multiple concurrent connections. This means you can access two FTP sites at once, conduct an Archie search while downloading a file from an FTP site, or perform any other combination. Don't feel like you can do only one thing at a time.

Once you have found a Bookmark and want to connect it to its accompanying FTP site, simply double-click the Bookmark. Anarchie then attempts to make the connection (fig. 10.4).

Fig. 10.4
Double-clicking the Info-Mac (Hawaii) Bookmark causes Anarchie to attempt to connect to Hawaii's Info-Mac mirror.

Up close with the Bookmark list and Archie windows

Almost all of your FTP surfing will be done from the Bookmark list and Archie windows. Therefore, it might be a good idea to get an overview of what these two windows look like and contain.

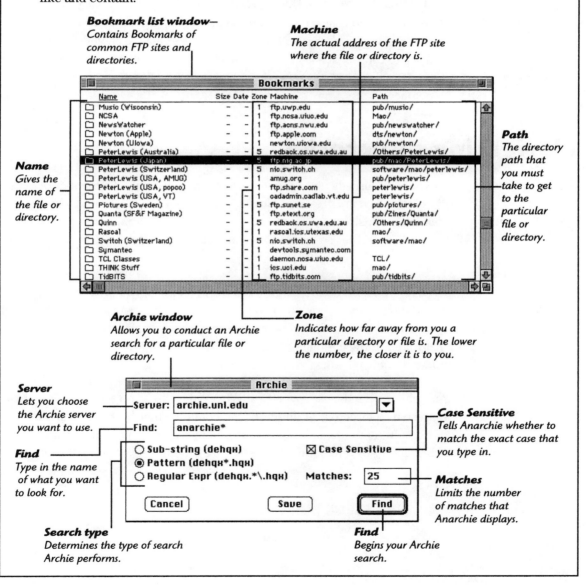

Bookmark list window—
Contains Bookmarks of common FTP sites and directories.

Machine
The actual address of the FTP site where the file or directory is.

Name
Gives the name of the file or directory.

Path
The directory path that you must take to get to the particular file or directory.

Archie window
Allows you to conduct an Archie search for a particular file or directory.

Zone
Indicates how far away from you a particular directory or file is. The lower the number, the closer it is to you.

Server
Lets you choose the Archie server you want to use.

Case Sensitive
Tells Anarchie whether to match the exact case that you type in.

Find
Type in the name of what you want to look for.

Matches
Limits the number of matches that Anarchie displays.

Search type
Determines the type of search Archie performs.

Find
Begins your Archie search.

Q&A

> ***Sometimes when I try to connect to a Bookmark, I get a strange message and then Anarchie tells me I can't connect. Am I doing something wrong?***
>
> Probably not. There are several reasons that you might fail to get a connection. Perhaps the FTP site is already full and won't allow any more users on. It's also likely that the FTP site is temporarily down, or isn't available during the times you're trying to connect. Sometimes an FTP site will even choose not to allow anymore anonymous connections. Usually, simply going to another site or trying to connect at a later time will result in a successful connection. Refer to the "The transcript" section at the end of this chapter for hints on how to find out more.

Navigating directories

As you have already discovered, FTP sites are made up of a number of directories that are arranged much like the branches of a tree. An understanding of this concept is crucial when you're navigating through an FTP site with Anarchie. To review this concept, see Chapter 4, "FTP Concepts and Culture."

Even if you are a relative beginner to the Macintosh, you probably already know about folders, how to open them, and how they work. You know that if you double-click a folder, a new window appears displaying the contents of that folder. If the contents of the newly opened window contain another folder, double-clicking that folder opens yet another new window.

Anarchie works the same way. With Anarchie, when you see a folder icon, it represents a directory. A directory can contain either files or subdirectories, or both. In Anarchie, a file is represented by a document icon, and a subdirectory by a folder icon (see fig. 10.5).

Fig. 10.5
This is the directory
/mirrors/info-mac/
game at
ftp.hawaii.edu.
Notice that
subdirectories are
represented by folder
icons and files are
represented by
document icons.

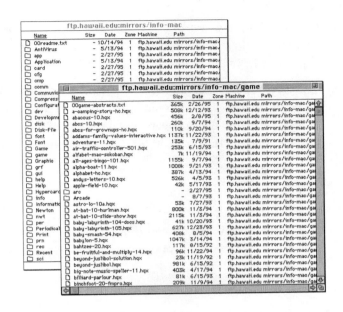

When you look at figure 10.5, also notice that the information in the directory window is the same as the Bookmark list window. There are a couple of slight differences. First, the window's title bar displays the directory name (i.e., /mirrors/info-mac/game). Second, notice that there is information provided in the Size and Date columns for files. File sizes are listed in terms of kilobytes (1,000 bytes), and the date indicates when the file was last updated on the FTP site. The rest of the information is identical.

Always look at the Date and Name columns before downloading a file. If there appears to be more than one file of the same name, the one with the most recent date is the newest version. Also, you will generally want to download a file with the highest number in the Name. If, for instance, you have a choice of downloading abcs-10.hqx or abcs-14.hqx, download abcs-14.hqx, as it is probably version 1.4, as opposed to version 1.0.

Navigating these directories is no different than using the Finder:

- **Opening directories**. Double-clicking a folder opens a new window displaying the contents of the subdirectory. This also allows for multiple windows to be open at the same time.

- **Navigating a directory**. You can use the scroll bars to move up and down within a directory just as you would with any other Macintosh window from the Finder.

- **Changing directories**. The multiwindow approach is particularly useful when you need to navigate multiple directories of an FTP site. There is no need to navigate one directory at a time—once a window is open, clicking the directory's window instantly activates that directory.

- **Closing directories**. Clicking a window's close box closes that directory.

If you have several windows open at once, you can close them all at the same time by holding down the Option key while clicking the close box.

Get a clue! Find the directories you want

How would you feel if you went into your local library to check out some books, only to discover that all the aisle markers, books, and catalogs were written in Latin? Needless to say, it would be tough to get what you wanted. Some people have reported the same feeling when navigating FTP directories for the first time. What's in a directory marked /app? /vir? /dev? Although these names can be confusing, there is a fairly standard way to label directories on FTP sites (see table 10.1).

Table 10.1   Common directory names on FTP sites

Directory name	Full name	Description
/app	Applications	Generally consists of computer applications of various types.
/comm	Communications	Contains communications software such as newsreaders, FTP clients, and so on.
/comp	Compression	Usually holds compression programs such as Compact-Pro on StuffIt Lite.
/dev	Development	Contains programs for software developers; rarely useful to recreational computer users.

Directory name	Full name	Description
/game	Games	Does this really need an explanation?
/grf	Graphics	Consists of files that have to do with graphics, including actual pictures, picture display programs, and the like.
/pub	Public	This is usually the main public directory and often acts as the root directory for software and files downloadable by anonymous users.
/util	Utilities	Contains that subgroup of programs that do highly specialized tasks and often include Extensions or Control Panels. Can also represent a directory with specific types of utilities. For instance, /graphicutils contains graphic utilities.
/vir	Virus	Contains virus detection and elimination software.

There are probably hundreds of other directory names out there. Fortunately, directory names are becoming more understandable. Directories labeled /text can be expected to have text files, /sound directories should contain sound files or utilities, and so on. If you know these common names, finding the right file is a lot easier.

!(Tip)

Knowing that directories are now more often represented by English words can help you with Archie searches, especially when you're not sure what you're looking for. Because Archie searches can also match directory names, a search for a category, such as Graphics, is likely to point you in the right direction.

Disconnecting from a site

There are right ways and then there are wrong ways to disconnect from an FTP site. Simply shutting off your computer while you're in the middle of an FTP session is a wrong way. There are a couple of ways to make a clean break from an FTP site.

The first is to open the File menu and choose Close. This closes the active connection. If you have more than one site open, make sure you click the window representing the site from which you wish to disconnect. You can also disconnect from an FTP site by clicking its close box. If you have many directories from a site open, you can hold down the Option key while clicking the close box. This closes all active windows and disconnects.

Where have I been? What have I done?

There will be times, both as a beginner and as an advanced user, when you'll want to be able to find out exactly what you've seen and where you've been. Anarchie gives you two ways to do this.

The log

A very helpful feature of Anarchie is its **Log** function. Anarchie keeps a running account of where you've been and what you've done. To view this information, open the Windows menu and choose Show Log. A listing of everything you have done while using Anarchie appears.

There is one added feature that makes this function even better. The log entries are **hot**. That is, you can double-click a log entry, and Anarchie repeats that function. This is particularly helpful if you have downloaded a file or accessed a directory and forgotten how you got there. Simply find the log entry, double-click, and you'll be there in no time!

One thing that Anarchie *doesn't* do is delete log entries automatically—you must do that yourself. If you use Anarchie a lot, this file can get quite large rather quickly. After you get a feel for how big it can get, you may decide to keep the entire record and not delete any log entries. If it begins to get too cumbersome or difficult to navigate, however, you can delete log entries.

 (Tip)

We recommend that you make a habit of checking the log after every Anarchie session. By making it a habit, you can keep your log entries down to those you want to keep and prevent the log file from getting too big.

To delete items from the Log window, you can click, Shift+click, or ⌘+click to choose one entry or multiple entries for deletion (see fig. 10.6). Once you select the items you want to delete, open the Edit menu and choose Clear. The selected log entries are deleted.

Fig. 10.6
These four selected items will be deleted after you open the Edit menu and choose Clear.

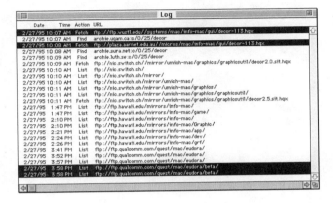

The transcript

As you become a more advanced user, there may be times when you need to get more detailed information about where you've been. Perhaps you'd like the IP address of a machine you've logged in to, or perhaps you'd like to find out exactly why your login wasn't accepted.

This is what the **Transcript** window is for. To view the transcript, open the Window menu and choose Show Transcript. A listing of all system commands received during your Anarchie session appears.

Remember that most FTP sites run on that strange operating system with the funny name—UNIX. Because Anarchie is sort of a middleman between you and UNIX, you don't actually get a chance to see what exactly happens when you perform a certain function. The session transcript gives you this information.

For instance, if you try to log in to a certain site and you are told that you cannot connect, you can go to the Transcript window to find out why your connection was refused.

Unlike the log, however, a session transcript only keeps track of what you've done during a particular Anarchie session. Once you quit, the transcript is wiped out and you start from scratch the next time you use Anarchie.

11

Getting and Sending Files

It's never as easy as it looks, right? Wrong. Anarchie makes uploading and downloading as easy as pointing and clicking!

Well, this is what it's all about. You've waited to start uploading and downloading files so you can become a part of the Information Superhighway. Now you can fill your hard drive with all those great programs and files and even contribute some of your own.

If you're like most people, though, you may be a little nervous. After all, these are computers we're talking about, right? Well, with Anarchie, you can download the files you want simply by pointing and clicking. And uploading your files to an FTP site is just as easy.

Getting a file from there to here

You are probably most interested in downloading files for your own use. Although many people do upload files (how else would they get on FTP sites?), a large majority of FTP users download almost exclusively, and so that's what we'll talk about first.

Before you do anything else, though, you need to choose an FTP site to go to. For instance, let's say that you want to get the latest version of Eudora. From your Bookmark list window, double-click the Eudora folder. Anarchie attempts to connect you to the appropriate site. Once you are connected, a directory window appears that gives you a listing of the available files and subdirectories.

?Q&A

I see a lot of files that have the extension .fat or .ppc in them. Are these special files?

Yes. Last year, Macintosh introduced its PowerPC-based **PowerMac** computers. However, since the PowerMacs make use of a different type of microchip, special programs needed to be written to take full advantage of the superior capabilities of this powerful computer. **PPC** files work exclusively on PowerMacs—don't try to use them on any other kind of Macintosh. Although **FAT** files work on standard 68K Macintoshes, they are best utilized by a PowerMac. Applications written for this computer are called **fat applications**. If you are using a PowerMac, always get a FAT file if it's available.

Once you've located the file you want, you are ready to begin your download. Double-click anywhere on the name of the file you want to download and let Anarchie do the rest.

While the file is being downloaded, a progress window appears telling you how much of the file has been downloaded and how much time remains (see fig. 11.1). The bar indicating how much of the file has been downloaded is accurate. However, the time needed to download the file is just an estimate and can't always be taken literally.

Fig. 11.1
Double-click the name of the file you want to get and Anarchie begins downloading it to your hard drive. Anarchie also keeps you informed of the progress of your download.

Progress indicators

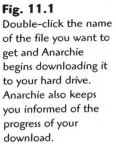
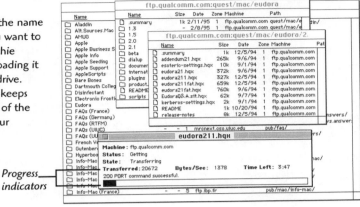

Where do I put it?

As Chapter 10, "Connecting to FTP Sites with Anarchie," pointed out, where you want to save your files is up to you. Anarchie's default for the Save Files option is the Desktop. Although you can save files wherever you want, keep in mind that all locations are not created equal.

Many users choose to save files to the Desktop. There are several reasons why you might want to keep the Desktop as the destination for your downloaded files. First, the Desktop allows you to quickly and easily access the files and see if they'll be useful to you. This helps you avoid the hassles of opening several folders to get to the file. Second, you can easily throw away files on the Desktop if you don't want them, and they can be quickly moved to a more permanent location if you decide to keep them.

Others like to create a folder on their Desktop called something like *Downloads* or *Anarchie*. This can be beneficial in that your Desktop won't get crowded with lots of files. If you want to do this, first create the folder on your Desktop and name it. Then go into the Anarchie configurations and change the Save Files setting to your newly created folder.

To set your Save Files option:

1 Open the Edit menu and choose Preferences.

2 Double-click the button next to the Save Files option. At this point, you will see a standard selector window appear.

3 Find the folder you want to download files to. Click the name of the folder.

4 After you click the folder, a button called **Select FolderName** will highlight at the bottom of the selector window. Click this button and you're done.

If you've already selected a different default folder, you can switch it back to the Desktop. Choosing the Desktop as the location to save files can be a little tricky if you don't know how. From the selector window, scroll down until you see an icon that isn't highlighted, such as the Trash icon. You must click next to one of these icons to get the Select Desktop Folder button to appear (see fig. 11.2). Clicking this button then selects the Desktop.

Fig. 11.2
After clicking an empty space next to a deselected icon, you have the option of choosing the Desktop as the location for saved files.

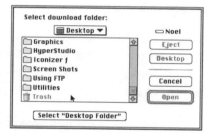

Look, but don't touch

In your travels to FTP sites, there are occasions when you may want to open a file in a simple word processor. For instance, many large files and applications available on FTP sites have an accompanying text file that provides a description or other valuable information. Viewing this file first can often save you a lot of time.

You can always download this text file and then open it. Anarchie also gives you the option of automatically downloading and viewing such a document in one easy step. To view a document, simply click the file name, open the FTP menu, and choose View Selection. Anarchie then temporarily downloads the document and opens it in your default word processor (probably TeachText or SimpleText). You can then read the document before deciding on your next action (see fig. 11.3).

Fig. 11.3
This document describes all of the different files available in this Eudora directory. The default word processor used here is SimpleText.

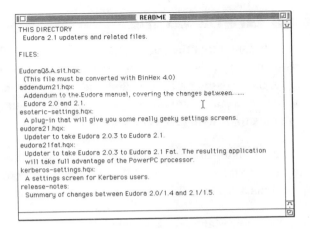

```
THIS DIRECTORY
  Eudora 2.1 updaters and related files.

FILES:

EudoraQ&A.sit.hqx:
  (This file must be converted with BinHex 4.0)
addendum21.hqx:
  Addendum to the Eudora manual, covering the changes between.....
  Eudora 2.0 and 2.1.
esoteric-settings.hqx:
  A plug-in that will give you some really geeky settings screens.
eudora21.hqx:
  Updater to take Eudora 2.0.3 to Eudora 2.1.
eudora21fat.hqx:
  Updater to take Eudora 2.0.3 to Eudora 2.1 Fat.  The resulting application
  will take full advantage of the PowerPC processor.
kerberos-settings.hqx:
  A settings screen for Kerberos users.
release-notes:
  Summary of changes between Eudora 2.0/1.4 and 2.1/1.5.
```

⊗<Caution> This function works seamlessly on almost every Macintosh. However, if you do not have a default set, this function may not work. If this is the case, you must set one. Unfortunately, Anarchie won't let you set the default—you must obtain a copy of Fetch (another FTP program) and set it from that application. To configure this setting, open the Customize menu in Fetch and choose Suffix Mapping.

A rose by any other name...

For a number of reasons, there will be occasion when you download two files with the same file name. As an example, let's assume that you are downloading the README files from a number of different applications. There's only one problem—they're all called README! As you know, Macintosh won't allow more than one file with the same name to exist in one place.

It's a good thing that Anarchie offers a simple way to get around this problem. When you're downloading files, Anarchie automatically looks at the location that you're downloading to and determines if the name of the file you're getting already exists there. If it does, Anarchie renames the duplicate file.

Let's continue with our example for a moment. After downloading one README file, you find another one you'd like to download and you do so. Anarchie renames the second one README #1. If you download another one, it is named README #2, and so on.

It's all Greek to me

So you finally found that file you've been looking for—at least you think you have. Problem is, it doesn't really look like you think it should. For some reason, you didn't expect it to be called Widgetts1.4-50.sit.hqx, and now you have this uncomfortable sinking feeling in the pit of your stomach. How are you ever going to turn that mess into something that actually works?

What you are looking at is a file that has been compressed and encoded. In order to fit more information on FTP sites and to allow for faster downloads, most programs are generally compressed so that they take up less space.

This usually requires an extra step when downloading files from FTP sites— usually. With Anarchie, though, even this extra step is eliminated as long as you have a copy of StuffIt Expander on your Macintosh. For instructions on how and where to get StuffIt Expander, see Chapter 10, "Connecting to FTP Sites with Anarchie."

Macs do windows

There's a good chance that you may want to use Anarchie to download DOS, Windows, or other types of files onto your Macintosh. Perhaps you have SoftWindows installed on your Macintosh and you'd like to download some applications to use in Windows. Whatever the reason, you're going to need to get some different decompression and decoding utilities to help.

One common method of encoding files is called **UUEncoding** which, although it is primarily a UNIX utility, is used to compress all types of files. To **UUDecode** files (that's computerese for decoding a UUEncoded file) on your Macintosh, you should have a utility called **UUUndo**. This file can be found at **mac.archive.umich.edu** in the /util/compression directory under the name uuundo1.05b.sit.hqx.

A common method of compression for IBM compatibles is **ZIP**. Zipped files usually have a .zip file extension. A good Macintosh utility for uncompressing zipped files on a Macintosh is unzip2.01, which also can be found in the /util/compression directory at **mac.archive.umich.edu**.

These two utilities will increase your power and flexibility to utilize even more of what's available on FTP sites.

⓵ (Tip)

> **Drop Stuff with Expander Enhancer** is an addition to StuffIt Expander that allows you to quickly and easily manage more Internet file types. You can find it at **ftp.switch.ch /mirror/info-mac/Compress-Translate/** (which is another place you can find StuffIt Expander). The file is drop-stuff-with-ee-352.hqx.

Every time you download a file, Anarchie looks for a copy of StuffIt Expander. When it finds one, it automatically calls the program and uses it to decompress and decode the program you are downloading.

❌ <Caution>

> StuffIt Expander handles the most common Macintosh compression and encoding schemes such as .hqx, .cpt, and .sit. However, if you download a different type, such as a PC .zip file or a UNIX .tar file, StuffIt Expander won't handle them.

You'll still have some cleaning up to do, however. In the process of decoding and decompressing your files, StuffIt Expander leaves the compressed and encoded files hanging around on your computer. If you set your file destination to be the Desktop, you'll see them there. Always make sure that you throw these files in the Trash to avoid clutter and to save disk space.

I know it's here somewhere

It finally happened. This friend of yours who is an absolute Net guru came up to you yesterday and told you, "Man, you've *got* to check out this new FTP site—it's great!" He then hands you a scrap of paper with some words scribbled on it and leaves you scratching your head.

What will you do? The site he's given you isn't in your list of Bookmarks, and he didn't give you a file name you could search for using Archie. But you really want to look at this site. Can you do it using Anarchie? Of course you can—and it's easy.

If you have the name of an FTP site (and perhaps a directory path and file name), but can't find it in the Bookmarks (and can't or don't want to bother going through an Archie search), Anarchie offers another way:

1 Open the FTP menu and choose Get. A dialog box asks you for information on where you'd like to go.

2 If you only have the name of an FTP site, type it in where Anarchie asks for the Machine and then click the List button (see fig. 11.4).

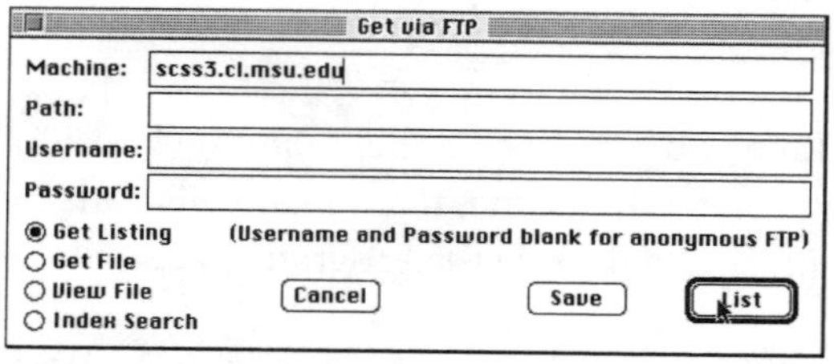

Fig. 11.4

Typing in the name of an FTP site and clicking the List button gets you into an unfamiliar FTP site for browsing.

```
┌──────────────────── Get via FTP ────────────────────┐
│  Machine:  │ scss3.cl.msu.edu                      │ │
│  Path:     │                                       │ │
│  Username: │                                       │ │
│  Password: │                                       │ │
│  ● Get Listing    (Username and Password blank for anonymous FTP) │
│  ○ Get File                                          │
│  ○ View File      [ Cancel ]      [ Save ]   [ List ]│
│  ○ Index Search                                      │
└──────────────────────────────────────────────────────┘
```

3 If you have a directory path (like /pub/mac), type it in where Anarchie asks for the Path and click the List button.

4 If you have an actual file name, type that in at the end of the path (for example, /pub/mac/netscape.sea.hqx). Then select the Get File radio button and click the Get button (fig. 11.5).

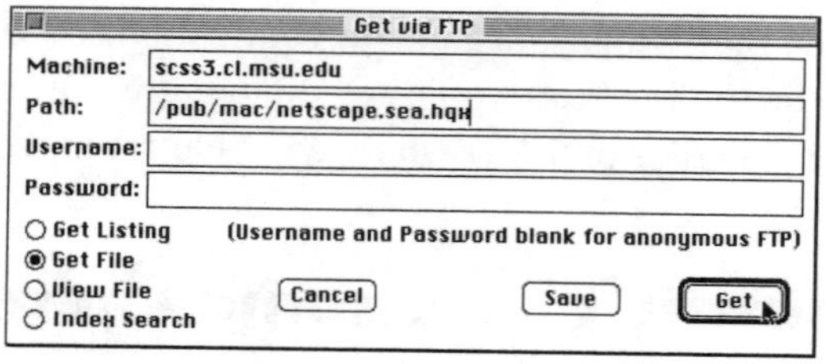

Fig. 11.5

If you add a path and a file name, Anarchie goes out to the FTP site and automatically downloads the desired file for you.

```
┌──────────────────── Get via FTP ────────────────────┐
│  Machine:  │ scss3.cl.msu.edu                      │ │
│  Path:     │ /pub/mac/netscape.sea.hqx             │ │
│  Username: │                                       │ │
│  Password: │                                       │ │
│  ○ Get Listing    (Username and Password blank for anonymous FTP) │
│  ● Get File                                          │
│  ○ View File      [ Cancel ]      [ Save ]   [ Get ] │
│  ○ Index Search                                      │
└──────────────────────────────────────────────────────┘
```

The more, the merrier

You finally hit the mother lode. An FTP site with all the things you've only dreamed of. You've been looking in one directory for a mere two minutes and you've already found five files to download.

The problem is, they're all pretty big and you know it will take awhile to download them all. You'd like to just tell Anarchie to download all five and go do something else instead of coming back after each one has been downloaded and sending the download command again.

Well, the solution is, you can download them all together. In fact, you have different ways of doing it.

Select all the files and download them at once

The first way of selecting multiple files to download is the same as selecting log entries for deletion. Simply Shift+click or Control+click the files you'd like to download (see fig. 11.6).

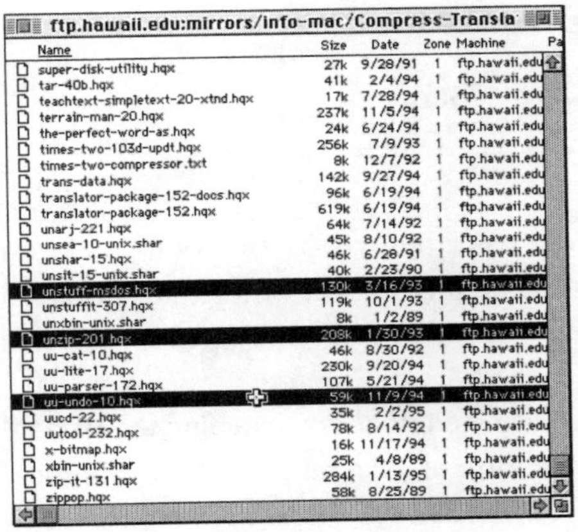

Fig. 11.6
Selecting multiple files at once downloads them to your machine one at a time in consecutive order.

When you've selected all the files, simply double-click one of the selected files and Anarchie begins downloading them one at a time. As soon as the first has been downloaded, Anarchie begins downloading the second one. This is probably the best method to use, since it allows you to download as many files as you want.

You also can use the drag-and-drop method. First, Shift+click or Control+click to select the files you want to download. Then drag one of the files to your Desktop or a folder. After you release the mouse button, all the files begin to download.

Start downloading files while you keep looking

The other way is slightly different. Once you've determined which files you'd like to download, double-click the first one and it'll begin to download. After it has started, click in the directory window again and double-click the next file you want to download. Repeat these steps until all files are being downloaded (see fig. 11.7).

Fig. 11.7
Selecting one file at a
time allows all files to
be downloaded at
once.

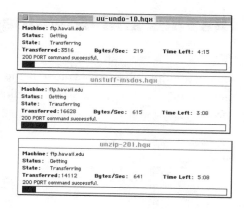

You can use this process when you're browsing a directory and want to begin downloading a file while looking for others. We don't recommend that you choose more than a few files for download at a time when using this method.

**{Note}**

Even though it may seem that downloading the second way is faster than the first—it isn't. You can only transfer so much data through your phone line, so transferring three files at once causes each file to download 1/3 as fast as downloading one file. However, since the first method allows you to download more files with fewer steps, use it whenever you can.

Getting a file from here to there

What if you found a really neat file on some obscure FTP site in Norway that's almost impossible to log in to, and now you'd like to make that file available on a local or more accessible FTP site? Or, suppose you just finished compiling all of the space shuttle logs and want to share them with the world? Can you do it?

Well, the answer is, it depends. Some anonymous FTP sites are very low on space and severely limit what can be uploaded to their systems. Others don't allow uploads at all. Many, however, do allow users to upload files to their FTP sites. As with downloading, uploading files using Anarchie is easy.

Before uploading files, always check the FTP site for any distribution restrictions. Also, check the FTP site to make sure that a copy of the file you want to upload isn't already there.

What a drag

With Anarchie, uploading files is as easy as dragging and dropping. Although you can upload a file by opening the FTP menu and choosing Put, there's really a much easier way.

With any directory window in Anarchie open, simply click the file and then drag and drop it on the directory you'd like to upload the file to. If the site accepts the upload, the transfer will be successful—if not, it won't.

As you read the next several sections, you'll realize that there is a little more to a completely successful upload to FTP than meets the eye. It would be a very good idea to open the Transcript window while doing uploads; the messages captured in that window can prove to be very useful.

A bigger drag

Just as you can download multiple files at once, you can also upload multiple files at once using basically the same methods. First, you can simply select all the files you'd like to upload and drag them to the directory they're to be uploaded to. This method uploads the files one at a time in order.

As with downloading, you can also select one file, drag it to the upload directory, select another file and drag it to the upload directory, and so on until all files are being uploaded.

The same comments apply to uploading as to downloading, as well. Both methods succeed in uploading the files equally quickly, and it's probably not a good idea to upload more than a few files at a time. With this in mind, let's learn a little more about uploading.

Where do I upload to?

You may be thinking that an FTP site administrator would have a tough time keeping up with all the new files if anybody could just upload to any of the site's directories—which might number in the hundreds.

If you are, you're right. Keeping track of uploads to an FTP site this way proves to be a logistical nightmare on even a modest-sized FTP site.

As you also might have guessed, site administrators have a way around this little dilemma. Most of them set up a special directory to receive uploaded files. The most common name given to this directory is /incoming. Most FTP sites that allow uploads of any type have an /incoming directory in its root directory. Always upload to this directory if it is available.

It disappeared!

You've just completed your upload, and you log back in to the FTP site to see your newly uploaded file. You go to the /incoming directory and…Hey! Waitaminit! It isn't there! What happened? Well, it's still there—you just can't see it.

Most FTP sites that accept uploads don't instantly put the file online. The site checks the file for viruses, determines what directory it belongs to, possibly informs you of the site's plans, and *then* actually puts the file on the site. While this whole process is occurring, the file stays hidden to anonymous users.

Who do I tell?

Through any of the above steps, it is quite likely that you'll need to talk to someone at the FTP site regarding your upload. Many FTP sites require that you e-mail the site administrator with information on your upload before they even consider putting it up permanently (see fig. 11.8).

Fig. 11.8
This FTP site requires you to contact the site administrator before the upload is accepted.

Most FTP sites ask you to contact them for one reason or another regarding your upload. In any event, it's just good etiquette to let them know what you're up to. You don't need to do anything fancy. Just send a simple note telling the administrator the name of the file you uploaded, where you uploaded it, and a short description of the file.

There are other reasons you may want to contact the site administrator. What if they don't have an /incoming directory and you'd like to find out whether they'll accept an upload? What if you uploaded a file two weeks ago and it still isn't on the site? For these or any of a number of other reasons, you'll probably need to contact someone in charge of the FTP site.

To do this, you usually need to use e-mail. Unfortunately, not all sites operate the same way. A couple of common e-mail addresses for FTP site administrators are listed below:

admin@*site.host.name*	Ex: admin@ftp.mcp.com
ftpadmin@*site.host.name*	Ex: ftpadmin@ftp.msu.edu
sysadmin@*site.host.name*	Ex: sysadmin@ftp.msu.edu

Remember when we told you it might be a good idea to open the Transcript window while doing an upload? This is the perfect reason why. When you do an upload, many sites actually tell you who you need to contact regarding your upload (refer to fig. 11.8).

Although it may be a while before you actually do any uploading on a regular basis, you might want to review this section occasionally to remain familiar with exactly how it's done. Knowing how to upload is yet another piece of information that makes you more knowledgeable about FTP and the Internet.

12

Adding Bookmarks in Anarchie

In this chapter:

- Why do I need new Bookmarks?

- Okay, I need Bookmarks, show me how create them

- How do I save Bookmarks?

- I want to change a Bookmark. What do I do?

- Can I set up Bookmark lists?

- You mean I can customize Bookmarks?

Let's face it, the Information Superhighway is no different than Route 66— you've got to have a map to get you where you want to go.

Most of us have taken a trip at some point in our lives—a vacation, an excursion to see a seldom-visited family member or a spur-of-the-moment ride in the country. There have undoubtedly been times when we've been lost, discovered a memorable spot, or run across a road that we had never seen before.

Whether you take a shortcut using that newly constructed road, or discover a Bed and Breakfast that you just *know* you have to visit again, you need a way to make sure you remember where you went so you can go there again. Most of us draw a new line on our atlas, put a red dot on the map, or perhaps even scribble instructions on a piece of paper and put it in the glove box.

This is an everyday example of how all of us attempt to remember where we've been and where we're going. We're always experiencing new things and seeing new sites. If we had to remember all of these things depending solely on our memory, it wouldn't take long to get lost.

And, let's face it, the Information Superhighway is no different than Route 66—you've got to have a map to get you where you want to go. In fact, the amount of information and different sites available with FTP is so staggeringly large that we would be hopelessly lost if we *didn't* have ways to keep track of where we were. It would be like trying to drive from Los Angeles to New York without a map or road signs to follow.

Does the face of FTP ever change?

With Anarchie, the **Bookmark** is the tool you use to help keep track of new roads and memorable spots while cruising FTP sites. In fact, this points to the main reason for using Bookmarks—to help us remember these sites, directories, and files. It has been estimated that the size of the Internet doubles every six months. It's easy to see that this means new sites, files, and information become available every day.

❋ *{Note}* Even if no new FTP sites were ever added to the current number available, you'd still find sites, directories, and files that were new to *you* and you'd still need Bookmarks. Even if you were to explore all that's out there at this moment, you'd spend months' worth of 8-hour days to get to all of it.

New sites aren't the only results of change on the Internet. Just as roads are rerouted and businesses move to better locations and more modern facilities, FTP sites change location or restructure their sites to meet the various demands and needs of such a dynamic environment.

When this happens, you'll know it. You'll access one of your favorite sites one day, only to be told that a file isn't available or that a directory path isn't valid—the electronic version of a road block.

When this happens, you'll need to do some experimenting to find the file's new location or directory path. Once you've found it, it'll be handy to have a bookmark to update so that you don't have to go through all that work again.

⊗<Caution> Companies go out of business every day, and so do FTP sites. If you can't find a familiar site, directory, or file, it's possible that it simply no longer exists. Don't take too much time trying to track down a change—consider the possibility that it simply may not be there any more.

X marks the spot

So you've found a new place that you want to come back to later. It's now time to create a Bookmark that will help you get there.

It doesn't matter whether you arrive at a destination via an Archie search, or by opening the FTP menu and choosing Get. Once you've found a site, directory, or file you want to save, you might want to mark it for later use. The process for doing so is always the same.

Many people are affiliated with a university, company, or other business that maintains an FTP site. Many of these sites probably aren't included in the list of Bookmarks that are prepackaged with Anarchie (see fig. 12.1).

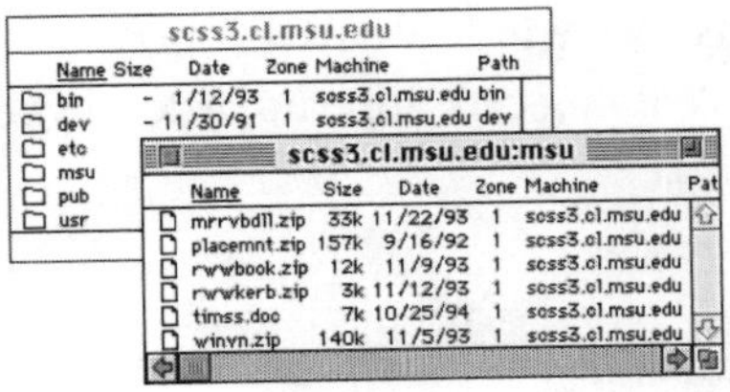

Fig. 12.1
This FTP site at Michigan State University has files that are useful to people who access the Internet through the MSU system.

This is a very common type of "first Bookmark" for many users. Such sites often have software that's specifically designed for a local system or unique use to the system's community.

①(Tip) When you get your account, find out if the system you're on maintains its own FTP site. If there is one, it may have a lot of useful material.

Saving your Bookmark

Saving a Bookmark in Anarchie is very easy. After you've found the site, directory, or file you want to mark, you're ready to go on. Make sure you select exactly what you want to save as the Bookmark. There's a slightly different method of selection depending on what you want to mark.

(Tip)

> Think about how you want to save a particular Bookmark. For instance, if you find an FTP site that contains a document that changes every week, you'll probably want to save the file as the Bookmark. However, if you simply find a neat site that looks good to browse, save the entire site.

Marking a site

If you want to mark an entire FTP site and not any particular directory or file in it, the process is simple and quick.

1 Make sure that the root directory window is selected. Don't click any of the directories, because that selects a particular directory within the window.

2 With the root directory window active, open the File menu and choose Save Bookmark. A dialog box appears, asking you to name the Bookmark (see fig. 12.2).

Fig. 12.2
Anarchie suggests a name for every Bookmark you save. When marking a site, the default name is the FTP site name. Simply type in a different name to call it something different.

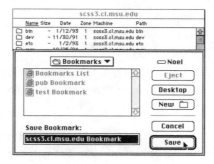

3 By default, Anarchie uses the FTP site name—for instance, star.sun.moon.edu Bookmark. You can either accept the default name or provide one of your choosing at this point.

4 Anarchie also automatically attempts to save the new Bookmark in the Bookmarks folder. We recommend that you save all of your Bookmarks to this folder. If you want to rename it and place it somewhere else, you can—it's up to you.

5 After you have accepted the name and location of the Bookmark, click the Save button and you're done.

When you save a bookmark this way, a new Bookmark file is created in addition to the default one. After you have created several of these Bookmarks, you'll probably want to combine them all into a **Bookmark list**. The process for doing this is explained in the section "A whole lotta Bookmarks."

Marking a directory or file

Marking a directory or file is similar to marking a site, but with one minor difference—you must actually select the directory or file you want to mark. To do this, just click the file or directory before opening the File menu and choosing Save Bookmark (see fig. 12.3).

Fig. 12.3
Saving a directory or file as a bookmark allows you easy future access.

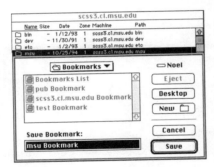

As with saving a site, Anarchie suggests a default name and location for the Bookmark. You can name it whatever and place it wherever, but we recommend that you save all your Bookmarks in one location.

Editing your Bookmark

What if you already have a Bookmark saved and you want to simply change it rather than create a whole new one? Anarchie lets you do it.

1 First, while holding down the Option key, open the File menu and choose Edit Bookmark. If you don't hold down the Option key, the Edit Bookmark choice isn't displayed when you access the File menu—so make sure you do this.

2 Next, a dialog box appears asking you to select the Bookmark you want to edit. After you select the Bookmark for editing, the next window allows you to edit the information in the Bookmark (see fig. 12.4).

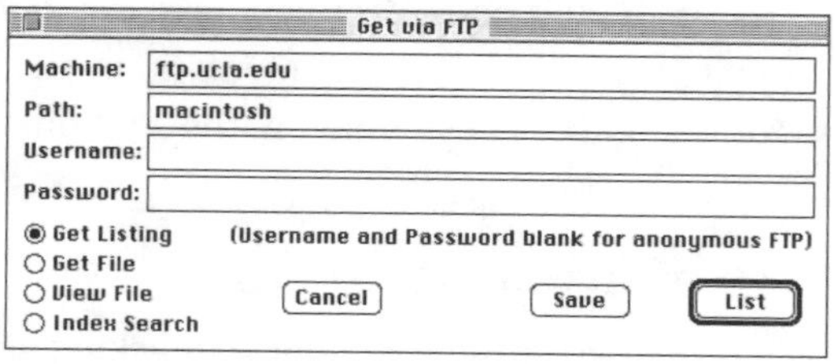

Fig. 12.4
This FTP site changed the name of its Macintosh default directory from mac to macintosh, so typing in the name of the new directory makes the appropriate changes to the Bookmark.

3 From this window, you can change the site name, path, file, or any other information you want. After you finish editing the Bookmark, click Save.

Find it faster

While editing a Bookmark, you may have noticed that one of the radio buttons was labeled **Index Search**. You may be wondering what exactly an index search is. Even if you aren't, we're going to tell you.

Some FTP sites let you find a file on their site by asking it to search for the file. In other words, if somebody tells you that they found the file widgets2.0 on **yakov.wow.su.gov** but didn't tell you where on the site the file was, it might take awhile to find it on your own. Even with the help of Archie, you might never be able to find the file.

But if that FTP site supports index searching, you can tell the site what file you're looking for and it automatically locates it for you. If this happens to you, simply type in the name of the file and choose the Index Search option while editing a Bookmark or while getting a file.

Bear in mind that many FTP sites do not support index searching, so you may have limited success with this option. Try doing one, though—after all, it can't hurt—most FTP sites just return an error telling you that the command was not understood.

Changing information usually changes the default name Anarchie attempts to save it as. If you want to save the changed Bookmark as a new one, accept the name Anarchie prompts you with. If you want to save it under the original Bookmark name, type in the old name and tell Anarchie to replace the old Bookmark with the new one.

Using your Bookmark

Once your Bookmark is saved, you can return to it at any time. When you're ready to use it, open the File menu and choose Open Bookmark. A dialog box appears that lets you select the Bookmark you want to use. Select the Bookmark by double-clicking it.

After you begin using Bookmarks, you'll appreciate the importance of keeping all of them in one folder. It can be rather annoying to have to change folders every time you want to use a different Bookmark.

A whole lotta Bookmarks

After you've used FTP for a while, you'll probably accrue quite a few Bookmarks. It may seem that you're spending more time than you should going from one Bookmark to another. One of the first questions you'll ask yourself is, "Why can't I just put all of my new Bookmarks in a list like the one that popped up the first time I used Anarchie?"

The answer to this question is that you can. Once you know how to update your Bookmark list, you'll probably want to do it on a regular basis, as it's the only way to give you instant point-and-click access to all your Bookmarks from one window.

Adding Bookmarks to the list

To add Bookmarks to your current Bookmark list, you need to make use of both the Finder and Anarchie. However, it's still really as easy as dragging and dropping, because Anarchie does most of the work for you.

Let's assume that you've saved all of your Bookmarks in the Anarchie Bookmark folder we recommended and that you want to add two of those Bookmarks, scss3 Bookmark and ssa Bookmark, to your Bookmark list.

1 First, create a new folder on the Desktop using the Finder. Close all open windows and click on the Desktop. From the Finder, open the File menu and choose New Folder. A new folder called untitled folder appears on the Desktop. You don't need to rename this folder.

2 Next, open the Anarchie Bookmark folder, select the Bookmarks you want to add to the list, and drag them onto the folder you just created. *Make sure* that you also select the current Bookmark file (which should still be called Bookmarks unless you changed it) along with the new ones you want to add.

3 Drag and drop the entire folder onto the Anarchie 1.4 application. A window opens displaying all of the Bookmarks you chose, including the new ones (see fig. 12.5).

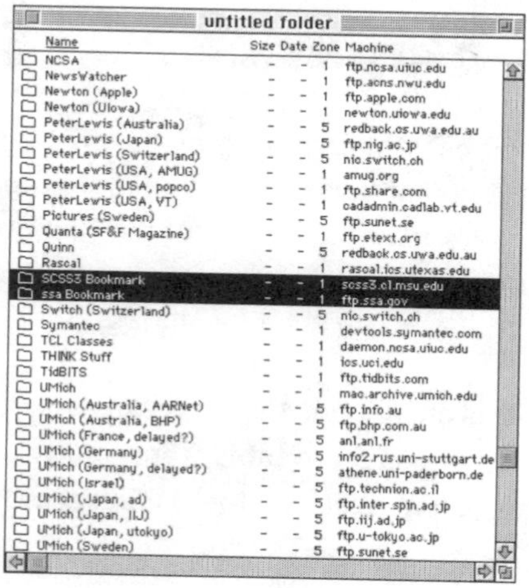

Fig. 12.5

When you place all the Bookmarks you want to include in a single list in a folder and drag and drop it on Anarchie, a new Bookmark window including the additions appears.

4 Finally, open the File menu and choose Save Bookmarks. Save the file under any name you choose, and you're done. The next time you open the Bookmarks, your new list includes all of the old Bookmarks plus the ones you just added.

Q&A

> **Can I save a group of Bookmarks without saving the whole list?**
>
> Sure. Just follow the steps above, selecting only those Bookmarks you want to use in your new list. Don't include the current Bookmark file as suggested in step 2.

Deleting Bookmarks from the list

As you know by now, the Bookmark list that comes with Anarchie is rather large and contains a lot of Bookmarks. After you've used it for a while, you'll probably decide that some of the existing Bookmarks aren't very useful to you. Perhaps they're outdated, or they're in the wrong time zone for you to access them properly.

For these reasons and possibly others, you'll eventually want to delete Bookmarks from your list. Although deleting Bookmarks is easy, it may seem a little counter-intuitive at first. Whereas with most Macintosh applications you select items and then choose to delete them, with Anarchie you select items and then choose to *keep* them.

This is how it works:

1 With your Bookmark list window open, open the Edit menu and choose Select All. Notice that all of the Bookmarks are selected.

2 ⌘+click those items you want to delete. When you're done, only those items that you want to keep are selected (see fig. 12.6).

 **<Caution>**

> You can't choose to keep one item using Anarchie. You must choose *at least* two items to keep, otherwise Anarchie simply saves the selection as a single Bookmark rather than as a Bookmark list.

Fig. 12.6
Select the items you
want to keep and
⌘+click to deselect
those items you want
to delete. Only those
items selected are kept
in the new Bookmark
list.

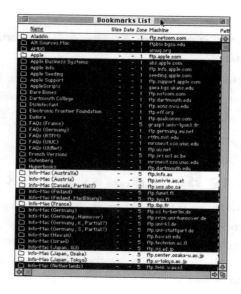

3 Once you select all the items you want to include in the new Bookmark
list, save them. Open the File menu and choose Save Bookmark. Name
the Bookmark list, and you're done.

For mature audiences

When making a Bookmark, be aware of an "advanced" feature. Until now,
we've assumed that you'll want to access only anonymous FTP sites.
Anarchie automatically supplies a login of anonymous and your e-mail ID for
all of your Bookmarks.

However, there will be times when you won't want this default information
supplied when you log in. Some FTP sites don't accept an anonymous login.
They may require you to enter **guest**, **ftp**, or some other specialized term at
login. In these cases, the default anonymous login that Anarchie supplies
doesn't get you in. To access these sites, you'll need to provide this login
information when saving your Bookmark.

Let's assume that the FTP site you want to log in to only accepts a login ID
of **guest**. You need to let Anarchie know this when saving the Bookmark
for that FTP site. The process is easy. When providing the information to

Anarchie, type **guest** in the Username text box before saving the Bookmark. The next time you use that Bookmark, Anarchie provides the correct login ID.

The information in this chapter can get you into just about any FTP site available to the general public. Using Bookmarks allows you to easily access new sites and get to familiar ones with a click.

13
Finding Files with Anarchie

Can't find a file or program? Don't worry, you have a travel guide ready to map the way for you!

Do you know the *Rime of the Ancient Mariner*? A sailor looks at the vast ocean surrounding him and laments, "Water, water everywhere, but not a drop to drink." With FTP, there are certainly times when you feel like that old sailor—there you are, surrounded by an ocean of files, directories, and applications, yet you can't find what you want.

This is where an electronic travel guide called **Archie** comes into play. Archie is the primary **search engine** for finding information on FTP sites (see fig. 13.1).

Plain English, please!

A **search engine** does just what it sounds like it should do, it searches for things. Archie is a search engine for FTP, just as Veronica is a search engine for Gopher.

Fig. 13.1
This is one of the more popular Archie servers located at the University of Nebraska at Lincoln (**archie.unl.edu**).

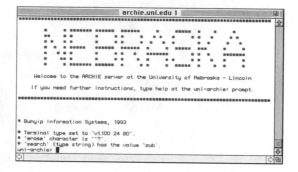

{Note} | You should check out Chapter 4, "FTP Concepts and Culture," for more about Archie and how it works.

Files, files everywhere...

Fortunately, Anarchie gives you access to this helpful guide that can find virtually anything on FTP if you know how to look. Anarchie has built-in access to Archie to allow you to do quick searching at the same time that you're downloading files.

{Note} | When connecting to an Archie server using Anarchie, you will never actually see Archie as it appears in figure 13.1. Instead, Anarchie provides a simple Archie interface to make things easier.

Conducting a search using Anarchie is fast and easy. Although this chapter covers different functions of searching, all the functions begin with the same step—displaying the Archie window. To do this, open the File menu and choose Archie (see fig. 13.2).

Fig. 13.2
The Archie dialog box lets you find practically anything that's available via anonymous FTP.

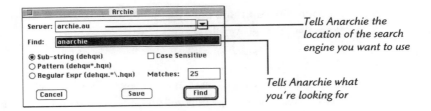

Tells Anarchie the location of the search engine you want to use

Tells Anarchie what you're looking for

There are two items that you will pay the most attention to—the **Server** and the **Find** options. Since these two options often determine the speed and success of your search, you need to make sure you use them correctly.

The Server option allows you to tell Anarchie which Archie server you want to use. This can be very handy. For instance, if you want to search for a particular file both in Europe and North America, you can choose to search using two different servers. (Remember that Anarchie lets you do more than one thing at a time!) You may also find that a particular Archie server is often busy and may want to choose a different one so that you can complete a search.

The Find option is where you enter the term you want to search for. Enter just about any word or **argument** you want to. We'll discuss the different types of Finds you can do a little later in this chapter (see the "Searches using Anarchie" section).

66 *Plain English, please!*

In computerese, an **argument** doesn't refer to a disagreement between you and the computer! It's a general term used to describe a phrase or element used by a computer. If you conduct a search for **anarchie**, *anarchie* is your argument. 99

Getting the latest Archie servers

Like everything else on the Internet, Archie changes with time. Better and new Archie servers appear while others disappear. When you're using the Internet, and especially FTP, it's always good to have the most up-to-date information. Anarchie once again comes through by making sure you can find the most current Archie servers.

To update your Archie servers, simply open the Edit menu in Anarchie and choose Fetch Server List. This accesses the Archie server list at the University of Texas. Once the correct file is retrieved (Anarchie does this automatically), be assured that you are accessing the latest Archie servers.

(Tip)

We recommend that you update the servers before conducting Archie searches with Anarchie for the first time. Since updating the servers is not a time-consuming step, we also recommend that you make a habit of updating the servers every couple of weeks.

Searches using Anarchie

This is where the rubber meets the road. It's time to get out on the Information Superhighway with Archie, your interactive, electronic travel guide. After reading Chapter 4 and the beginning of this chapter, you should have enough background information to start conducting useful Archie searches so that you can find what you need using Anarchie.

Whether you conduct a simple or complex Archie search, the results you get always consist of the same information. Always pay attention to whether the search results consist of files, directories, or both. Directories can often contain unexpected, but beneficial, files that are related to what you searched for to begin with.

It's also a good idea to pay attention to any numbers that appear in file names. Generally, the higher a number, the more recent it is. For instance, say you search for *Anarchie* and get, among others, two hits named Anarchie-130.sit and Anarchie-140.sit. You'll probably want to retrieve the one with the higher number, as it probably represents a more recent version of the software.

Archie search results

Notice that this window looks just like your Bookmark Window.

Lets you know how far away a particular machine is from your location—a higher number indicates it's farther away than a lower number.

Tells you when the file or directory was last updated.

The domain name of the machine where the match was located.

The name of directories that will contain the argument used in the Archie search.

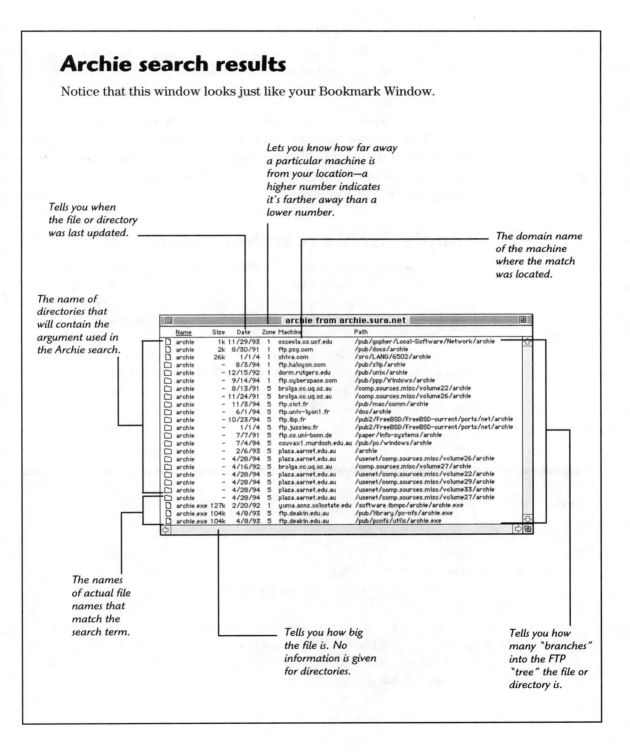

archie from archie.sura.net

Name	Size	Date	Zone	Machine	Path
archie	1k	11/29/93	1	osceola.cs.ucf.edu	/pub/gopher/Local-Software/Network/archie
archie	2k	8/30/91	1	ftp.psg.com	/pub/docs/archie
archie	26k	1/1/4	1	shiva.com	/src/LANG/6502/archie
archie	-	8/3/94	1	ftp.halcyon.com	/pub/slip/archie
archie	-	12/15/92	1	dorm.rutgers.edu	/pub/unix/archie
archie	-	9/14/94	1	ftp.cyberspace.com	/pub/ppp/Windows/archie
archie	-	8/13/91	5	brolga.cc.uq.oz.au	/comp.sources.misc/volume22/archie
archie	-	11/24/91	5	brolga.cc.uq.oz.au	/comp.sources.misc/volume26/archie
archie	-	11/3/94	5	ftp.ciot.fr	/pub/mac/comm/archie
archie	-	6/1/94	5	ftp.univ-lyon1.fr	/dos/archie
archie	-	10/23/94	5	ftp.ibp.fr	/pub2/FreeBSD/FreeBSD-current/ports/net/archie
archie	-	1/1/4	5	ftp.jussieu.fr	/pub2/FreeBSD/FreeBSD-current/ports/net/archie
archie	-	7/7/91	5	ftp.cs.uni-bonn.de	/paper/info-systems/archie
archie	-	7/4/94	5	csuvax1.murdoch.edu.au	/pub/pc/windows/archie
archie	-	2/6/93	5	plaza.aarnet.edu.au	/archie
archie	-	4/28/94	5	plaza.aarnet.edu.au	/usenet/comp.sources.misc/volume26/archie
archie	-	4/16/92	5	brolga.cc.uq.oz.au	/comp.sources.misc/volume27/archie
archie	-	4/28/94	5	plaza.aarnet.edu.au	/usenet/comp.sources.misc/volume22/archie
archie	-	4/28/94	5	plaza.aarnet.edu.au	/usenet/comp.sources.misc/volume29/archie
archie	-	4/28/94	5	plaza.aarnet.edu.au	/usenet/comp.sources.misc/volume33/archie
archie	-	4/28/94	5	plaza.aarnet.edu.au	/usenet/comp.sources.misc/volume27/archie
archie.exe	127k	2/20/92	1	yuma.acns.colostate.edu	/software.ibmpc/archie/archie.exe
archie.exe	104k	4/8/93	5	ftp.deakin.edu.au	/pub/library/pc-nfs/archie.exe
archie.exe	104k	4/8/93	5	ftp.deakin.edu.au	/pub/pcnfs/utils/archie.exe

The names of actual file names that match the search term.

Tells you how big the file is. No information is given for directories.

Tells you how many "branches" into the FTP "tree" the file or directory is.

⊕(Tip)

> You can often tell how recent a file's version is by looking at the date column. More recent dates often indicate a newer version.

It isn't as necessary to pay a lot of attention to the path or even the machine name. You can always make a bookmark out of a good site, directory, or file for later reference. It's a good idea, though, to make a note of this information so that you can learn some of the common directory- and file-naming conventions used on the Internet.

Simple Archie searches—substring

A **simple search** usually consists of one term and directs Archie to look for files or directories that contain that term. Keep in mind that the Archie search engine looks at FTP directories as well as file names. This is important to remember when deciding what you're going to search for.

For instance, if you're looking for a category of application or file, you may want to use a search term that's likely to reflect the directory such a file would be in. In other words, if you're looking for an application to compress files, you might choose to search for *compress* or *comp*.

Getting a URL

A new standard for Internet addressing is emerging with the increased use of the World Wide Web—the **Uniform Resource Locator (URL)**. Basically a URL is a way of identifying different locations on the Internet.

Let's assume that you find a really neat file or directory that you'd like to tell a friend about (it'll happen, trust me). There's an easy way to get that information without writing down machine names, paths, and file names. Hold down the Option key, open the Edit menu, and choose Copy URL.

This copies that file, directory, or site name onto your Clipboard. Now you can just paste it into an e-mail message, word processor, or other text file.

!)(Tip)

Remember that shorter terms produce more results that have nothing to do with what you're looking for. Searching for *comp* produces the hit compute-1.68b.zip, but searching for *compress* doesn't. Always use terms that eliminate as many irrelevant hits as possible.

Besides, searching on Archie for a generic term can surprise you by producing an actual file or application that you want. For example, if you're looking for a shareware program that plays different sound files, you might search for the term *sound*. Doing so will likely locate files with "sound" in the title, as well as directories titled "sound" (see fig. 13.3).

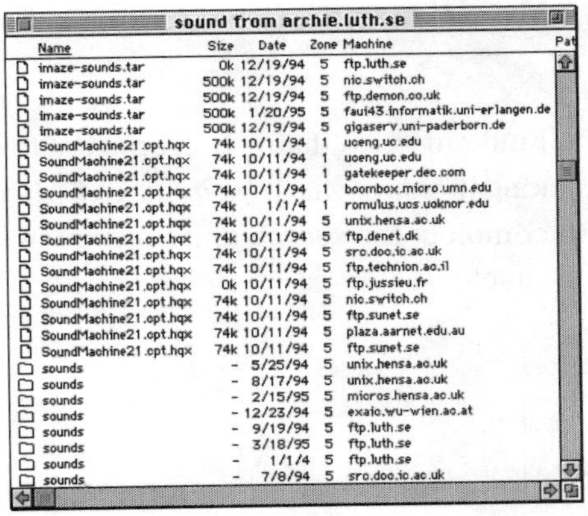

Fig. 13.3
A search for the term *sound* locates both directories and sound utility files.

Conducting a simple search is, well, simple:

1 Open the File menu and choose Archie.

2 Select the Archie server you want to use by clicking on the arrow to open the drop-down list and then clicking the server you want. You can also manually type in the name of an Archie server if you like.

3 Type the search term in the Find text box.

4 Double-check to make sure the Sub-string radio button is selected and click Find (see fig. 13.4).

When using a simple search term, there are often a *lot* of hits. This means that if you select a low number of matches to display, you'll probably miss a lot of useful matches. We recommend that you set the Matches setting to at least 100 when conducting a substring search. This means the search will take a little longer, but you get a lot more to choose from.

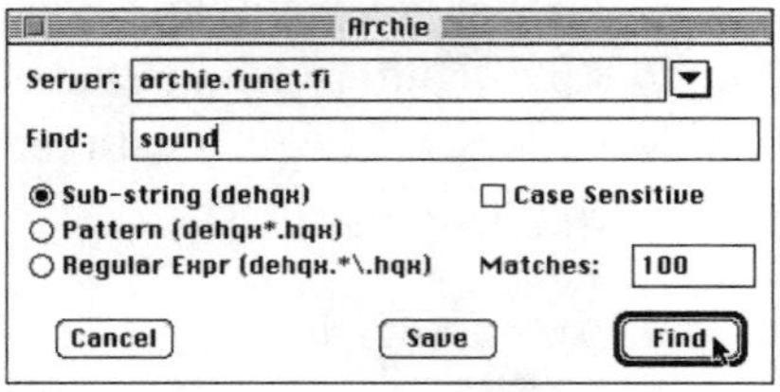

Fig. 13.4
When you have chosen your Archie server, provided the search term, and selected the Sub-string search option, you are ready to tell Anarchie to begin looking.

After you click the Find button, a dialog box appears telling you how much progress you're making in your search (see fig. 13.5). This box tells you how long it may take to complete the search and how much information is being transferred to your machine.

Fig. 13.5
Anarchie lets you know how much progress you're making in your Archie search.

Pay attention to this dialog box. If it appears that nothing is being transferred (no "packets" are being sent) after a couple of minutes, you may want to abort and try again. To gauge progress, look for the number of Packets Received and Chunks Received to go up and the Finish Guesstimate time to go down.

Complex searches

A simple search isn't the only way to query Archie for information. You can use more sophisticated methods for more sophisticated needs. The **regex search** was mentioned briefly in Chapter 4. Basically, Anarchie allows you to conduct a regex search two different ways—with the Pattern option or the Regular Expr option. We'll focus mainly on the **pattern search**, but also briefly explain a full regex search.

Pattern search

Suppose you want Archie to return only hits that are .sea files. Or perhaps you know the name of a piece of software, but don't know the current version and want to conduct a quick search.

Just make use of the **pattern search**. A pattern search lets you use **wildcards**. Wildcards are explained in detail in Chapter 4, "FTP Concepts and Culture." As a brief overview:

- A wildcard is a character used to represent an unknown character.

- The * wildcard takes the place of an unknown quantity of unknown characters. For example, the term *hi** could represent either "high" or "history."

- The ? wildcard takes the place of one character. For instance, the term *hi??* can represent "high," but not "history."

You will probably use the * wildcard more than the ?. You must have a very specific search in mind to make proper use of the ? wildcard.

A common way to use a wildcard is to eliminate hits that may contain applications from other platforms. Let's assume that you still want to find a sound utility, but don't want to bother searching through directories or looking at utilities that only work on PCs.

Because you know that a very common Macintosh extension is .hqx, you might conduct a pattern search for *sound*.hqx*. The results from this search contain only files that can be used on a Macintosh and differ a great deal from the results produced by a simple search (see fig. 13.6). You will also notice that this type of search eliminates matching directories.

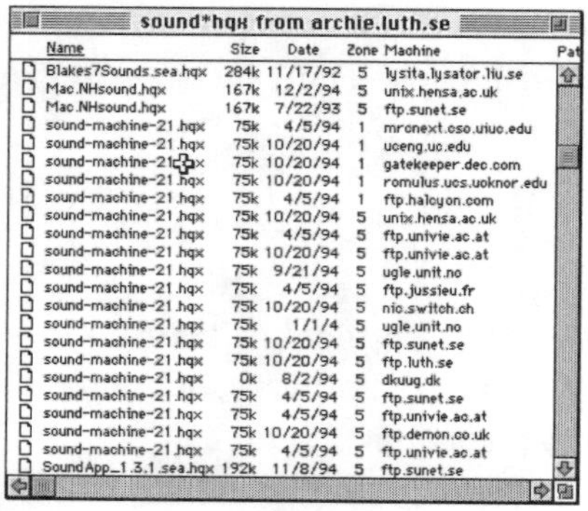

Fig. 13.6
Conducting a pattern
search restricts results
to only those types of
files that you want to
see.

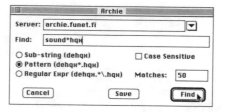

Although the search type is more complex, the process really isn't:

1 Open the File menu and choose Archie.

2 Select the Archie server you want to use.

3 Type the search term, including any wildcards, in the Find text box.

4 Select the Pattern radio button to conduct the complex search, and click Find (see fig. 13.7).

Fig. 13.7
After you have selected
the Archie server and
provided the search
term with wildcards,
Anarchie will find only
those hits that match
your search criteria.

This type of search is more precise than most simple searches. You probably don't need to look for 100 matches. Usually, 25 to 50 matches suffice and allow you to find what you're looking for.

Regular expression searches

As was mentioned earlier, the * is in fact a regular expression, and Anarchie makes use of this character in a pattern search. However, there are different regular expressions that can be used in an even more complex way. The most common ones are listed in the table:

Element	Definition
.	Matches any single character
*	Matches zero or more occurrences of the preceding character
[ ]	Lets you specify a range or set of characters
^	Matches anything except the character following it
\	Lets you tell Archie to include the special character following it (like ^) in the file name instead of interpreting it as a special character

If you want to specify a pattern of characters that Anarchie can use to find matching file names, use the Regular Expr option in the Archie window. You do this by simply clicking the Regular Expr radio button. This is not a search type that you'll need to use very often, but you might find it useful for doing something like searching for the most recent version of a file. A regular expression search lets you do things like look for file names that contain a version number greater than the current one—for instance, a search for a number greater than 6.

66 *Plain English, please!*

A **regular expression** lets you look for file names that match patterns of ASCII characters. For example, you can specify the first part of a file name and then give a range of values for the version number. Or, you can look for all files that contain the letters *archie* and end in *hqx*. 99

When using the Regular Expr search, enter the character pattern that you want Anarchie to search for. You can use ranges of letters and numbers, and special characters to build your search string. Some examples of the ways in which regular expressions might be used are:

- [0-9] matches any number
- [abcd] matches any one of the characters a, b, c, or d
- [[^]a-zA-Z] matches any nonletter
- [0-9]* matches any number of numbers
- .* matches any number of any characters

As an example, the search *jpeg.*[0-9]* matches any file name that contains a string that starts with "jpeg." and ends in a digit, with any number of other characters in between. If you know that the Anarchie distribution file has the version number in the middle of the file, and you want to see if there is a version higher than 1.3, you can use the search *anarchie-1[^0-3]** to find only version 1.4 and above.

Comparing search types—examples

In order to bring all of this together, it might help to compare a simple and complex search in terms of results to help you better understand the difference between the two.

Let's assume that you're looking for a self-extracting archive of Anarchie for a friend. You can find such a file with either a simple or complex search. However, it probably takes longer and may require more attempts to use a simple search, whereas a complex search can direct you to such a file immediately.

Let's say that you try both. For your simple search, you just search for *anarchie*. Since you're looking for a self-extracting file, you conduct your complex search using the term *anarchie*sea*.

❶(Tip)

> Remember that most software contains numbers indicating its version number somewhere in the name, usually between the application name and the extension. Therefore, searching for *anarchie*sea* is much more effective than searching for *anarchie.sea**.

As you can see in figure 13.8, the search results are quite different. The complex search produced only a few hits, all of which matched what you were looking for. On the other hand, the simple search produced only one hit out of dozens that matched what you wanted.

Fig. 13.8
The complex search produced only relevant hits. The simple search produced more, but fewer relevant, results.

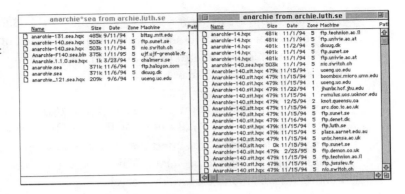

Again, it's important that you take a minute to think about how you want to conduct a search before you begin. Think of ways to narrow a search down to make your queries as fast and effective as possible. As with anything, it takes practice to figure out what works best; but by starting with these basics, you'll be off to a good start.

Retrieving a file that Anarchie finds

After you've completed a successful search, Anarchie displays a window with the query results. You can proceed to use this window just as you would a Bookmark.

If your search produces a directory, clicking the directory opens the folder. You can then proceed to download files or follow subdirectories as you wish. If you want to download a file found in the search, simply double-click it and it downloads. All instructions and procedures for downloading apply to getting files from an Archie search, as well.

Aborting a query

There will be times when you'll want to stop a query before it's done. For instance, if a search is taking too long and you want to stop, or you decide to look for something else, you may want to abort your search.

There are two ways to abort a query—each method produces slightly different results. The first way is simply to click the close box of the Archie search window. Do this any time and your search is aborted immediately. You see no results of an aborted search.

The second method to abort a query is to press ⌘ (the standard abort sequence for all Macs). Unlike clicking the close box, however, any results produced at the time of the abort are displayed in a new window. This can be helpful if you're conducting a long search and want to see if the file you're looking for was found early in the search.

Keep in mind that Archie is a tool much like any other. If used correctly, it can make your endeavors much more enjoyable and fruitful. Once you've had some time to experiment with Archie, you'll find it an indispensable ally on the Net.

Part IV:

FTP and Archie from the Command Line

Text-Based Access to FTP

In this chapter:

- What do I have to do to run FTP?
- Show me how to connect to an FTP server
- That file looks cool, can I download it?
- I want to share a file. How do I upload it?

FTP from your command-line account has been a tried and true friend, with few changes, for 20 years.

This book focuses mostly on using FTP through a graphical user interface (GUI). You can't always use a graphical interface to FTP, however, because many Internet service providers only give you access to a command-line account. If you connect to a command-line account through a terminal interface, you can fall back on the old reliable **ftp command** to do everything that the fancy graphical interfaces let you do. It's just a little less intuitive.

Instead of starting your FTP application and then pointing and clicking while the application does all the hard work, you have to learn the FTP commands that the graphical applications actually use to connect to the FTP server. Using FTP from the command line is not that difficult once you learn the commands.

Getting to the `ftp` command

If your command-line account (or **shell account**, as some providers call it) is running on a UNIX or VMS based host, it should be simple to use the `ftp` command. Almost every Internet provider has an `ftp` command built into their system. To use the ftp command, just type **ftp** at your system prompt. The ftp prompt then replaces your system prompt:

```
% ftp
ftp>
```

Now you can connect to any FTP server on the Internet.

❓Q&A

How do I use ftp if my account is menu-based rather than command-line?

Some Internet providers give you a text-based menu interface to your account. If you have a menu-based account, you will probably be able to find FTP as one of the entries on your menu. To use FTP, you just select it from the menu and then enter the information that you are prompted for:

- The FTP server you want to connect to

- The account you want to log in to on the FTP server

- The password for the account. If you're logging in to an anonymous FTP server, you may only have to press Enter as the system may default the password to your Internet e-mail address (your address should be in brackets at the end of the password prompt if it is used as the default).

Once you enter the information, you connect to the FTP server. You may go directly into a standard ftp program where you can enter the commands described in this chapter. However, your provider may be running a customized ftp program that limits the commands you can enter, or requires you to use special commands.

Usually, a customized ftp program has a help feature that explains the commands to you. It may even give you an overview of the commands when you first start the program. If you have any problems using your provider's ftp program, contact your provider for help.

Connecting to a site

Your next step is to connect to the Internet host that has the files you want. To connect to an FTP server, you need to tell the ftp program the server's name or its IP address. Once ftp knows where you want to go, it connects to the server and asks you for an account name and password to use on the server. If you get through all these steps successfully, you're ready to get your files.

Host names and IP addresses

Host names are found in e-mail addresses and are also used when connecting to Internet hosts to use Internet services (such as the FTP). A host name is made up of several words separated by periods. The host name bigmachine.bigcorp.com is used here to illustrate the parts of a host name. The rightmost word, for example, specifies the **domain** of the machine (which in this case is "com," indicating that it is a commercial site). Working to the left in the host name, you come to the word "bigcorp." This part of the host name specifies the institution that owns the machine.

Any words to the left of the institution name are assigned within the institution. Small organizations usually have only a single word (specifying the name of an individual machine at the organization) to the left of the institution name. Sometimes, in large organizations you may find more words to the left of the institution name. These usually designate departments or groups within the organization.

For example, you might have a host name like x.dev.bigcorp.com which would identify a

machine named "x" in the "dev" group (perhaps development) in the company "bigcorp." The leftmost word in a host name is always the name of an individual machine.

The host name is really just a convenient way for people to refer to hosts. The host name represents the **IP address** of the host, which is the address that Internet software needs to get information to or from the host. The IP address is a unique number assigned to identify a host on the Internet. This address is usually represented as four numbers between 1 and 254 separated by periods, for example, 192.58.107.230.

Most software translates automatically between the host name and the IP address so that you don't have to remember which numbers represent which machines. There occasionally may be times when the system software that translates the host names is not working. If you know the IP address for the FTP server you want to connect to, you can enter this and connect to the server even if the name translation software is not working.

To connect to a server you have to open it

The command that you use to connect to a server is open *host_name*. For example, if you want to connect to the FTP server **ftp.sei.cmu.edu**, enter **open ftp.sei.cmu.edu**.

!(Tip)

> When you first start ftp, you can connect to an FTP server by following the `ftp` command with the name of the server. For example, if you want to connect to the U.S. Senate's FTP server, type **ftp ftp.senate.gov**.

If everything goes well, you get a message saying that you're connected to the server, followed by the login prompt for that server. Figure 14.1 shows you what a successful connection to a server looks like.

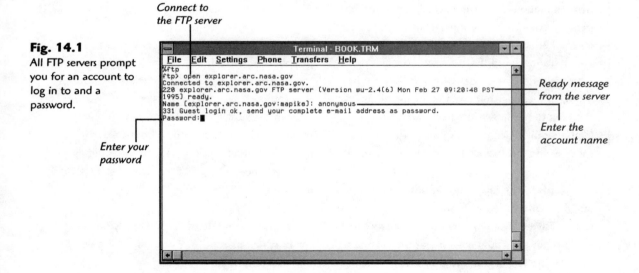

Connect to the FTP server

Fig. 14.1
All FTP servers prompt you for an account to log in to and a password.

Ready message from the server

Enter the account name

Enter your password

Sometimes FTP connections fail

Things don't always go well when you try to connect to an FTP server, and you may fail to talk to the server. There are a number of reasons why this might happen. For example, the server you tried to connect to may be down, or you may have mistyped the name. Or the server may exist, but only allows connections from specific hosts. In any case, you get an error from ftp indicating why the connection failed. Here are some examples of different types of failed connections:

Restricted access

```
ftp> open ftp.disney.com
Connected to ftp.disney.com.
421 Service not available, remote server has closed
connection
ftp>
```

Machine unavailable (down)

```
ftp> open ftp.mpc.com
ftp: connect: Connection timed out
ftp>
```

Nonexistent host

```
ftp> open ftp.bigcorp.com
ftp.bigcorp.com: unknown host
ftp>
```

 **{Note}**

When an FTP server responds to any command from your ftp program, it returns a message number at the beginning of the response. If you want to find out more about what these message numbers mean, you can look at the Internet document RFC959, which describes how FTP works. You can find this document on the anonymous FTP server **ds.internic.net** in the directory /rfc in the file rfc959.txt.

Any of these error messages might mean simply that you have the host name wrong. Check to see if you have the right host name for the FTP server. If the host name is correct, here are some suggestions for what to do in response to the different errors:

- If you see a `Connection timed out` message, just wait awhile and try again.

- An `unknown host` message might be an indication that the FTP server no longer exists. Try to find out if the server has been renamed, or use another FTP server that has the same information as the one that no longer exists.

- Check with the maintainer of the FTP server if you see a `Service not available` message. If you don't know who maintains the server, address your mail to the site's postmaster. For example, the postmaster's address for the machine ftp.bigcorp.com (a fictitious server) is postmaster@bigcorp.com.

❶ *(Tip)*

Do you know the name of a site, but not the name of the FTP server? Before asking someone at the site, try two things. First, try to ftp to the main part of the site name. Many sites automatically connect you to their FTP server, or they give you a list of the servers you can connect to.

For example, if you want to find FTP servers at Carnegie Mellon University and you know that their domain name is cmu.edu, try opening that host. It tells you that it doesn't support anonymous FTP, and then it gives you a list of some of the FTP servers on campus.

A second way to find the name of an FTP server is to add "ftp." to the beginning of the domain name. For example, if you know that Microsoft has the domain name microsoft.com, try to ftp to the host **ftp.microsoft.com** (which is a real server).

You need to log in after you connect

Once you've successfully connected to the FTP server, you'll need to log in to an account on the server. The ftp program prompts you for an account name and password.

If you're connecting to an anonymous FTP server, use the account name **anonymous**. Then you'll need to enter a password. Many anonymous FTP servers allow you to enter anything as a password. Most request that you use your Internet mail address; some enforce the use of an Internet address as the password.

You can also use ftp to log in to a personal account if you have one on the remote host. To log in to a personal account, enter your account name and your password to complete the login.

Once you're successfully logged in, the server sends a welcome message, and then you are returned to the ftp prompt. Figure 14.2 shows a successful login.

Fig. 14.2
The welcome message from the FTP server **explorer.arc.nasa.gov** is an example of what you may get when you successfully log in to a server.

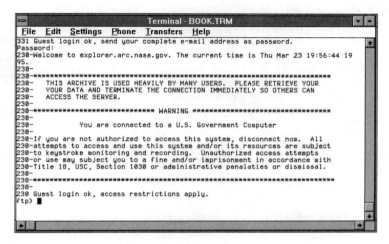

```
                         Terminal - BOOK.TRM
File  Edit  Settings  Phone  Transfers  Help
331 Guest login ok, send your complete e-mail address as password.
Password:
230-Welcome to explorer.arc.nasa.gov. The current time is Thu Mar 23 19:56:44 19
95.
230-
230-*******************************************************************************
230-     THIS ARCHIVE IS USED HEAVILY BY MANY USERS.  PLEASE RETRIEVE YOUR
230-     YOUR DATA AND TERMINATE THE CONNECTION IMMEDIATELY SO OTHERS CAN
230-     ACCESS THE SERVER.
230-
230-************************** WARNING **************************
230-
230-          You are connected to a U.S. Government Computer
230-
230-If you are not authorized to access this system, disconnect now.  All
230-attempts to access and use this system and/or its resources are subject
230-to keystroke monitoring and recording.  Unauthorized access attempts
230-or use may subject you to a fine and/or imprisonment in accordance with
230-Title 18, USC, Section 1030 or administrative penalties or dismissal.
230-
230-*******************************************************************************
230-
230 Guest login ok, access restrictions apply.
ftp> █
```

❷Q&A

What should I do if my login fails?

Error messages are unavoidable. One appears whenever you make a mistake logging in to an FTP server. Here are how you can handle a couple of the more common login failures.

When you try to log in as *anonymous* and the server doesn't let you (its quota of anonymous logins has been met), you get an error message, followed by the ftp prompt. At this point, although your login failed, you're still connected to the FTP server. To disconnect from this server and try another one, enter the close command. Now you can open a connection to another server.

What if you accidentally typed in the account name "anonymouse" when you tried to log in to the FTP server? Your login fails, but you are still connected to the server. If you want to try to log in again, type the user command at the ftp prompt. The ftp program prompts you for an account name. Now you can type **anonymous** correctly. To avoid the account prompt altogether, type the account name immediately after the user command (for example, enter the command **user anonymous** at the ftp prompt).

Finding what you want: listing directories and files

What do you do once you've connected to an FTP server? If you don't know the directory structure of the server, get a listing of the server's directories. Most FTP servers put you in the server's top-level directory when you first connect (some others put you in a subdirectory). You can use two commands to see what's in this (or any other directory): the `dir` and the `ls` commands.

The `dir` command gives you an alphabetical listing of the current directory (see fig. 14.3). The listing shows the complete information about each item in the directory. The listing will look somewhat different, depending on the operating system of the FTP server, but gives you as much information about the directory items as is available.

The `ls` command gives you a short listing of the current directory (see fig. 14.4). It can be easier to scan a short listing because the file and directory names are at the beginning of the line and you don't have to sort through extraneous information.

Local and *client* have different meanings when you're using a command-line account

Early in the book, we introduced you to the idea of *clients* and *servers*, and *local* and *remote* machines. When you are connected to a command-line account, the notion of **local** and **client** are slightly different.

The machine where your command-line account lives is the machine that runs the client programs (like the ftp program). When you're doing anything in FTP that refers to the local host, it refers to the machine that is running the FTP

client—the machine where your command-line account lives.

The computer that you're using to dial in to your command-line account is just acting as a terminal. It sends what you type to your account and displays any output from your account on your screen. Your computer doesn't run any programs (except for the communications program you use to dial in to your account), nor can you directly FTP files to or from it.

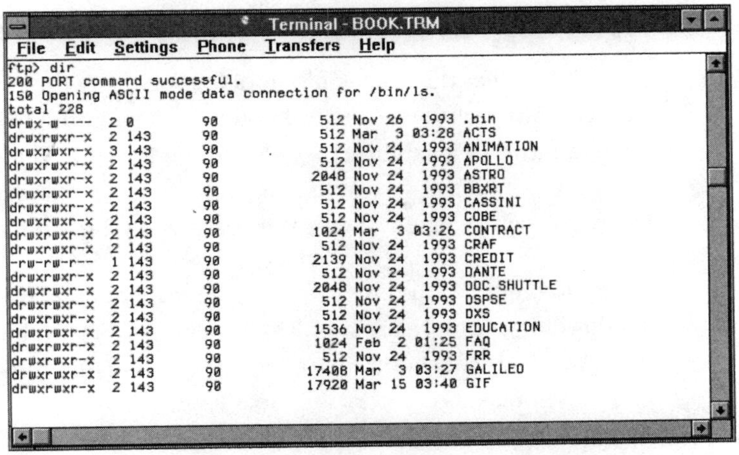

Fig. 14.3
The list you get from a UNIX host with the dir command shows whether an item is a file or directory, its protection, the date it was last modified, and the size.

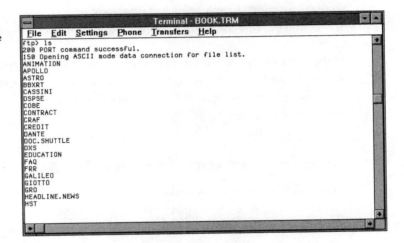

Fig. 14.4
In a short directory like this one, you can find what you need fast.

On the other hand, this listing doesn't tell you what you're looking at in the directory, so you don't know if the directory entries are files or subdirectories. Also, the items in this listing are not necessarily in alphabetical order.

How to get around in directories

When you're getting ready to transfer files, you need to make sure that you're in the proper directories on both the FTP server and on your account. The ftp program has commands to let you move around on the server and on your local account.

Moving around the FTP server

It's unlikely that the files you're looking for are in the top-level directory of a server. Most servers group related files in subdirectories. You probably have to move to a subdirectory to find the files you want. To move to a subdirectory on the server, use the `cd` command. For example, to move to the subdirectory msdos, enter the command **cd msdos** at the ftp prompt.

After moving to a subdirectory, do a directory listing to see what's in that subdirectory. If there are no files that interest you in the current directory, see if there are any subdirectories in the listing that look interesting. Move to an interesting subdirectory and do a listing there.

You can keep moving through the server's directory structure by doing a directory listing at each level and then moving to the next subdirectory you're interested in. You can continue this process until you find the files you want.

Once you're familiar with the directory structure of a server, you can give the complete path name to move quickly to a subdirectory several levels down. For example, the command **cd pc/win/winsock** moves you three levels down in the directory structure.

Moving around in your local account

Before you transfer a file, make sure you're in the proper directory on your local account. When you download files, ftp transfers them to the current local directory. Your current local directory is the directory that you were in when you started the ftp program. If you want to save the downloaded files to another directory, you need to change your local directory. Remember that "local directory" here refers to the directory on your command-line account, not a directory on the computer you used to dial in to your account.

You can set your current local directory from inside ftp with the `lcd` command. Just follow the `lcd` command with the path to the directory where you want to store downloaded files. You can give a **relative address** to move to a directory below the current one, or you can give an **absolute address** to move to any directory in your local file structure. An absolute address begins with a slash that tells ftp to start at the top of your local machine's file structure, while a relative address starts with the name of a directory directly under your current directory.

When you use a relative address, ftp looks in the current directory for the directory that you want to move to. Say your current local directory is /usr/users/mapike. You can use relative addressing to move down two levels to the directory /usr/users/mapike/games/zork. To move to the zork directory, you would use the command **lcd games/zork**.

When you use an absolute address, ftp starts at the top of the directory structure for your local machine to find the directory you want to move to. Say your current local directory is /usr/users/mapike. To move out of that directory to the directory /usr/projects/sources, you would use the command **lcd /usr/projects/sources**.

If you enter the lcd command without specifying a local directory, ftp uses your home directory as the local directory.

❝ Plain English, please!

Your **home directory** is the directory that you start in when you log in to your command–line account. ❞

Getting what you came for: downloading a file

Now you've connected to a server, you've navigated through the directories, and you've finally found a file you want to download. How do you do that? The ftp program lets you move a file from the FTP server to your command-line account. After you've done this, you need to use your communications software to move the file to the computer that you use to connect to your command-line account.

Transferring a file to your command-line account

It's easy to move a file from the FTP server to your local account. The command that ftp uses to download a file is get (or you can use recv). Simply follow the get command with the name of the file that you want (and, optionally, with the name you want to store the file under on your local account). For example **get pkz204g.exe pkz.exe** moves the file pkz204g.exe from the FTP server to a file called pkz.exe on your local account.

The get command requests that the FTP server send you a copy of the file you requested. The copy is stored in the current directory on your local file system. If you don't specify a file name for the local copy, it's stored with the same name it had on the server. When ftp is finished transferring the file, it tells you the transfer was successful and gives you information about the transfer (see fig. 14.5).

✱ {Note}

To get a file, you must move into the directory on the FTP server where the file is stored. You cannot specify a full path, either absolute or relative, to the get command. You get the error message No such file or directory when you try to use the get command this way, even if you've specified the path to the file correctly.

Your disk space may be limited

When you transfer files to your command-line account, you probably will have a limited amount of disk space (possibly only a few megabytes) that you can use for file storage. Sometimes your account provider will let you store more than your allotted amount, but will charge you a monthly fee for the extra storage space.

You probably don't want to store the files on your command-line account anyway. You most likely want to transfer them to the computer that you are using to dial in to your command-line account. Once you transfer the files to your computer, delete them from your command-line account to make room for new files and to avoid extra storage charges.

Fig. 14.5
When ftp finishes transferring a file, it tells you the name of the local and remote file, the size of the file in bytes, and how long the transfer took.

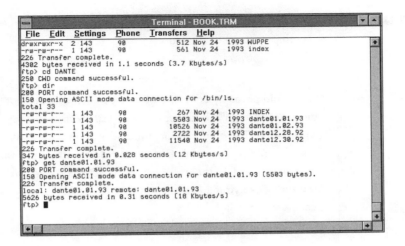

By default, ftp doesn't check to see if you already have a file in the your current local directory with the same name as the one you are downloading. If you download a file with the same name as one already in your local directory, the one in the local directory is overwritten.

You can prevent ftp from doing this, however. Type the runique command at the ftp prompt to tell ftp to append a dot (.) and a unique number (starting with 1, and going as high as 99) to the end of the file name. For example, if you had a file called project.txt and tried to download a file with the same name, ftp would name the downloaded file project.txt.1. The runique command is a toggle; type it again to turn it off.

Is a text file different than a picture?

Transferring a file seems simple enough. But wait! Make sure you use the right **type** to transfer the file so that the file isn't corrupted. By default, many ftp programs have the transfer type set to **ASCII**, assuming that you are transferring text files. You can change the type to **binary**, however, if you want to download something other than a text file. This includes program files, image files, zipped files, and so on. To change the type to binary, simply enter the binary command at the ftp prompt.

⊗<Caution> If you try to download binary files in ASCII mode, you may end up with a corrupted copy of the file.

❶(Tip) You should probably enter the **binary** command as the first thing you do when you connect to an FTP server. Text files usually transfer with no problem in binary mode. There are rare circumstances when the remote server and your local system store end-of-line characters differently. ASCII mode is necessary in this case to translate the end-of-line characters properly. You might as well try transferring everything in binary mode and use ASCII mode only if a problem occurs with text files.

Can I look at a file before I transfer it?

One thing that you might want to do occasionally is look at the contents of a file rather than store the file to your disk. This is particularly useful if you're retrieving an index file that tells you what files are in the current directory. To display the file on your screen instead of saving it, put a space followed by a dash (-) after the get command. For example, the command **get index.txt-** displays the file index.txt on your screen.

The only time you may run into a problem is when the file you're displaying is very long. The information quickly scrolls off your screen as the file is displayed. If you're using an interface (like Windows Terminal) that saves a certain number of lines from your terminal session, you can scroll back through the information that was displayed from the file and read it at your leisure.

Or, you can see if your system has **pause output** and **resume output** commands. Many systems use Ctrl+S to pause output to the screen, and Ctrl+Q to resume output. (If these don't seem to work for you, you might want to ask your system administrator if there are commands like these for your system.) As the information is flashing by, you have to press Ctrl+S to stop it. Then press Ctrl+Q to let what you've read go by, and press Ctrl+S to stop it again. It takes a lot of practice to use the commands fast enough that you don't miss a lot of information.

The best solution to this problem is if your system has a pager program like **more**. If you pipe the file you're retrieving through more, you can view the file one page at a time. To use more, enter the command **get index.txt |more**.

 Plain English, please!

When you **pipe** something to a program, you take the output of a command and direct it to be used as the input for the program you are piping to. So, for example, instead of saving the file that the get command is sending you, you can send the text of the file to the more program, which will display it on your screen a page at a time. The vertical bar (|) indicates that a pipe should be used. The output of the command will be sent to the program following the vertical bar.

It's important to omit the dash, and not to put a space between the vertical bar and the word more. When ftp begins displaying the text, you can view it the way you view anything piped through more. Press the **space bar** to go to the next page of output. Type **Q** to quit and return to the ftp prompt.

Downloading multiple files

You've found an FTP server that has lots of files you'd like to download, and you're not looking forward to typing in dozens of get commands. Well, there might be a shortcut you can use to transfer those files. ftp has an mget command that lets you download multiple files with one command. You can give the mget command a list of the files you want to transfer, or you can use wildcards to specify groups of files with similar names.

If you want to download several files that have very different names, you can give a list of files to the mget command and it downloads all of those files to your local account. For example, the command **mget wndstrm.txt wvp_vid.txt** downloads the two files wndstrm.txt and wvp_vid.txt. You must put a space between the file names—the command doesn't work if you put commas between the names. Since you are transferring multiple files, you don't have an option of specifying the names that the files are saved under on your local account—the names will be the same as they are on the FTP server.

If you want to download several files that have similar names, you can use wildcards to specify a pattern that the filename should match. The most useful wildcard character is "*" which matches any number of any characters. You can also use "?" to match any single character.

For example, the command **mget *.zip** downloads all files with the extension ".zip". The command **mget wsarch0?.zip** downloads all files beginning with "wsarch0" followed by any single character, and ending with ".zip". The names of the files stored on your local account will be the same as they are on the FTP server.

By default, when you use the `mget` command, ftp asks you to confirm the transfer before each file. This can be useful if you want to transfer all but one or two files that have similar names. You can use a wildcard to specify a large group of files to transfer, and then just answer no when ftp asks if you want to transfer the files you don't want.

Moving files between your personal computer and your command-line account

You successfully transferred a file from an FTP server to your command-line account, but this isn't really what you wanted to do. You really wanted to transfer the file to your personal computer—the one that you're using to dial in to your command-line account. Or maybe you want to take a file off your personal computer and put it on an FTP server. You can do either of these things, as long as the service provider and the communications software you use understand the same **transfer protocol**.

 Plain English, please!

A **transfer protocol** is the set of commands that a computer uses to send and receive information. In order for two computers to communicate, they must be using the same protocol.

There are a number of different transfer protocols in use today—**xmodem**, **ymodem**, **zmodem**, and **kermit** are some of the most common ones. What you will need to do is find out what communications protocol is available on your command-line account, and get a communications package for your personal computer that uses the same communications protocol. Once you're sure both machines have the same communications protocol, you should be able to transfer the file.

One of the communications protocols that is available on many UNIX systems is the kermit protocol. There are kermit applications available for DOS, and many Windows communications programs support the kermit protocol. A better protocol that you can use if your account has it is the xmodem protocol. To find out what protocol is available to you, you will probably need to ask your system administrator.

Getting a file to your personal computer

After you've gotten a file from an FTP site and put it on your command-line account, it shouldn't be too difficult to move it to your personal computer. Here's an example of the steps you'll probably need to go through, no matter what protocol you are using:

1 If you are not already logged in, log in to your command-line account in the usual way.

2 Tell the communications program on your personal computer what type of transfer protocol you are using. There is probably a Settings item in the menu bar of your communications program. Open the Settings menu and look for something like "File Transfer" (see fig. 14.6). Choose this entry.

Fig. 14.6
The Crosstalk communications program has a File Transfer item under the Settings menu that lets you set up your transfer protocol.

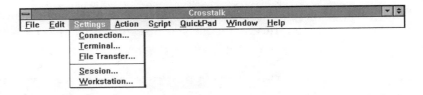

3 The Settings dialog box should let you choose your communications protocol. If you are using kermit to transfer files, you will need to set the transfer type (see fig. 14.7).

Transfer protocol

Fig. 14.7
When you use kermit as your transfer protocol, the communications software on your personal computer defines whether the file transfers should be binary or text.

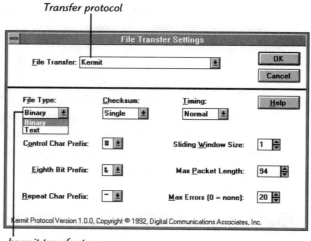

kermit transfer type

4 Start the transfer program from your command-line account. For example, if you are using kermit to send the file wsarch07.zip, use the command **kermit -s wsarch07.zip**.

If you are using xmodem, use the command **xmodem -sb wsarch07.zip**. You should use one of the following switches to tell the xmodem command what type of transfer you are doing:

- **-sb** indicates xmodem is sending a binary file.

- **-st** indicates xmodem is sending a text file.

- **-sa** indicates xmodem is sending an Apple Macintosh text file.

5 Now tell the communications program on your personal computer to receive the file you are sending. There is probably a menu item called Action or Transfer that lets you select a Receive File item (see fig. 14.8).

Fig. 14.8
The Crosstalk communications program has a File Transfer item under the Action menu that lets you send or receive files.

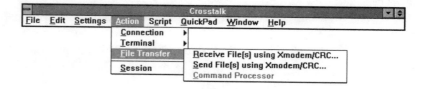

6 You should then get a dialog that lets you specify where to store the file on your local file system. Once you've filled in this dialog, select OK. Your file transfer should start. You'll probably get dialog that shows you the status of your file transfer (see fig. 14.9).

Fig. 14.9
The Crosstalk communications program has a dialog box that lets you know how many bytes have been transferred, how fast the file is being transferred, and whether any transfer errors have occurred.

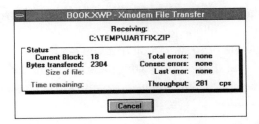

This is a very rough outline of the procedure you use to transfer files to your personal computer. How your file transfers work will depend on what transfer program is available on your command-line account, and what type of communications software you use to connect to your account. If you have any problems, ask your system administrator for help.

Sending a file from your personal computer to your command–line account

Maybe you've developed a program for your personal computer that you'd like to distribute as shareware. Or maybe you've got some pictures that you'd like to upload to an FTP site. The first thing you'll need to do is send the files from your personal computer to your command-line account. The steps you need to follow are very similar to the steps outlined in the previous section, "Getting a file to your personal computer."

When you are ready to send a file to your command-line account, follow steps 1, 2, and 3 in the section above. Step 4 is where the main difference in the transfer procedure shows up. You will be telling your command-line account to wait to receive a file. For example, if you are sending the file maphorse.gif to your command-line account using kermit, enter the command **kermit -r maphorse.gif**. If you are using xmodem, enter the command **xmodem -rb maphorse.gif**. You should use one of the following switches to tell the xmodem command what type of transfer you are doing:

- **-rb** indicates xmodem is receiving a binary file.

- **-rt** indicates xmodem is receiving a text file.

- **-ra** indicates xmodem is receiving an Apple Macintosh text file.

To complete the file transfer, follow steps 5 and 6 from the preceding section (except that you'll be looking for a "send" menu item instead of a "receive" item). The file browser dialog that you get in step 6 will let you find the file that you want to send from your personal computer. Once you've transferred the file to your command-line account, you can upload it to an FTP server.

 (Tip)

> Remember to delete the file from your command-line account once you've uploaded it to an FTP server so that you don't waste your disk space allotment.

Sharing your files: uploading them to an FTP server

ftp isn't limited to retrieving files from FTP servers. If the FTP server allows you to, you can upload files from your machine to the server. Before you do this, you need to worry about all of the same things that you did when you retrieved a file. You should:

- Set the transfer type to binary

- Make your current local directory the one that has the file you're going to transfer

- Navigate to the directory on the FTP server where you want to store the file

Once you've done all this, you're ready to go.

The command that ftp uses to upload a file is put (most ftp programs also let you use send). Simply follow the put command with the name of the file that you want to upload (and, optionally, with the name you want to store the file under on the FTP server). For example, the command **put pkz204g.exe pkz.exe** will move the file pkz204g.exe from the current directory on your local account to the current directory on the FTP server.

The put command tells the FTP server to store the copy of the file you are sending in the current directory on the FTP server. If you don't specify a file name for the remote copy, it is stored with the same name it had on your local system. Remember that you need to have permission to write to the directory on the FTP server in order to upload files to it.

(!) (Tip)

> If an anonymous FTP server allows you to upload files, it probably has a directory with a name like "incoming." You may find the incoming directory under a public area (often /pub) on the server.

(X) <Caution>

> By default, ftp doesn't check to see if the FTP server already has a file in the current directory with the same name as the one you are transferring. If you transfer a file with the same name as one already in the directory, the one in the directory is overwritten.
>
> You can prevent ftp from doing this, however. Type the sunique command at the ftp prompt to tell ftp to append a dot (.) and a unique number (starting with 1, and going as high as 99) to the end of the file name. For example, if a file called project.txt existed on the FTP server and you tried to upload a file with the same name, ftp would name the uploaded file project.txt.1. The sunique command is a toggle, so type it again to turn it off.

Like the mget command, there is an mput command that lets you upload multiple files to the FTP server with one command. You can again enter a list of files, or use wildcards to specify a group of files with similar names.

Saying good-bye to ftp

When you've finished transferring files on a server, close your connection to the server. FTP servers usually allow a limited number of connections, so if you don't close the connection you prevent others from using the server. If you want to close your connection and exit the ftp program, enter the bye command (or you can use quit) at the ftp prompt. This returns you to your system prompt.

If you want to close the connection to the current server, but want to remain in ftp so that you can connect to other servers, use the `close` command (or `disconnect`). You can then use the `open` command to connect to another FTP server.

A summary of other ftp commands

There are a few other ftp commands that you might need or want to use while perusing an FTP server. The following table is not a complete listing of all other ftp commands, but a summary of some you may find useful:

ftp command	Description
bell	Sounds a beep (bell) when a file transfer is completed.
cdup	Changes directories on the FTP server to the one above the current server.
delete *remote_file*	Deletes the file *remote_file* from the current directory on the FTP server if you have permission.
help *command*	Gets information about a particular ftp command (if *command* is omitted, a list of all ftp commands is shown).
mkdir *dir*	Creates the directory *dir* on the FTP server if you have permission.
prompt	Toggles whether ftp asks if you want to transfer each file when doing an `mget` command.
pwd	Prints the name of the current directory on the FTP server.
rename *old_name new_name*	Renames a file in the current directory on the FTP server if you have permission.
rmdir *dir*	Removes the subdirectory *dir* from the current directory on the FTP server if you have permission.
verbose	Tells ftp not to report to you the success of transfers, the local and remote file information, or the sizes of files transferred.

15

Archie Searches from a Command Line

Archie from the command line may not be as friendly as a graphical Archie, but it can still get you to the files you need.

I f you connect to the Net with a terminal interface, you can't use a graphical Archie client. Don't worry, though, because you can still do Archie searches as long as you can use Telnet from your Internet account. And once you learn the commands you need, using an Archie server from the command line is a breeze.

Connecting to an Archie server

First things first: connect to an **Archie server**. You can connect to any Archie server and use a command-line interface to search the Archie databases if your Internet account lets you use Telnet. **Telnet** is the Internet service that you use to log in to an Archie server (or any other Internet host, for that matter).

Most UNIX-based Internet accounts give you access to the telnet command. This command enables you to use programs or log in to accounts on other Internet hosts. Type the telnet command followed by the name of the Archie server you want to connect to (for example, **telnet archie.internic.net**). If you have any trouble, ask your system administrator for help.

Is there an easier way to use Archie?

Some Internet accounts (mainly UNIX accounts) have a built-in command that starts Telnet and connects to an Archie server. To see if your UNIX system has a command like this, type **archie** at the command prompt. You should get the help information for your system's archie command.

To use the UNIX archie command, you must specify all of the information you need to send to the Archie server as part of the command. You can set your search type and the Archie server that you want to use from the command line, as well as enter the search string.

The problem with using this type of Archie command is that you get no feedback (error messages, login messages, and so on). If the command fails, you don't know what the problem is. Even if it's working, you don't know until the search is complete. If nothing is happening, there might be a problem, or your search request might just be waiting in the queue (there's nothing to tell you how long you'll wait). Another problem with this type of command is that when the results are returned, they fly past on-screen. You can solve this problem by writing out the results to a file or by piping the command through a pager such as **more**. (See the "Can I look at a file before I transfer it?" section

in Chapter 14 for more information on using the more program.)

Here are some examples of the UNIX archie command using the most common command line switches (the different type of searches referred to in these examples are described in more detail in the section "Search types" later in this chapter):

- **archie –c pkz –m 200** does a case-sensitive substring search on "pkz" and returns the first 200 matches.

- **archie –s pkz |more** does a case-insensitive substring search on "pkz" and pipes the results through the more pager.

- **archie –e pkz204g.exe –o results** does an exact match (the default search type) on "pkz204g.exe" and writes the matching files to the file "results."

- **archie –r wsarch0[^1-6].zip –h archie.internic.net** connects to the Archie server **archie.internic.net**, then does a regular expression search looking for the latest version of the WSArchie distribution file (where the last digit of the file name is greater than 6).

- **archie –L** returns a listing of available Archie servers and indicates the current one.

You can connect to any Internet Archie server using Telnet. Pick one that's geographically close to you since it's likely to be physically closer to you on the network and should give you a faster response time. The following table lists names and locations of some of the Archie servers.

Archie server	Location
archie.internic.net	New Jersey
archie.unl.edu	Nebraska
archie.ans.net	New York
archie.rutgers.edu	New Jersey
archie.sura.net	Maryland
archie.au	Australia
archie.cs.mcgill.ca	Canada
archie.th–darmstadt.de	Germany
archie.wide.ad.jp	Japan
archie.switch.ch	Switzerland
archie.doc.ic.ac.uk	United Kingdom

❋ {Note}

There are two ways to get a complete list of the Archie servers available to you. First, if you're connecting to an Archie server using Telnet, type **servers** at the Archie prompt. This gives you a list of all available Archie servers. If you have an `archie` command on your UNIX system, use the `archie -L` command to get a list of available servers.

❶ (Tip)

During peak hours (generally from 9:00 a.m. through 6:00 p.m.), it may be better to pick a site overseas that is in the middle of their night. Sites such as these may have less traffic than local sites and may respond faster.

When you enter the `telnet` command, you'll probably get a message saying that your host is trying to connect to the Archie server. A welcome message appears when your host successfully connects to the Archie server (see fig. 15.1). The Archie server asks you to log in to an account name. Type **archie** as the account name (no password is required). You're now ready to do an Archie search.

Fig. 15.1

When you connect to an Archie server, you get a welcome message from the server and a login prompt.

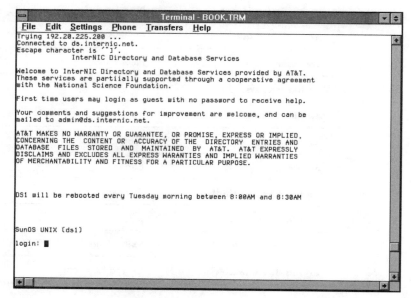

```
                      Terminal - BOOK.TRM
 File  Edit  Settings  Phone  Transfers  Help
Trying 192.20.225.200 ...
Connected to ds.internic.net.
Escape character is '^]'.
             InterNIC Directory and Database Services

Welcome to InterNIC Directory and Database Services provided by AT&T.
These services are partiially supported through a cooperative agreement
with the National Science Foundation.

First time users may login as guest with no password to receive help.

Your comments and suggestions for improvement are welcome, and can be
mailed to admin@ds.internic.net.

AT&T MAKES NO WARRANTY OR GUARANTEE, OR PROMISE, EXPRESS OR IMPLIED,
CONCERNING THE  CONTENT OR  ACCURACY OF THE  DIRECTORY  ENTRIES AND
DATABASE  FILES  STORED  AND  MAINTAINED  BY  AT&T.  AT&T EXPRESSLY
DISCLAIMS AND EXCLUDES ALL EXPRESS WARANTIES AND IMPLIED WARRANTIES
OF MERCHANTABILITY AND FITNESS FOR A PARTICULAR PURPOSE.



DS1 will be rebooted every Tuesday morning between 8:00AM and 8:30AM



SunOS UNIX (ds1)

login: █
```

✱ {Note}

All the figures in this chapter were done using a Windows terminal program. However, the pictures in this chapter are valid for whatever type of terminal interface you use, it doesn't matter if you connect to your account from a Macintosh terminal program, or from an actual ASCII terminal—the commands you type and the results you see will be as pictured.

❓ Q&A

Why can't I connect to the Archie server I've picked?

The server may be down or may no longer exist. Or, the server may have so many people using it that it can't accept any more connections. Try connecting to a different server, or wait awhile before trying this server again.

Simple Archie searches

After you connect to an Archie server, enter a few commands to set up your search and you're on your way. Just tell Archie what type of search you want to do and how to display the results.

Archie normally displays all files it finds in one large chunk. This causes the information to scroll quickly off your screen if there is more than one page. You can use the pager command to read what appears on-screen more easily. Type **set pager** at the Archie prompt to tell Archie to send only one page of information to your computer at one time. Press the space bar to move to the next page.

Archie lets you specify how closely a file name must match the search string you enter. The "Search Types" section later in this chapter explains all the different degrees of matching you can tell Archie to use. The simplest search that returns the most results is the **substring case-insensitive search**. Archie returns any file name that contains the character string you enter, regardless of whether the case of the characters matches the case of the search string. To do this type of search, type **set search sub** at the Archie prompt.

 (Tip)

> By default, Archie returns the first 95 matches it finds in its database. You can tell Archie to change this value if you want to see more or fewer matches. For example, if you want to see the first 200 matches, enter the command **set maxhits 200** at the Archie prompt.

Once you've set up the pager and your search type, you're ready to do a search. Enter find followed by the name (or part of the name) of the file you are interested in. Searches are entered in a queue in the order they're received. The server tells you what your position is in the search queue. It also gives the estimated time of completion of your search, usually in minutes and seconds (see fig. 15.2).

Fig. 15.2
Once you've con-
nected to an Archie
server, only a few
commands are
necessary to start
your search.

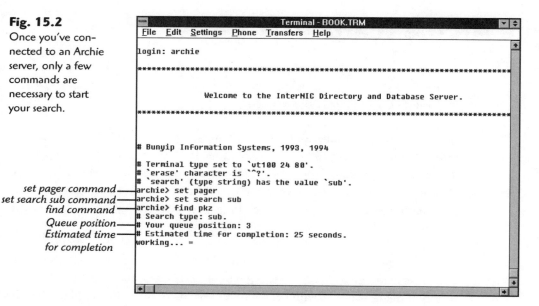

set pager command ——
set search sub command ——
find command ——
Queue position ——
Estimated time ——
for completion

```
login: archie

********************************************************************

              Welcome to the InterNIC Directory and Database Server.

********************************************************************


# Bunyip Information Systems, 1993, 1994

# Terminal type set to `vt100 24 80'.
# `erase' character is `^?'.
# `search' (type string) has the value `sub'.
archie> set pager
archie> set search sub
archie> find pkz
# Search type: sub.
# Your queue position: 3
# Estimated time for completion: 25 seconds.
working... =
```

🅀 **Q&A**

> **What should I do if the Archie server tells me I'm number
> 956 in the queue and my search will take several hours?**
>
> Luckily, it's not difficult to cancel a search on an Archie server. Any time you've
> started a search and you want to cancel it, simply press Ctrl+C. This will put you
> back at the Archie prompt. If you do find that your search is going to take a
> long time, you may want to exit this server and try one that's less busy.

Understanding the search results

After Archie finishes searching its database for files that match what you are
looking for, it displays the results a page at a time if you set pager when you
connected to the server (see fig. 15.3). For each matching file, Archie displays
several pieces of information that can help you find the file and then download it with FTP:

- The computer where the file is located, including the host name and
  Internet IP address numbers for the host

- The last time that the Archie server connected to this host system to
  update its database

- The location of the matching file (generally a directory on the host machine) and information about the matching file, such as the full name, the size of the file, and when the file was created

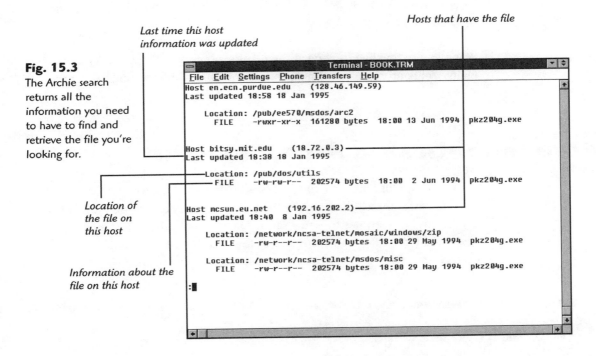

Fig. 15.3
The Archie search returns all the information you need to have to find and retrieve the file you're looking for.

Last time this host information was updated

Hosts that have the file

Location of the file on this host

Information about the file on this host

Which matching file should I retrieve?

Once you have a list of matching files from Archie, how do you decide which one to try to retrieve with FTP? Look at the date that this Archie server last connected to the FTP server to update its database. This date can be important, because the file may have been deleted from the FTP server after the Archie server updated its database. If the date displayed for the last update is more than a few weeks old, you may want to choose a different matching file.

If several FTP servers are available that have the file you want, it doesn't make a lot of difference which one you get the file from. Choose a server that you have a good chance of connecting to easily—one that doesn't have a lot of traffic, for example.

If you have pager set, Archie presents the results one screen at a time. Press the space bar to move to the next screen. Press the Enter key to move forward one line. Press the B key to move back a page. Note the names of the servers that have a recent copy of the matching file. Later, connect to one of these anonymous FTP servers to retrieve the file.

When you're finished looking at the results, press the Q key to get back to the main Archie prompt. You can do this at any time while viewing the search results.

More sophisticated Archie searches

If you know a lot about the file names you are searching for, you can reduce the number of matching files Archie returns to you. You can do more sophisticated Archie searches by being more specific about the files you are searching for. Archie can either match the search string you enter more closely or search for a **character pattern**.

Using help in Archie

Archie has a help feature you can use to get information about different commands. To get a list of the Archie commands, type **help ?** at the Archie prompt. Once you use the help command, Archie leaves you in its help system rather than returning you to the Archie prompt.

To get information about one of the commands, just type the name of the command at the help prompt. The Archie server will give you information about the command, using pager to keep the text from quickly scrolling by on your screen. To exit help, type a period (.) and then press Enter. You may need to do this several times to get back to the Archie prompt if you are several levels into the help system.

Search types

If you know the exact (or almost exact) name of the file you want, you can tell the Archie server to narrow its search. You can search for files that match your search string exactly; you can specify partial matching; and you can specify whether the uppercase and lowercase letters in your search string must match those in the file name exactly. You also can tell the Archie server to search for a particular pattern of characters using a **regular expression**.

> **66** **Plain English, please!**
>
> A **regular expression** lets you look for file names that match patterns of ASCII characters. For example, you can specify the first part of a file name, then give a range of values for the version number. Or, you can look for all files that contain the letters "win" and end in "zip". Regular expressions are explained in the "Regular expression" section later in this chapter. **99**

The following table tells you about the different types of searches that you can do. You'll need to tell the Archie server what type of search you're doing before you do your first search. To set your search type, enter the command `set search` followed by one of the search names. For example, to do an exact search, you would enter **set search exact** at the Archie prompt before you do your search. When you log in to the server, it should tell you what the default search type for that server is. If you want to change the type of search you are doing, just enter a new `set search` command before doing your next search.

Search type	Description	Example
sub	Archie returns any files it finds whose names contain the search string)upper- and lowercase letters are ignored).	**find arch** returns any files whose names contain the string "arch". example, wsarch06.zip and Archive.idx would both match.
subcase	Archie returns any files it finds whose names contain the search string with the case of the letters matching exactly.	**find arch** returns only the files whose names contain the string "arch" with the exact capitalization. For example, wsarch06.zip would match, but Archive.idx would not.

continues

Search type	Description	Example
exact	Archie returns any files it finds whose names exactly match the search string (including case).	**find wsarch06.zip** returns only files with this exact name.
regex	Archie returns any files it finds that match the regular expression specified.	**find wsarch0[^1-6].zip** returns files that begin with "wsarch0" followed by a number greater than 6, then by ".zip".

Search examples

The following sections give you examples of how to specify the different search types, and what types of file names will match for the different search types.

Exact matches

If you want Archie to find only files that match your search string exactly, use the command `set search exact`. When you enter the `find` command, enter the exact spelling (including capitalization) of the full file name. For example, use the command **find pkz204g.exe** to find a copy of the PKZIP distribution file. This search type is most useful if you know the exact name of the file you are looking for.

Substring case-insensitive

To do a search that ignores the case of letters in the matching file names, use the command `set search sub`. When you enter the `find` command, you can enter just a part of the file name you are looking for, not worrying about the case of the characters you enter. This type of search returns the largest number of matches. For example, **find win** returns a list of all files that contain the letters "win" in their names, whether upper- or lowercase.

Substring case-sensitive

To search for a file name that contains your search string with the case of the letters matching exactly, use the command set search subcase. When you enter the find command, you can enter just a part of the file name you are looking for. Archie then returns only file names that contain the letters in your search string with the case of the letters matching the search string exactly. This type of search lets you narrow the search some if you know the exact case of at least part of the file name. For example, **find win** returns a list of all files that contain the lowercase letters "win" in their names.

Regular expression

If you want to specify a pattern of characters that Archie can use to find matching file names, use the command set search regex. This is not a search type that you'll need to use very often. But you might find it useful for doing something like searching for the most recent version of a file. A regular expression search lets you look for file names that contain a version number greater than the current one.

When you enter the find command, enter the character pattern that you want Archie to search for. You can use ranges of letters and numbers and special characters to build your search string. The following table lists the most common regular expression elements.

Element	Definition
.	Matches any single character
*	Matches zero or more occurrences of the preceding character
[ ]	Lets you specify a range or set of characters
^	Matches anything but the character following it
\	Lets you tell Archie to include the special character following it (like ^) in the file name instead of interpreting it as a special character.

Some examples of the search pieces you might use are:

- [0-9] matches any number.

- [abcd] matches any one of the characters a, b, c, or d.

- [^a-zA-Z] matches any nonletter.

- [0-9]* matches any number of numbers.

- .* matches any number of any characters.

The command **find win.*[0-9]** matches any file name that contains a string that starts with "win" and ends in a digit, with any number of other characters in between. If you know that the WSArchie distribution file has the version number at the end of the file, and you want to see if there is a version higher than 6, you can use the command **find wsarch0[^0-6]** to find only versions 7 and above of the file.

If you want to search for a file name that contains one of the characters that has a special meaning in the regex search (like a "*"), precede the character with a backslash (\\) in the search string.

●(Tip)

> When you're building your search string for a file name, you usually don't have to put a backslash in front of a "." in a file name because the special character . will match any single character, including the ".".

Exiting Archie

Once you're done searching the Archie database, type **quit** at the archie prompt. This disconnects you from the Archie server, and puts you back to your system prompt. From here, you can start FTP and connect to one of the FTP servers that has the file you want.

Part V:

FTP from the World Wide Web

Chapter 16: FTP Access through Mosaic and
Netscape

16

FTP Access through Mosaic and Netscape

The World Wide Web gives you more visual access to FTP— more interesting than just scrolling through lists of files and directories!

In this chapter:

- A little info about the WWW and FTP
- How do I access FTP servers through the WWW?
- Using Netscape and Mosaic to look at FTP servers
- How to retrieve files with Netscape and Mosaic

The World Wide Web, one of the newest services on the Internet, gives you the easiest way of looking at FTP servers (see the "What is the World Wide Web?" sidebar later in this chapter). It shows you more information and is easier to use than either a graphical FTP program or a command-line account. And it's more fun!

When you look at an FTP server from a World Wide Web browsing application (like Netscape or Mosaic), you see a graphical representation of the server's file and directory structure. It looks a lot like folders on a Macintosh, or a directory tree in the Windows File Manager. You can quickly change directories by clicking a folder. You also can retrieve files and save them to your computer, or view the files directly from the World Wide Web browser.

Plain English, please!

A **browser** is an application that lets you view and download World Wide Web documents. Most browsers also act as a graphical interface to other Internet services. 99

WWW FTP limitations

The WWW gives you a nice graphical interface to FTP. You can just point and click to look in directories and transfer files (see fig. 16.1). Your WWW browser hides all the commands that it uses to talk to the FTP servers.

Address of current FTP server and directory

Fig. 16.1
Netscape uses icons for directories and different file types on FTP servers, and lets you click the text next to the icons to view directories and retrieve files.

Directories

Unknown files

Text files

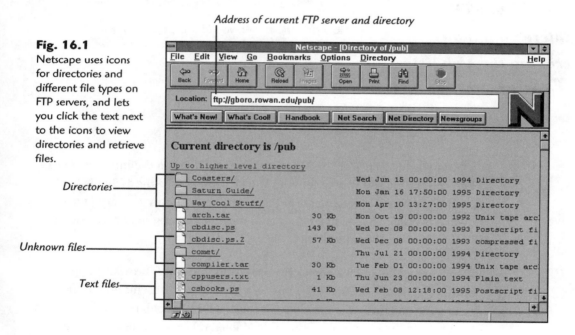

There are limits to using FTP from the WWW. First, you can only connect to anonymous FTP servers from the WWW—you can't connect to FTP servers that require you to log in to an account. Also, the only FTP commands that you can use are the commands to change directories and retrieve files. If you need to do anything else (like set the file transfer type or change user IDs on the FTP server), you should use a regular FTP program like WS_FTP. You also can't use a WWW browser to upload files to an anonymous FTP server.

Another difference is that when you connect to an FTP server using an FTP client, you have a permanent connection open to the FTP server. When you use the WWW to connect to an FTP server, you release your connection after every command to the FTP server. This means that your FTP transactions can be a little slower because you have to establish a new connection to the server every time you change directories or retrieve a file. Also, if the FTP server becomes busy, you may find that you can't connect to it the next time you try to change directories or retrieve a file.

What is the World Wide Web?

Over the first 20 years of its existence, the Internet was used mainly by the academic and research communities. Most of those people were very computer literate, so they didn't care if the Internet services were a little hard to use. In recent years, more non-computer experts began using the Internet. People began to design graphically oriented interfaces to the different Internet services to make them easier to use.

Around 1990, the researchers at the European Laboratory for Particle Physics wanted to go even further in making the Internet easy to use. They wanted to have one interface that let them move between documents and access all the Internet services quickly. What they designed was a **hypertext** system (which evolved into a **hypermedia** system) that let them link documents together and access Internet services with a simple addressing scheme. This system became known as the **World Wide Web** (or **WWW** for short).

 Plain English, please!

Hypertext is text that contains links to other files. You can activate the links (usually by clicking on them) to open the referenced documents.
Hypermedia is like hypertext except you can access all type of files (pictures, sound, animations) using links, not just text files.

Just what is a URL?

One of the neat things about the WWW is that you can access almost any file on the Internet if you have the right address for it. These WWW addresses are called **URLs** (short for **Uniform Resource Locator**). A URL points you to a document on the Internet. But it does more than just tell you the name of the host where you can find the file and the directory path to the file. It also lets you specify the Internet protocol that you use to retrieve the file.

You can have URLs that let you look at WWW documents (using the **http** protocol), documents on Gopher servers (using the **gopher** protocol), or documents on FTP servers (using, what else, the **ftp** protocol). You can even read UseNet news with many of the Web browsers. In this book, however, we're just concerned about how to use Web browsers (in particular, Netscape and Mosaic) to connect to FTP servers.

Let's look at a URL for a document on an FTP server. We want to look at a document called wvp_vid.txt, in the directory /pub/Coasters/Reviews, on the FTP server **gboro.rowan.edu**. To look at this document using a Web browser, you tell the browser to open this URL:

ftp://gboro.rowan.edu/pub/Coasters/Reviews/wvp_vid.txt

The ftp: tells the Web browser that it will be talking to an FTP server to get the document. This is followed by two slashes (required), the FTP server name, and the directory path to the file.

If you tell a Web browser to open this URL, it will retrieve the file wvp_vid.txt and display it for you. However, you don't need to give the address of a specific file in your URL. You can also give a path to a directory, and the browser will show you the contents of that directory (for example, **ftp:// gboro.rowan.edu/pub/Coasters/Reviews** will show you a listing of the Reviews directory). Or you can just use the FTP server name (for example, **ftp://gboro.rowan.edu**), and the browser will show you the top-level directory for that server.

FTP links in a Web page

While you're looking through a WWW document, you may find links to files on anonymous FTP servers. In many cases, you wouldn't even know you were connecting to an FTP server—you just click the link, and the Web browser loads the document for viewing. You can find out where the link is pointing by looking at the URL for the document. Many browsers show you the link's URL in the status bar when you place your cursor over the link. And most browsers display the URL of the current document, so you should be able to see the URL after you load the document. A URL that connects to an FTP server will begin with the characters "ftp:".

When you click a link to an FTP server, your browser should try to retrieve the file for you. The browser displays the file if it's a file type that the browser can display (either directly or with an external viewer). Even when the browser doesn't know how to display the file, you can use the browser to transfer this file and save it directly to disk instead of trying to display it. (See "Getting files" later in this chapter.)

Connecting to FTP sites

You can connect to an FTP server from a WWW browser by just opening a URL that specifies the FTP protocol and the name of the FTP server. You simply open the File menu and choose the appropriate Open command (for Mosaic the command is Open URL, and for Netscape it's Open Location). This gives you a dialog that lets you enter the URL for the FTP server (for example, **ftp://rtfm.mit.edu**). When you use this most basic URL, you get the top-level directory for that FTP server (see fig. 16.2).

Fig. 16.2
The top-level directory for the FTP server **rtfm.mit.edu** (displayed here using Mosaic) has some files and directories in it. The funny icons are files of a type Mosaic does not understand.

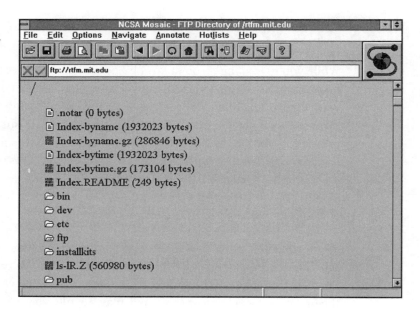

Although some Web browsers only show you the names of the files and directories at the FTP server, most of them give you a lot more information. Some browsers use different icons to represent files containing text, graphics and animations, and most use a folder icon to represent directories. Often, you will get additional information such as the size of the file and the last time it was modified. As you see in figure 16.2, Mosaic shows you an icon for each directory entry and gives you the name and size of each file. On the other hand, Netscape gives you a lot more information about the contents of a directory (see fig. 16.3).

**{Note}**

Netscape was recently upgraded so that when you connect to an FTP server, the Welcome message for that server is displayed at the top of the directory listing. Most browsers (including Mosaic) don't have a feature like this.

Navigating directories

Navigating directories in most Web browsers is a pretty simple process. To look at the contents of a subdirectory, all you need to do is click the link for that subdirectory. To move back to higher level directories, you have several options.

Web browsers all have some type of Back command that takes you to the last place you were. Usually the browser uses a left-pointing arrow on an icon for the Back command (both Netscape and Mosaic do this). You can almost always get to the Back command from a menu item, too:

- In Mosaic, open the Navigate menu and choose Back.

- In Netscape, open the Go menu and choose Back.

Most browsers also give you another way to move to the next higher directory level. After you move down from the top-level directory, you can usually find some type of link at the top of your directory listing that takes you to the directory a level above the current one (see fig. 16.3). Click this link to move up to the parent directory.

Fig. 16.3
Netscape lets you go to the directory above the current one with the Up to higher level directory link.

Link to parent directory

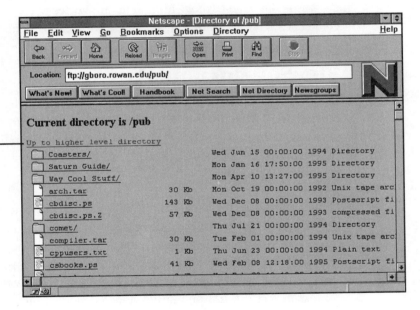

{Note} ___

Remember that the Back command takes you back to where you last were. That is, it might take you up or down in the directory series, depending on what your last stop was. For example, you can move down to a lower directory and then back up using the "Up to higher level directory" link. Then the Back command would take you down to the lower directory, not to the directory above the current one. On the other hand, the "Up to higher level directory" link at the top of the directory listing always takes you to the directory above the current one.

There is one other browser command that lets you move to directories you've recently visited. Web browsers all have some type of Forward command. You can use this command when you back up to a directory you've already visited. The Forward command then takes you to the lower directory you moved back from. Usually the browser uses a right-pointing arrow on an icon for the Forward command (both Netscape and Mosaic do this). You also can almost always get to the Forward command from a menu item:

- In Mosaic, open the Navigate menu and choose Forward.
- In Netscape, open the Go menu and choose Forward.

Going forward can be a confusing concept, but the basic idea is that to go forward, you have to have gone back from somewhere. You can use the Forward command to move around in directories you've already visited and come back from, but you can become somewhat lost when you do this.

Viewing documents

One of the things that the WWW is designed for is viewing documents. You can use a Web browser to go to an FTP server and look at files without saving them to your local disk. (Saving files is covered in the next section, "Getting files.") To view a document on an FTP server, simply click the document in the directory listing.

If the file you are viewing is plain text or a WWW document (often a file with an extension .htm or .html), your browser will load the document for you to read. However, if the document contains some type of nontext information (a graphic or sound file, for example), your Web browser probably will not be able to display it directly. Most browsers let you define viewers for these nontext files (see the "Configuring viewers" sidebar on the next page).

 Plain English, please!

A **viewer**, sometimes called a **helper application**, is an external program that you use to display a nontext file when you try to load that file with a Web browser. Most viewers are simply programs that you put on your computer to handle different types of files. Viewers let you play sound files, look at graphic files, play movies, etc.

There is one thing that you should keep in mind when trying to view nontext files. If you don't have a viewer for the type of file you are loading, you may be wasting a lot time. Most browsers download a file before checking to see if you have a viewer for it. These files are usually very large and take a long time to load. Once the browser has loaded the file, it often just throws it away if it can't find a viewer for it. This can be a very frustrating experience.

{Note} Netscape does allow you to configure a viewer for that file or save it to disk if it finds you don't have a viewer configured for that file type.

(Tip) Most browsers have some type of abort command to stop the download. If you realize that you're transferring a file that you don't have a viewer for, you can simply abort the download. In Netscape, click the stop sign in the toolbar; in Mosaic, click the spinning globe.

Configuring viewers

Although configuring viewers for a browser is usually not that difficult, complete coverage of the steps is beyond the scope of this book. However, a quick discussion of the general steps is given here.

Most browsers have some type of configuration dialog box (often called a **Preferences dialog box**) that you can open from one of the items on the menu bar. The configuration dialog boxes usually have a section that pertains to viewers (or helper applications, as Netscape calls them).

You'll need to tell your browser what viewers it should use for the different file extensions. These are the general steps:

1 Enter the extensions for the file type that you need a viewer for. For example, you might enter .wav for a particular sound viewer, or .mpg and .mpeg for an MPEG movie viewer. (Netscape and Mosaic have lists of file types that you can select from.)

2 Then enter the location of the viewer on your machine: for example, c:\apps\mpegplay.exe. (Netscape and Mosaic have Browse options that let you look through your directories for the location.)

3 Click OK (or whatever option your Preferences dialog box has).

When the browser finds a file with a particular extension, it looks in its configuration information to see if there is a viewer that will handle files with that extension. It then starts the viewer with the file it has just downloaded.

Getting files

The purpose of an FTP site is to let you download files. And most Web browsers have no problem doing this. Instead of downloading a file to view it, browsers let you download a file from an FTP server directly to your computer. You can also save the file you're currently viewing.

Saving the file you're currently viewing is a simple procedure for most browsers:

- In Netscape, open the File menu and choose Save As. This opens a Save As dialog that lets you specify where to save the file on your local disk. You can also specify the format in which the file is saved. If you are reading a text file from an FTP server, be sure to choose Plain Text for the file type.

- In Mosaic, open the File menu. Choose Save as Text if you are viewing a text file (which is likely if it's from an FTP server). This will also bring up a dialog box that lets you specify where to save the file on your computer.

What if you don't want to bother viewing a file—you just want to transfer it from the FTP server to your local disk? Most browsers let you do this without too much trouble. You can load a file directly to disk whether its link is part of a directory listing for the FTP server you're looking at, or whether the link is an FTP URL embedded in a WWW document.

Both Netscape and Mosaic have two ways of letting you load a file directly to disk:

- One way is to place your cursor over the file in the directory list (or the link with the embedded FTP URL) and Shift+click.

- The other way is to click the right mouse button while your cursor is over the link. In Mosaic, choose Load Anchor to Disk from the pop-up menu. In Netscape, choose Save This Link As from the pop-up menu.

Either of these methods will bring up a Save As dialog box that lets you specify where the file should be stored.

 **{Note}** Unless you specify otherwise in the Save As dialog box, your Web browser should save the file on your local disk in the same format as it exists on the FTP server. Web browsers usually use binary mode for all FTP transfers.

Keeping track of favorite sites

When you've found an FTP server that you like, most WWW browsers make it easy to mark that server so that you can quickly return to it. You do this by making lists of the FTP server URLs. Mosaic calls its lists **hotlists**, while Netscape calls them **bookmarks**. Once you have the lists, you can just select an item from a list to quickly load it.

Making lists of URLs

Netscape makes it easy to keep lists of URLs. While you are viewing an FTP server you want to mark, simply open the Bookmarks menu and choose Add Bookmark. This command writes the title and URL of the current FTP server and directory as the last item in your bookmark file, and shows the item at the end of your Bookmarks menu.

Mosaic's hotlist feature works in a similar manner. While you're viewing an interesting FTP server, open the Navigate menu and choose Add Current to Hotlist. This writes the title and URL of the directory you're viewing to the end of the current hotlist (you can also press the Add to Hotlist icon, which looks like a plus sign next to a little piece of paper on fire).

 **{Note}** Both Netscape and Mosaic let you keep multiple bookmark or hotlist files, and let you designate one of them as the current hotlist or bookmark file. It's beyond the scope of this book to discuss how to create and use the different files.

Quick access to your favorite FTP sites

Bookmarks allow you to access documents quickly. You simply open the Bookmarks menu and select any of the bookmarks that appear at the end of the menu. Netscape loads the directory information for the FTP server associated with that bookmark.

Mosaic's hotlists also make for quick access to URLs. Simply open the menu item for the hotlist you're interested in, and select the FTP server you want to connect to. Mosaic loads the directory information for the FTP server associated with the item.

Part VI:

The Best FTP Resources

17

The Best Sources of Software and Computing Information

In this chapter:

- Where are the most up-to-date files and sites?
- Where to find files of all kinds
- Where to find applications for Windows and DOS
- Where to find applications for Macintosh
- Special tips for using FTP sites

So now you know how to use FTP. The next thing you need is a list of the best places to find files.

Anonymous FTP lets you get to collections containing more software than you could ever use. Put simply, the FTP sites around the world contain several *terabytes* of goodies. (That's several thousand gigabytes or several million megabytes.) And all of it is free for the taking. You don't need an account at the site, and you don't need a secret password. It's all done anonymously.

But how do you find the FTP site with the stuff you want? With terabytes of data, downloading it all and sorting through it isn't an option. Archie helps, but not all anonymous FTP sites list their files in Archie. Even some of the sites that do list their files don't update Archie frequently enough to remain current. So, although Archie can help you find some of the sites and some of the files you need, it's incomplete and often out of date.

That's where this chapter and Chapter 18 come into play. This chapter tells you where to find the major software collections for Windows and Macintosh applications. Specifically, you find sites with the shareware, freeware, public domain, and demonstration software for every type of application you can imagine.

◉ {Note}————
All of the FTP sites listed in this chapter allow anonymous login using the username **anonymous**. If a password is requested, use your e-mail address unless instructed otherwise by the login directions at the site.

Windows software

The Internet FTP sites are loaded with gigabyte after gigabyte of shareware, freeware, and public domain software. Just one site, the Center for Innovative Computing Applications (CICA), has enough Windows software to more than fill a CD-ROM. So if you want more software for exploring the Internet, something to spruce up your Windows desktop at the office, or to have a little fun in the evening with a game, spend a few minutes browsing these FTP servers. There's bound to be something there you can use.

◉ {Note}————
Keep in mind that with shareware you can get the software for free, but the developer usually asks you for a small donation or registration fee if you use and like the software. You, or your company, should pay this fee for two reasons. First, the shareware developer can't go on developing new software if no one pays for the software they use. Second, if the license agreement states you must pay to continue using the software, you are violating the license and the law when you don't pay.

CICA

Address: **ftp.cica.indiana.edu**

If you only visit one Windows anonymous FTP site this year, visit the Center for Innovative Computing Applications (CICA). This site is to Windows shareware what the Library of Congress is to books. If it's out there, CICA has it. The following table lists some especially interesting directories. Of particular interest here is /pub/pc/win3/winsock; it has a few dozen megabytes of Internet-related programs for use with Windows Sockets.

Interesting CICA subdirectories under /pub/pc/win3

access	fonts	patches	symantec	vbasic
atm	games	pdoxwin	toolbook	video
bcpp	icons	printer	tp	winsock
demo	listings	programr	truetype	winword
desktop	misc	sdl	uploads	wpwin
drivers	nt	sounds	util	wrk
excel				

Alternates for a busy site

The bad news is that everybody knows what a great site CICA is, so it is always very busy. In the past two months, I've tried to log on there a few dozen times and connected only once or twice. Most of the time, I get the following message:

```
530-Sorry! We have reached maximum
    number of connections (75).
530-Please retry again later, or
    connect to a mirror site:
```

You might get a different error message depending on the client software you use.

Because this is such a good source of software, several other FTP sites have set up mirror sites. (These mirror sites provide the same information and materials as the original site.) The following table lists some of the U.S. mirror sites and the directory that contains the mirror of CICA.

CICA mirrors

Address	Directory
wuarchive.wustl.edu	/systems/ibmpc/win3
archive.orst.edu	/pub/mirrors/ftp.cica.indiana.edu (link to .ftp.nws.orst.edu/pub/mirrors/ftp.cica.indiana.edu)
gatekeeper.dec.com	/pub/micro/msdos/win3 (link to /.f/micro/msdoc/win3)
ftp.cdrom.com	/pub/cica (link to /.5/cica)
mrcnext.cso.uiuc.edu	/pub/win3
ftp.pht.com	/mirrors/cica (link to /.2/cica)
mirrors.aol.com	/pub/cica (link to mir01/CICA/pub)

SimTel

address: **oak.oakland.edu**

If you want to find software for almost any topic you can think of, from the Bible to sports, check out the SimTel software collection. SimTel claims to be the largest collection of MS-DOS and MS-Windows programs on the Internet (over 11,000 files). There are dozens of directories in both the DOS and Windows file structures, containing software in such diverse areas as astronomy, genealogy, and music. In addition, there are more mundane applications like spreadsheets and Windows Sockets utilities.

Most of this software is shareware and public domain. The two file collections can be found under the directories:

- /SimTel/msdos

  This is the SimTel collection of DOS software.

- /SimTel/win3

  This is the SimTel collection of Windows software.

The SimTel collection is mirrored by a number of sites, including **wuarchive.wustl.edu** (/systems/ibmpc/simtel/) and **ftp.uoknor.edu** (/mirror/simtel). For more information about the collection and its mirror sites, read the file README.description under either the DOS or Windows directories.

The best of the rest

There are a number of other FTP sites that have software for particular applications, or otherwise specialized software collections. Some of the best sites are listed here.

NCSA

address: **ftp.ncsa.uiuc.edu**

Here's another site you really shouldn't miss. The National Center for Supercomputing Applications (NCSA) is the home site for NCSA Mosaic. It's also another very busy site. In addition to the Mosaic files themselves, you'll find viewers to use for Mosaic (for viewing pictures, listening to sounds, or watching multimedia movies), and information about HTML (the language that WWW documents are written in).

You can also find the Mosaic software and many of these viewers and documents utilities at CICA and its mirror sites, as well as the Washington University and Sunsite sites described later in this chapter.

Directories to check out at this site are:

- /Web/Mosaic/Windows

    This is where to find the main NCSA Mosaic program. There's also a copy of Win32s here, if you need it.

- /Web/Mosaic/Windows/viewers

    Here, you'll find programs to use with Mosaic to view pictures and movies, listen to sounds, view PostScript, and more.

- /Web/html/Windows

    This contains several public domain and shareware utilities for creating Web documents with HTML.

For a thorough discussion of Mosaic, the World Wide Web, and HTML, check out the Que book *Special Edition Using the World Wide Web and Mosaic*.

Washington University at St. Louis

address: **wuarchive.wustl.edu**

Here's another big, popular site. As with CICA, you need a little bit of luck and good timing to get connected, but it's worth the effort. The following list tells you a little about what you can expect to find there:

- /systems/ibmpc

  This contains software for PCs running DOS and Windows.

- /packages/NCSA

  This is a mirror of the NCSA directories that contains Mosaic and related files.

- /packages/www

  Here, you'll find more software for use with the World Wide Web, including Cello and Lynx.

Walnut Creek

address: **ftp.cdrom.com**

WOW! When I logged in to this site, the message stated that it has 30 gigabytes of files online. You could spend the next few weeks looking around this site and not see it all. Walnut Creek CD-ROM sells low-cost CD-ROMs. These are usually huge collections of shareware and public domain materials. They put hundreds or thousands of these on a CD and sell it for a fraction of what you would spend in online charges downloading. Their CD-ROMs include a full set of the software found in CICA's Windows collection, a UNIX collection, several game collections, and much more. The following is a quick list of some of the interesting directories:

- /pub/cica

  This is a mirror of the CICA site at Indiana.

- /pub/os2

  This is a collection of files for OS2 users.

- /pub/doom and /pub/doom2

  This is a collection of software and documents for use with the game Doom.

- /pub/gutenberg

  This is a mirror of the Project Gutenberg files.

 **{Note}** You can order CDs from Walnut Creek by calling 1–800–536–3373 or by sending e-mail to **order@Mail.Coast.NET**. A WWW Forms Interface for ordering CD-ROMs is also available at **http://www.coast.net/SimTel/**. The SimTel collection CD can save you money if there is a lot of software at the site you'd want to download. Currently priced at $34.95, this CD saves you time. The CD is updated every few months, so you get the most recent versions of the software (you can also get a yearly subscription with quarterly updates for $79.95).

The OAK software repository

address: **oak.oakland.edu**

This is an especially good site because it is easy to get connected. It allows up to 400 anonymous FTP logins at once (compared to only 75 at CICA). When I logged in to write this, there were only 116 users logged in. You shouldn't have trouble getting connected (until everyone else reading this book tries!).

What does this site have? Here are a couple of hot choices that will keep you busy for a while:

- /pub/msdos

  Contains roughly 200 subdirectories with DOS programs, utilities, programmers' tools, games, and so forth.

- /pub/msdos/windows3

  Contains about 700 files with a total of about 125M of Windows 3.x shareware.

University of Illinois at Urbana-Champaign

address: **ftp.cso.uiuc.edu**

This is a nice "little" site with some good files. It doesn't have anywhere near the number of files that some of the big sites do, but it's well maintained and easy to log on to. That makes it worth a look. Here are some examples of what you might find useful:

- /pc/exec-pc

  According to the description at the site, this is an "Index & sample of most interesting files from World's Largest BBS."

- /pc/pcmag

  This contains *PC Magazine* files. The description says that the collection at wuarchive (Washington University at St. Louis, described earlier in this chapter) is more up to date, but—if you don't need the most recent collection—this site is easier to log on to.

Sunsite

address: **sunsite.unc.edu**

This is an excellent server run by the University of North Carolina. It's a major center for information about Sun Microsystems, Inc. There is also a good collection of files for DOS and Windows users. Among the interesting directories are the following:

- /pub/micro/pc-stuff

  Here, you'll find programs and documentation for DOS and Windows systems. There is also a great collection of WAV sounds in the /sounds subdirectory.

- /pub/packages/infosystems

  This contains subdirectories for Mosaic (a good place to look if NCSA is busy), WWW information, Archie, FTP, Gopher, and other Internet tools. You can also find client and server software here.

- /pub/sun-info

  There are many subdirectories here full of information about Sun systems.

Microsoft

address: **ftp.microsoft.com**

Without looking, you'd probably guess that this is one of the greatest sites for software on the Net. After all, Microsoft is the reigning king of software. You'll find a lot of drivers and patches for Windows (the 3.11 Windows update is worth a look), Word, Excel, and other desktop applications. You'll also find information about their products; the Microsoft TechNet Knowledge Base has frequently updated answers to common and uncommon problems with Microsoft products. There are also some great resources for developers. And, given Microsoft's reputation, this site probably will just get better. Here's a brief guide to its directories:

- /bussys

  This is the Business Systems directory, which includes subdirectories for LAN software, Mail, SQL, and WinSocks.

- /deskapps

  This is Microsoft's bread and butter. Here you'll find subdirectories for Access, Excel, PowerPoint, Word, Office, and games, to name a few.

- /developr

  This contains developer tools and information on BASIC, developer utilities, the Microsoft Developer's Network, Microsoft Systems Journal, OLE, 32-bit developers kits, Microsoft Certification, and Visual Basic. This is a real developers' playground.

- /Softlib

  Check out the instructions and index for the software library here and then proceed to /Softlib/mslfiles for the files themselves.

- /peropsys

  This is home of the Microsoft "cash cows" DOS and Windows. You can even get information about Windows 95 in the /peropsys/win_news directory.

Macmillan Computer Publishing

address: **ftp.mcp.com**

Okay, so technically, this isn't a software site. Macmillan (Que, which publishes this book, is a part of Macmillan) publishes books about every major software package for personal computers and quite a few others. Publishing over 600 books a year, this company collects more computer information than any other. So, at this site, you'll find software that has been included with Macmillan's computer books and other software of interest to our readers.

- /pub/que/net-cd

  Here, you'll find copies of much of the software that's on the CD included with the books *Special Edition Using the Internet,* Second Edition, *Special Edition Using the World Wide Web with Mosaic,* software from other Internet books, and software that couldn't be included on the CDs. Que updates this directory periodically as new versions are released to make it easy to find the latest versions of software covered in these books.

Other good software sites

The Net contains many other software sites. The following table lists addresses for some of the more useful or interesting sites.

Other sites with useful software

Site	Directory	Description
ftp.qualcomm.com	/quest/windows/eudora	Eudora manufacturer
ftp.utas.edu.au	/pc/trumpet	Home of all the Trumpet software, including the Trumpet Winsock and News Reader
ftp.uml.edu	/msdos/games	A collection of DOS games
ftp.law.cornell.edu	/pub/LII/Cello	Home of the Cello WWW browser
boombox.micro.umn.edu	/pub/gopher	Big Gopher archive with documentation and software
titan.ksc.nasa.gov	/pub/win3/winvn	Home of the WinVN newsreader

Mac software

The Internet FTP sites are loaded with gigabyte after gigabyte of shareware, freeware, and public domain software. Just one site, Info-Mac archive, has enough Macintosh software to more than fill a CD-ROM. So if you want more software for exploring the Internet, something to spruce up your Mac desktop at the office, or to have a little fun in the evening with a game, spend a few minutes browsing these FTP servers. There's bound to be something there you can use.

✴ *{Note}*
Keep in mind that with shareware you can get the software for free, but the developer usually asks you for a small donation or registration fee if you use and like the software. You, or your company, should pay this fee for two reasons. First, the shareware developer can't go on developing new software if no one pays for the software they use. Second, if the license agreement states you must pay to continue using the software, you are violating the license and the law when you don't pay.

Info-Mac

address: **sumex-aim.stanford.edu**

If you only visit one Mac anonymous FTP site this year, visit the Info-Mac archives at Stanford (or one of the mirror sites listed later in this section). This site is to Mac shareware what the Library of Congress is to books. If it's out there, Info-Mac has it. The following table lists some especially interesting directories.

Interesting Info-Mac subdirectories under /info-mac		
AntiVirus	Application	Communication
Communication/MacTCP	Compress-Translate	Configuration
Development	Disk-File	Font
Game	Graphic	Graphic/Quicktime
Graphic/Utility/Utility	Help	Hypercard

continues

continued

Incoming	Information	Newton
Periodical	Print	Recent
Science–Math	Sound	TextProcessing
UserInterface		

Of particular interest here is /info-mac/Communication/MacTCP; it has a few dozen megabytes of Internet-related programs for use with MacTCP.

(!) (Tip) —
America Online has an Info–Mac mirror that is available to its subscribers only.

Alternates for a busy site

The bad news is that everybody knows what a great site Info-Mac is, and it is always very busy. Many times, especially during the day, your anonymous login attempt will fail and you'll get the message System load too high for connection attempt. During working hours (8–5 Pacific time), it limits the site to 75 anonymous logins. If you're caller 76, you'll have to try again.

Because this is such a good source of software, several other FTP sites have set up mirror sites. (These mirror sites provide the same information and materials as the original site.) The following table lists some of the U.S. mirror sites and the directory that contains the mirror of Info-Mac.

US Info-Mac FTP mirrors

Address	Directory
ftp.hawaii.edu	/mirrors/info-mac
mrcnext.cso.uiuc.edu	/pub/info-mac
grind.isca.uiowa.edu	/mac/infomac (link to /3/mac/infomac)
wuarchive.wustl.edu	/systems/mac/info-mac
ftp.orst.edu	/pub/mirrors/sumex-aim.stanford.edu/mac/info-mac (link to .ftp.nws.orst.edu/pub/mirrors/sumex-aim.stanford.edu/mac/info-mac)
ftp.pht.com	/mirrors/mac/info-mac (link to /.2/mac/info-mac)
ftp.uu.net	/systems/mac/info-mac

 **{Note}**

For a complete list of mirror sites (including international mirrors, mirrors accessible via the World Wide Web, and information about how often the mirror updates its files) go to the /info-mac/Help directory at Info-Mac (or one of the mirrors listed in the preceding table) and retrieve the file mirror-list.txt. Only the most reliable sites are listed in the table.

UMich

address: **mac.archive.umich.edu**

This is another huge Macintosh file archive site. According to the readme file here, there are over 6,000 Mac files. All of the Mac files are in the /mac directory. If you're looking for additional Mac Internet software, check out /mac/util/network and /mac/util/comm.

This site has become so popular that it now enforces restrictions on the number of users. During "business hours," the site only allows 10 connections. During evenings and early mornings, 30 connections are allowed. In the dead of night (11 p.m.–4 a.m. EST), it allows 60 connections. The site also allows 60 connections on weekends. There are quite a few mirror sites as well. One of the easiest to connect to is **archive.orst.edu** in the /pub/mirrors/archive.umich.edu/mac directory.

The best of the rest

There are a number of other FTP sites that have software for particular applications, or otherwise specialized software collections. Some of the best sites are listed here.

NCSA

address: **ftp.ncsa.uiuc.edu**

Here's another site you really shouldn't miss. The National Center for Supercomputing Applications (NCSA) is the home site for NCSA Mosaic. It's also another very busy site. In addition to the Mosaic files, you'll find viewers to use for Mosaic (for viewing pictures, listening to sounds, or watching multimedia movies) and information about HTML (the language that WWW documents are written in). Directories to check out at this site are:

- /Web/Mosaic/Mac

  This is where to find the main NCSA Mosaic program.

- /Web/Mosaic/Mac/Helpers

  Here, you'll find programs to use with Mosaic to view pictures and movies, listen to sounds, view PostScript, and more.

⊛ {Note} You can also find the Mosaic software and many of these viewers and document utilities at Info-Mac and its mirror sites.

⊛ {Note} For a thorough discussion of Mosaic, the World Wide Web, and HTML, check out the Que book *Special Edition Using the World Wide Web and Mosaic.*

Washington University at St. Louis

address: **wuarchive.wustl.edu**

Here's another big, popular site. You need a little bit of luck and good timing to get connected, but it's worth the effort. Here are some of the things you'll find:

- /systems/mac/macintosh

  Here you'll find a large collection of Macintosh software divided into over two dozen directories.

- /systems/mac/info-mac and /systems/mac/umich.edu

  These directories contain mirrors of the Info-Mac and UMich archives described elsewhere in this section.

Walnut Creek

address: **ftp.cdrom.com**

WOW! When I logged in to this site, the message stated that it has 30 gigabytes of files online. You could spend the next few weeks looking around this site and not see it all. Walnut Creek CD-ROM sells low-cost CD-ROMs. These are usually huge collections of shareware and public domain materials. They put hundreds or thousands of these on a CD and sell it for a fraction of what you would spend on online downloading charges. Their CD-ROMs include Info-Mac 4, which has most of the software found in the Info-Mac collection, a UNIX collection, several game collections, and much more. The following is a list of some of the more interesting directories:

- /pub/mac/umich

  This is a mirror of the UMich site.

- /pub/gutenberg

  This is a mirror of the Project Gutenberg files.

⊛ {Note} — You can order CDs from Walnut Creek by calling 1–800–786–9907 or sending e-mail to **orders@cdrom.com**. The Info–Mac collection CD-ROM is an excellent buy if you spend a lot of time downloading software for your Mac from one of the Info–Mac sites. Currently priced at $49.95, this CD saves you time. The CD is updated every few months, so you get the most recent versions of the software.

Macmillan Computer Publishing

address: **ftp.mcp.com**

Okay, so technically, this isn't a software site. Macmillan (Que, which publishes this book, is a part of Macmillan) publishes books about every major software package for personal computers and quite a few others. Publishing over 600 books a year, this company collects more computer information than any other. So, at this site, you'll find software that has been included with Macmillan's computer books, including the following:

- /pub/que/macnet-cd

  This contains copies of much of the software that's on MacNetCD included with *Special Edition Using the Internet with Your Mac*. Que updates this directory periodically as new versions are released to make it easy to find the latest versions of software covered in this book.

- /pub/software/macintosh

  Here you'll find more Macintosh software, primarily from Macmillan's Hayden imprint, which specializes in Macintosh topics.

Other good software sites

The Net contains many other software sites. The following table lists addresses for some of the more useful or interesting sites.

Other sites with useful software

Site	Directory	Description
ftp.qualcomm.com	/quest/mac/eudora	Eudora manufacturer
amug.org	/amug	Arizona Macintosh User's Group
ftp.apple.com	/dts	Apple's software FTP site
boombox.micro.umn.edu	/pub/gopher	Big Gopher archive with documentation and software

Internet and general computing resources

Where is the best place to go for Internet information? Well, other than this book and other books from Que, we recommend that you look on the Internet itself. Thousands of useful documents are available that should answer most questions and solve most Internet problems. This section describes some of the more useful sites.

InterNIC

address: **ds.internic.net**

No one organization really runs the Internet, but InterNIC is the closest thing to a governing body. InterNIC has several purposes, as set out by the National Science Foundation (NSF) charter that funds it. Its most visible role is assigning network addresses and domain names. It also keeps several important databases, including a WHOIS registry of domains and networks. But what does this FTP site have that is of interest to you? Try these directories for starters:

- /rfc

  RFC stands for Request for Comment. These are the working notes of the committees that develop protocols and standards for the Internet. They tend to be technical and of little practical use to anyone other than network engineers.

- /fyi

  FYI stands for For Your Information. These are a subset of the RFCs that tend to be less technical and more informational.

- /std

  STD represents the Internet Activities Board Standards. If an RFC becomes fully accepted, it becomes a standard and is designated an STD. These also tend to be technical.

{Note}

InterNIC also runs an Internet Referral Desk. This group answers questions and sends out information about the Net. The group will send you a list of providers in your area, pointers to information on the Net, and more. Contact them by using the following information:

Telephone:	800–862–0677
	908–668–6587
	619–455–4600
Fax:	619–455–3990
E-mail:	**info@internic.net**

continues

continued

Mail: InterNIC Information Services
                 General Atomics
                 P.O. Box 85608
                 San Diego, CA 92186-9784

⊛ *{Note}*_____| SURAnet, **ftp.sura.net**, mirrors many of these files, as does **ftp.near.net**.

UUNET

address: **ftp.uu.net**

UUNET is one of the main distribution centers for UseNet news. It is also a large service provider. It has one of the largest collections of Internet information to be found at any FTP site. The following directories are where you should start:

- /index

  Because this archive is so large, there is a separate directory for indexes of all its files. We highly recommend downloading a copy of the index if you plan to spend much time here.

- /inet

  This contains most of the information UUNET has about the Internet. This information is broken up by types into about a dozen subdirectories.

The best of the rest

In addition to Internet statistics and resources, anonymous FTP sites give you access to entertaining and philosophical computer topics, such as the effect the electronic revolution will have on your life. You can find anything from information about specific Internet services to discussions of security and privacy in cyberspace.

RTFM MIT server

address: **rtfm.mit.edu**

There are several good FTP servers at the Massachusetts Institute of Technology (MIT), but this is the one with all the answers. You'll want to look in the following directories to start:

- /pub/usenet-by-group

  This is one of the most useful directories on the Net. The subdirectories of this directory correspond to newsgroup names for many newsgroups. In these subdirectories, you'll find FAQs and other regular postings for each group.

- /pub/usenet-by-group/alt.answers

  This is the same concept as the preceding entry except that the **alt.answers** group is the home to FAQs for all the other alt groups. So, there are more subdirectories here for the alt groups and more FAQs.

- /pub/usenet-by-group/news.answers

  This is a superset of all the other directories with FAQs. You'll also find a lot of general information FAQs that aren't associated with a particular newsgroup.

- /pub/faq-maintainers

  This is a list (compressed in .Z format) of all the people who maintain a FAQ.

{Note} | **FAQ** stands for **Frequently Asked Questions**. These documents answer questions that are frequently asked in certain groups, usually newsgroups. Most active newsgroups have a FAQ. The FAQs serve to cut down the number of postings that ask the same questions. You'll also find FAQs for mailing lists, popular software, and other special interests. For example, NCSA maintains a FAQ on Mosaic because they developed the software. This cuts down on the number of questions posed to the developers.

Electronic Frontier Foundation (EFF)

address: **ftp.eff.org**

According to the EFF mission statement in the site's documentation, it exists to "ensure that the principles embodied in the Constitution and the Bill of Rights are protected as new communications technologies emerge." With that purpose in mind, EFF has assembled a large collection of information about the Internet to enable anyone who wants to make use of this technology to do so. Check out the following directories:

- /pub/Net_info

  This is the site's main directory for Internet information. You can find a wide range of information here.

- /pub/Alerts

  You'll find several documents here detailing recent government developments and decisions that affect freedom of information on the Internet.

Computer Professionals for Social Responsibility

address: **cpsr.org**

The Computer Professionals for Social Responsibility (CPSR) site has a very good collection of network security and privacy information. You'll find information about the well-publicized Clipper plan, as well as some more obscure files. Look in this directory:

- /cypherpunks

  There are about 20 subdirectories here that deal with all aspects of encryption and privacy.

 **{Note}** — This site is mirrored at **ftp.etext.org** in /pub/CPSR. Some of the files are mirrored at **aql.gatech.edu** in /pub/crypto.

Georgia Tech University

address: **aql.gatech.edu**

This site has a nice collection of zines. Take a look here at the cutting edge in magazine publishing. The site also has a mirror of the CSPR site's cypherpunk directory with some additions, which are listed below:

- /pub/Zines

  Here you'll find subdirectories for Future Culture, Internet Informer, and Voices from the Net.

- /pub/crypto

  This contains privacy and encryption files.

Other sites with Internet information

The following table contains a list of several additional sites that provide useful Internet information.

Other sites with useful Internet information

Site	Directory	Description
ftp.tis.com	/pub/PEM	FAQ and software for Privacy Enhanced Mail
cert.org	/pub	Computer and network security
ftp.near.net	/rfc	Mirror of the InterNIC rfc files
ftp.pica.army.mil	/pub/privacy/CPD	Computer Privacy Digest

18
FTP Sites Just for Fun

In this chapter:

- Government documents (and documents the government doesn't want you to know about!)

- Business, finance, and economics

- Entertainment, including transcripts of movies and TV shows, David Letterman's Top Ten lists, song lyrics, jokes, and so on

- Multimedia files (sound, graphics, and movies)

- Help for all your hobbies, like recipes, roller coaster reviews, genealogy information, and more...

There's bound to be an anonymous FTP site that has that triple chocolate cake recipe you're looking for.

The Internet gives you access to more than just terabytes of software. People put all kinds of things out on anonymous FTP servers, from pictures to chicken casserole recipes. And all of it is free for the taking. You don't need an account at the site, and you don't need a secret password. It's all done anonymously.

But you'd probably like an easy way to get to all of this stuff without having to look very hard, wouldn't you? Well, that's where this chapter comes into play. We've scoured the Net for good sites, asked co-workers and other Net addicts what their favorite sites are, and read hundreds of UseNet postings, FAQs, and other Internet documents about FTP sites. We've listed and described a few dozen of the best sites for a variety of different uses. From these few dozen sites, you should be able to find something about everything.

 *{Note}*_____ | All of the FTP sites listed in this chapter allow anonymous login using the username **anonymous**. If a password is requested, use your e-mail address, unless instructed otherwise by the login directions at the site.

Government and political information sites

Because it was the U.S. government that got the Internet going in the first place, it's no surprise that the government has many file servers with government information available to the public. Government servers dish up legislative and political documents, nonclassified military information, statistical information collected by various government branches, and more.

And it's not just the government that provides information about our elected leaders and various departments. Several other organizations have set up FTP sites that distribute information that sheds light on unusual government activities, political issues (and dirt!), and many other things.

Bureau of Labor Statistics public access server

address: **stats.bls.gov**

This site has a large collection of press releases and data about labor statistics. The data is probably not of much interest to the general reader, but the press releases might be. Check out the following directories:

- /pub/doc

    This contains the documentation for all of this site's information. If you want to make serious use of this site, you'll need to read this documentation.

- /pub/news.release

  Here's where you can find press releases about various labor statistics.

- /pub/time.series

  If you don't know what a time series is, you won't want to look in here. But if Box-Jenkins and ARIMA are part of your daily vocabulary, check out the subdirectories for Average Price Data, International Price Index, Local Area Unemployment Statistics, and much more.

Pencil FTP server

address: **pencil.cs.missouri.edu**

If the "Grassy Knoll" isn't just another suburban housing development to you, you'll want to check out this server. It has a large collection of documents related to the JFK assassination and the conspiracy theories surrounding it. Or maybe you're worried about what the military is doing in some Caribbean nation. Poke around in the /pub/map directory and get the inside scoop on this and a variety of other activist issues. There's a price to be paid for this inside scoop, though: this is a very slow server. You might want to check Wiretap (a site discussed in the "Internet Wiretap" section later in this chapter) first and see whether it has what you need before you look here. Here are a couple of interesting directories:

- /pub/jfk

  Pick your favorite conspiracy theory and have a good read. Most of the files here are in UNIX .Z format, so you'll need a conversion program to read them.

- /pub/map

  This is a collection of documents from nonmainstream political activist groups.

Sunsite

address: **sunsite.unc.edu**

Sunsite isn't just for byteheads. Here you'll find a good archive of political information, including many speeches by recent presidential candidates:

- /pub/academic/political-science/speeches

  Bush, Clinton, and Perot all have their words immortalized here. You'll also find speeches by candidates for a few offices other than president.

⊛ *{Note}* _____ | For related information, check out the directory /cpsr/clinton at **cpsr.org**, which was discussed in Chapter 17 in the "Computer Professionals for Social Responsibility" section.

UUNET

address: **ftp.uu.net**

There's more to UUNET's archive than Net info. You'll find this to be a good source of information about the federal government, as indicated in the item below:

- /government/usa

  Here you'll find political documents from the U.S. House, the Executive branch (just some transcripts of Saturday afternoon radio broadcasts), and an archive of U.S. Supreme Court opinions from the past few years. The Supreme Court files are stored in ASCII and WordPerfect formats.

⊛ *{Note}* _____ | **ftp.uu.net** has an eclectic collection of files. It's a great place to just wander around and find interesting information and pictures. Definitely try it.

Internet Wiretap

address: **wiretap.spies.com**

As U.S. citizens, we all have a right to see certain information as described in the Freedom of Information Act. But we can't always get to it for practical reasons. The Internet Wiretap makes a lot of this information easier to get to via the Internet. Here's where to look:

- /Gov

  This directory has numerous subdirectories with government documents. Look in Copyright, Economic, NATO, NAFTA, Patent, Platform, Treaties, several subdirectories that begin with GAO (Government Accounting Office), and several more that begin with US for various U.S. government departments.

U.S. Senate

address: **ftp.senate.gov**

This site didn't have much information on it when we first found it. It has grown quite a bit in the last few months, but it's still in the early stages of development. What is there is good, however; we should commend the senators who participate for their efforts. The directories listed below point to this information:

- /member

  Contains press releases and more for senators from about 20 states in this directory. Subdirectories are broken down by state and then by senator.

- /committee

  Contains reports, findings, and press releases from Agriculture, Labor, Dem-Policy, and Repub-Policy committees and a few more.

FedWorld

address: **ftp.fedworld.gov**

FedWorld is run by the National Technical Information Service (NTIS). FedWorld is designed to serve as a central source of federal government information in electronic format and to help find federal government information. (There's a three-hour-per-day login time limit, so use your allotment efficiently.)

- /pub/main

  Contains general interest information and introductions.

- /pub/commerce

  Contains documents from the Department of Commerce.

- /pub/ntis

  There are many documents here about federal regulations, technical and scientific reports, and programs dealing with communications technology.

- /pub/w-house

  Contains recent press releases, speeches, and more from the White House. (This also is available from the White House FTP server at **ftp.whitehouse.gov**.)

 **{Note}** When you connect to this site, start at the /pub directory, not the root directory. If you start at the root, you might just get an empty list.

University of Michigan

address: **red.css.itd.umich.edu**

This server at the University of Michigan has a collection of some of the weirdest political opinions and online zines around. Note that you might find some of the political opinions to be offensive.

- /pub/Politics

  This is the directory for most of the political documents. The site administrators make space available here for anyone who has political documents and asks for space. Files on anarchy and other unconventional politics are here. Don't be surprised by the way-out stuff you see.

- /pub/Zines

  This is a good collection of online publications.

Libraries

A large number of public and university libraries are on the Internet. You can get information on how to connect to those libraries. Some libraries even have part of their holdings available for online perusal.

Library of Congress

address: **marvel.loc.gov**

While you can't check out a book from the library's vast collection by downloading it, you can find information here about the library, how to find information in the library, and special services for visually and physically impaired patrons.

- /pub/exhibit.images

  Contains images from public exhibitions, such as "1492: An Ongoing Voyage" and "Scrolls from the Dead Sea: The Ancient Library of Qumran and Modern Scholarship."

- /pub/general.info

  Contains maps of the Library of Congress and other general information about the library.

- /pub/lc.online

  Contains information about using the library's online search feature, which is available via the Internet.

- /pub/nls

  Contains book listings and catalogs for the National Library Service for the Blind and Physically Handicapped (NLS).

- /pub/reference.guides

  Contains the text of reference guides, finding aids, and bibliographies produced by library staff.

Washington and Lee University

address: **liberty.uc.wlu.edu**

The directory /pub/lawlib provides access to a large amount of online information from W&L's law library.

UUNET library listings

address: **ftp.uu.net**

This site has information on how to contact libraries all over the world in the directory /doc/libraries. The library listings are grouped by geographical area. Most of the files here are in UNIX .Z format, so you'll need a conversion program to read them. For more information about UUNET, see the "UUNET" section earlier in this chapter.

Sunsite library listings

address: **sunsite.unc.edu**

The file /pub/docs/lib-catalogs.online/LIBRARIES.TXT contains listings of how to connect to and use a large number of libraries around the world. Most of them are university libraries, but there are also some public libraries in the list.

Business and finance sites

Business use of the Internet is growing. But, at this point, there is still a long way to go before you'll find the volume of business information on the Internet that you find in other categories. Still, there's more information than most people will probably ever need.

Data General Corporation

address: **dg-rtp.dg.com**

Data General operates this FTP site, which has a good collection of historical investment data about stocks, commodities, mutual funds, and more. Data General is in the process of reorganizing this site and collecting more information, so don't be surprised if it looks different when you visit. Right now, the main directory is /pub/misc.invest, and there are several subdirectories.

Patent Information on UUNET

address: **ftp.uu.net**

If you need information about patents, see /doc/patents. For more information about UUNET, see its other listings earlier in this chapter.

SURAnet

address: **ftp.sura.net**

There is a good collection of information here about the FDIC (Federal Deposit Insurance Corporation) in /pub/fdic. There is consumer information, press releases, and statistical data here, along with much more information.

FedWorld job listing

address: **ftp.fedworld.gov**

In addition to the volumes of information about the government (see the "FedWorld" section earlier in this chapter), this site has a listing of federal jobs available. This listing is in the /pub/jobs directory, sorted by state.

PRODUCT.COM

address: **ftp.product.com**

PRODUCT.COM is a worldwide provider of product information. Companies put product descriptions, press releases, and demos on this server for your access. Look in the /info directory and you'll find subdirectories full of information on books, computer hardware and software, furniture, services, and more.

Books

Anonymous FTP is a great resource to use to make electronic texts available to the Internet community. This section lists a few of the biggest and most interesting sites for electronic texts.

Project Gutenberg

address: **mrcnext.cso.uiuc**

Project Gutenberg is by far the most ambitious electronic text project going. The project has a goal of converting 1,500 classic book-length works in the public domain to electronic form by the end of the decade. It has a good start, as you can see from the collection. The main directory of interest here is /pub/etext.

 **{Note}**

This collection also is available on CD-ROM from Walnut Creek (see the info about Walnut Creek in Chapter 17).

Online Book Initiative

address: **obi.std.com**

Here's another group assembling a large collection of electronic texts. The /obi directory contains all of the files and subdirectories of interest. According to the site's self-description, the works range from Shakespeare and the Bible to novels, poetry, and more. There's about 250M of files here.

University of Maryland at College Park inforM

address: **info.umd.edu**

The directory /inforM/EdRes/ReadingRoom contains a variety of fiction, history, and philosophy for your reading pleasure.

Movies and entertainment

People seem compelled to collect and exchange trivia about the entertainers and shows that give us some relief from the mundane world. There are numerous sites that have plot synopses, scripts, and trivia for some of the most popular TV shows and movies.

 **{Note}**

You will find files at the sites listed here that contain information that may violate someone's copyright. Que Corporation, Macmillan Computer Publishing, and the author in no way support, encourage, or condone the use of illegally copyrighted materials on these sites.

Cathouse

address: **cathouse.org**

Here's a good repository of television, movie, and music fun. You'll find episode listings, episode summaries, and trivia for popular TV shows, including *Beavis and Butt-head* and *The Simpsons*. Some of the more interesting and unique material includes an archive of David Letterman's Top Ten lists and excerpts from classic *Saturday Night Live* scripts. All of this will be found in various subdirectories under /pub/cathouse/television. Other directories of interest include:

- /pub/cathouse/humor

  Contains jokes on a variety of subjects from many sources.

- /pub/cathouse/lyrics

  Song lyrics found here range from AC/DC to ZZ-Top. This is mostly rock-n-roll and pop, but you'll also find a few country artists, such as Alabama.

- /pub/cathouse/movies

  This is a database of movie information and scripts from a variety of blockbusters (*Star Wars* and *Terminator*), duds (*Army of Darkness*), and cult classics (Monty Python's *Life of Brian*).

- /pub/cathouse/rush.limbaugh

  Contains transcripts of the popular self-proclaimed moderate's TV and radio shows.

 Many of the files at this site are in UNIX .tar or .Z file format. You'll need a conversion program to read these files.

Internet Wiretap

address: **wiretap.spies.com**

Look in the /Library/Media directory for FAQs and other documents about films, TV, science fiction (Star Trek, in particular), and games.

Widener University

address: **ftp.cs.widener.edu**

The directory /pub/simpsons has a collection of information about *The Simpsons* TV show. You can find plot summaries, an episode guide, air dates for each episode, and information about the Simpsons pinball machine.

Georgia Tech University

address: **aql.gatech.edu**

This site has a nice collection of information about the *X-Files* television show. Text of a few episodes, some pictures, and some related UFO files make this a worthwhile visit. Look in /pub/xfiles.

Rutgers University Archives

address: **red.css.itd.umich.edu**

This collection used to be on the server **quartz.rutgers.edu**. You can now find it on one of the University of Michigan FTP servers. This collection has all sorts of information for the TV generation.

- /pub/tv-movies and /pub/Quartz/tv+movies

  There's information here on TV shows and movies. You'll find episode summaries, scripts, trivia, and more.

- /pub/journals/HToMC and /pub/Quartz/journals/HToMC

  This directory contains archives of the magazine published by the Holy Temple of Mass Consumption.

Pictures

There are probably hundreds of FTP sites that have pictures of everything from people's pets to spacecraft. Here are a few sites that'll give you a taste of what you can find.

 **{Note}**_____ Remember that you'll need some type of application to display any pictures you retrieve. LView Pro is a good shareware viewer available from many of the software FTP servers.

Finnish University and Research Network FUNET

address: **ftp.funet.fi**

Look in the /pub/pics/ directory for subdirectories full of space, sports, TV and film, mpeg, fantasy, comics, clip art, and other pictures.

 **{Note}**_____ You can log in here as **anonymous**, but they have also set up a special *pictures* account for anonymous login. If you have trouble with *anonymous* because too many other people are using the site, log in as **pictures**. Still use your e-mail address as a password.

NASA Explorer

address: **explorer.arc.nasa.gov**

Here's an interesting collection of images from various NASA spacecraft, including the Shuttle, Voyager, and Galileo. There are also directories with logs of space missions.

- /pub/space

  This is the main directory for this archive. The subdirectories here break it up by spacecraft. The individual spacecraft directories contain text files of mission logs.

- /pub/space/gifs

  This directory contains all of the images.

 **{Note}** For another similar site, see **ftp.gsfc.nasa.gov** and look in the /pub/images directory. There also are several sites with images of the Shoemaker-Levy comet's collision with Jupiter. One such site is **ftp.seds.lpl.arizona.edu** in the directory /pub/astro/SL9/images.

UUNET Faces

address: **ftp.uu.net**

This site has a few unusual nooks and crannies. Take a look at this directory:

- /published/usenix/faces

  Contains pictures of people's faces. You probably won't recognize most of the 5,500–6,000 faces, but for some reason their pictures are here anyway. Most of the files here are in UNIX .Z format, so you'll need a conversion program to read them.

Religion

Religion is an always popular, if controversial, topic on the Net. You can find online versions of major religious texts, as well as information about religious poetry and music.

Washington University at St. Louis

address: **wuarchive.wustl.edu**

The directory /doc/bible has a complete edition of the King James Bible, including cross references. There are versions for the PC and Macintosh—get the README file to understand how to use the archive.

Finnish University and Research Network

address: **ftp.funet.fi**

The directory /pub/doc/religion/judaism/tanach contains the Torah from the Tanach in Hebrew, the Prophets from the Tanach in Hebrew, and the writings from the Tanach in Hebrew. Also included is a program that displays Hebrew letters on a PC, and a Hebrew quiz for a biblical Hebrew language tutor.

The directory /pub/doc/religion/islam has a version of the Holy Qur'an.

⊛ {Note}⎯⎯⎯⎯ | /pub/doc/religion has subdirectories for many different religions (Buddism and Islam, to name a couple). Take a look around this site—it's another generally interesting site.

Food

Food is another popular topic on the Net. A few sites have collected recipes from the food-related UseNet groups. You can also find some information about brewing your own beer.

Digital Equipment Corporation

address: **gatekeeper.dec.com**

The directory /pub/recipes (linked to /.2/recipes) has many different recipes organized by title.

University of Miami

address: **mthvax.cs.miami.edu**

The directory /pub/recipes has old archives for the UseNet group **rec.food.recipes**. Recipes are organized by food type. Programs for indexing and reading the archives are also available for Macintosh and PC platforms; see the file /pub/recipes/readme for information. There is also a collection of homebrewing information in the directory /pub/homebrew.

Fun and unusual sites

All of the FTP resources aren't serious or easy to classify. This section presents a few sites where you can find some files that are fun, related to recreation, or just off the beaten path.

Doctor Fun

address: **sunsite.unc.edu**

The Doctor Fun cartoon sets the standard for Internet humor. The main archive for these is /pub/electronic-publications/Dr-Fun. You have to see these to appreciate them.

Baseball

address: **wuarchive.wustl.edu**

Take me out to the ball game—please. We might have been deprived of the World Series in 1994, but here's a site that has a collection of baseball files to cheer you up. Look in /pub/baseball to find schedules, stats, lyrics to "Take Me Out to the Ball Game," and—most important to ESPN fans—a list of nicknames made famous by Chris Berman.

Another good directory here is /multimedia/images, which has a good image collection.

Music

address: **ftp.nevada.edu**

The directory /pub/guitar has a large collection of guitar music.

❋{Note} This site asks you not to use it during business hours. It limits anonymous connections to 40 on weekends, 40 on weekdays from 8pm–6am, and 30 on weekdays 6am–8pm. All times are PST (to convert to GMT, subtract 8 hours). Try one of the mirror sites including **ftp.uu.net** in /doc/music/guitar or **ftp.uwp.edu** in pub/music/guitar for the guitar music collection. (You might have trouble accessing this second site with Anarchie. Fetch seems to work fine with it.)

Roller Coasters

address: **gboro.rowan.edu**

The directory /pub/Coasters has several subdirectories that contain reviews, pictures, and even a few movies of roller coasters from parks all over the world.

Genealogy

address: **ftp.cac.psu.edu**

The directory /pub/genealogy has a large amount of information on genealogy, including information on the PAF genealogy program, genealogy database programs, and text files relating to genealogy.

How to find more sites

This chapter has only scratched the surface of the FTP goldmine. If you want a more complete list of FTP sites, the following is where to look.

Perry Rovers maintains a file of FTP sites that he regularly posts to the **news.answers** UseNet newsgroup. Perry updates this list regularly, but once you get your initial copy from a newsgroup or FTP site, you probably won't want to get a new copy too often. It's big, roughly 560 pages in a normal font (12-point Courier), and about 800K, which will take a while to download unless you have a high-speed connection. It doesn't change that much from posting to posting.

Part VII:

Indexes

Action Index

Index

Action Index

Basics—FTP in Windows

When you need to...	You'll find help here...
Connect to a predefined FTP server	p. 77
Find an FTP program for Windows	p. 32
Get a copy of WS_FTP	p. 75, p. 33
Install WS_FTP	p. 75

Basics—FTP on the Mac

When you need to...	You'll find help here...
Connect using Bookmarks	p. 160
Find an FTP program for Macintosh	p. 37
Install Anarchie	p. 154
Make an alias	p. 155
Move within directories	p. 162
Register Anarchie	p. 156
Use Anarchie's log	p. 166
Use Anarchie's transcript	p. 167

Bookmarks in Anarchie

When you need to...	You'll find help here...
Create a Bookmark list	p. 189
Delete Bookmarks	p. 191
Edit a Bookmark	p. 187
Mark a directory or file	p. 187
Mark an FTP site	p. 186
Open a Bookmark	p. 189
Save a Bookmark	p. 186

Customizing Anarchie

When you need to...	You'll find help here...
Change the default file viewer	p. 172
Select a default download location	p. 171

Customizing WS_FTP

When you need to...	You'll find help here...
Change the default file viewer	p. 98
Create file association	p. 100
Set double-click options	p. 95
Set up your firewall information	p. 142

Getting files by FTP in Windows

When you need to...	You'll find help here...
Change the download directory	p. 94
Create a local directory	p. 94
Direct a download to a particular directory	p. 96
Download a file	p. 93
Execute downloaded files	p. 100
Move around in directories	p. 83
Retrieve multiple files	p. 103
Save multiple files with the same name	p. 102
Set up an FTP server profile	p. 110
Upload files	p. 104
Upload multiple files	p. 106
View a file	p. 98

Getting files by FTP on the Mac

When you need to...	You'll find help here...
Decompress or decode files	p. 174
Retrieve a file with a Bookmark	p. 169
Retrieve files without Bookmarks or Archie	p. 175
Retrieve multiple files	p. 176
View files	p. 172
Upload files	p. 179
Upload multiple files	p. 179

Searching for FTP files from Windows

When you need to...	You'll find help here...
Get a copy of WSArchie	p. 121
Install WSArchie	p. 122
Retrieve a file from the search results list	p. 129
Search for a file	p. 124

Searching for FTP files from the Mac

When you need to...	You'll find help here...
Abort a query	p. 207
Conduct a complex Archie search	p. 202
Conduct a simple Archie search	p. 200
Get a URL	p. 200
Retrieve a file that Anarchie finds	p. 207
Update the Archie servers	p. 197

Using FTP from the command line

When you need to...	You'll find help here...
Connect to an Archie server	p. 233
Connect to an FTP server	p. 213
Download a file	p. 221
Get a directory listing	p. 218
Move around in directories	p. 219
Set up an Archie search	p. 237
Start the FTP command	p. 212
Upload a file	p. 230

Using online services to FTP

When you need to...	You'll find help here...
Use FTP from America Online	p. 49
Use FTP from CompuServe	p. 44
Use FTP from NetCruiser	p. 40
Use FTP from Prodigy	p. 55

Using the World Wide Web to FTP

When you need to..	You'll find help here...
Change directories	p. 252
Connect to an FTP server	p. 251
Download a file to disk	p. 256
Keep track of favorite FTP servers	p. 257
Load a file into your Web browser	p. 254
Save the file you're currently viewing	p. 256

{ Index }

Symbols

jumping to another
directory (WS_FTP),
84-85
linked directories/files,
66, 84-85
listing (command line),
218-219
local directories
command line,
220-221
profiles, 116
names, 164-165
navigating
Anarchie, 164
browsers (WWW),
252-254
opening (Anarchie),
163
paths, 65-66
refreshing (WS_FTP),
89
relative addresses, 220
remote directories
conflicts with
WS_FTP, 112
profiles (FTP sites),
116
renaming (command
line), 232
root directory, 65
switching
Anarchie, 164
command line, 220
WS_FTP, 83, 96
uploading files to a
specific directory, 180
viewing
Anarchie, 162-164
command line, 232
WS_FTP, 83
disabling firewalls, 146
**disconnections from
FTP sites**
America Online, 54
Anarchie, 165-166
command line, 231-232
CompuServe, 49
NetCruiser, 44

timeouts, 89
WS_FTP, 89
**disk space limitations
(command-line
accounts), 222**
**disks, downloading
files to disks, 256-257**
**distribution restric-
tions, 178-179**
**Doctor Fun FTP site,
299**
**domains (Archie
searches), restricting,
134**
**double-clicking options
(WS_FTP), 95**
downloading files
alarms, 232
America Online, 54
Anarchie, 169-178, 207
binary files, 133
bookmarks, 169-176
canceling, 255
command line, 146-148,
221-226
CompuServe, 48
disk space limitations,
222
multiple files, 103-104,
176-178
NetCruiser, 44
passive transfer mode,
141-142
Prodigy WWW
browser, 56
prompts, 232
renaming files with the
same name, 102-103
to a disk, 256-257
to a specific directory,
96-97, 130, 171-172
transfer protocols,
226-230
truncated names, 102
with the same name,
173
WS_FTP, 93-104
WSArchie, 130-133
WWW, 255-257

**drag-and-drop method
for uploading files
(WS_FTP), 105**
**DropStuff with Ex-
pander Enhancer, 63**

E

e-mail, 13
addresses
administrators,
180-181
anonymous FTP
passwords, 81
host names, 213
sending
to administrators,
180-181
to postmasters,
26-27, 91-92
software
PEM (Privacy
Enhanced Mail),
281
Qualcomm FTP site,
270, 276
**Edit Bookmark com-
mand (File menu)
(Anarchie), 188**
Edit menu commands
Clear (Anarchie), 167
Copy Directory
(WSArchie), 137
Copy File (WSArchie),
137
Copy Host (WSArchie),
137
Copy Result
(WSArchie), 136
Copy URL (Anarchie),
200
Fetch Server List
(Anarchie), 198
Preferences
(Anarchie), 158
Select All (Anarchie),
191
editing bookmarks, 187

ports, 117-118, 140
post-processing
    (Fetch), 39
postmasters,
    contacting, 26-27,
    91-92
PostScript files, 59
PowerMac files, 170
PPC files, 170
PPP (Point-to-Point
    Protocol), 30
Preferences command
    (Edit menu)
    (Anarchie), 158
Preferences command
    (File menu)
    (Anarchie), 171
Privacy Enhanced Mail
    (PEM), 281
Prodigy WWW browser,
    55-56
    connecting to FTP
        sites, 55
    downloading files, 56
    starting, 55
    starting FTP sessions,
        55
    viewing files, 56
PRODUCT.COM FTP
    site, 292
profiles, 109-110
    advanced information,
        115-118
    creating, 110-114
    deleting, 118
    names, 110-111
    optional information,
        115-118
    saving, 114-115
    sharing, 118-119
Program Options dialog
    box (WS_FTP), 82, 88,
    91, 115
programs
    decompression, 175
    freeware, 32
    FTP programs, 30-40,
        49-54, 75, 153-154
    public domain, 32

shareware, 32
    see also software
Project Gutenberg FTP
    site, 292
prompt command, 232
protection (files), 129
protocols (transfer
    protocols), 226-230
Proxy OPEN firewalls,
    145
.ps files, 59
/pub directories, 165
public domain software,
    32
put command, 230
pwd command, 232

Q

Qualcomm FTP site,
    270, 276
queries (Anarchie
    searches), 207-208
question mark (?)
    wildcard, 71-72, 203
queues (Archie
    searches), 237-238
quit command, 231, 244
quoted commands,
    sending (WS_FTP),
    149-150

R

readme files, 59
recipes
    Digital Equipment
        Corporation FTP site,
        298
    University of Miami
        FTP site, 298
recv command, 222-223
refreshing directories
    (WS_FTP), 89
regex searches
    (Archie), 72
    Anarchie, 204-206
    command line, 241-244
    WSArchie, 135-136

registering Anarchie,
    156-157
regular expression
    searches, *see* regex
    searches (Archie)
relative addresses
    (directories), 220
religion
    Finnish University and
        Research Network
        FTP site, 298
    Washington University
        at St. Louis FTP site,
        297
remote machines, 63
    conflicts with WS_FTP,
        112
    profiles, 116
renaming
    directories, 232
    files, 173, 223, 231
Request for Comments,
    see RFCs
Restricted access error
    message, 215
restrictions, 18
    access, 64, 140-141
    directories, 87
    distribution, 178-179
    protection (files), 129
resume output
    command, 224
Retrieve command
    (File menu)
    (WSArchie), 129
retry options (pro-
    files), 117
RFCs (Request for
    Comments), 142
rmdir command, 232
Roller Coasters FTP
    site, 300
root directory, 65
routers, 140
RTFM FTP site, 279
rules (Archie
    searches), 69-70
runique command, 223
Rutgers University
    Archive FTP site, 295

S

substring searches
(Archie), 69
 Anarchie, 200-202
 command line, 237-238,
 241-243
 WSArchie, 135
**Suffix Mapping
 command (Customize
 menu) (Fetch), 173**
sunique command, 231
**Sunsite FTP site, 268,
 286, 290**
SURAnet FTP site, 291
switching directories
 Anarchie, 164
 browsers (WWW),
 252-254
 command line, 220
 WS_FTP, 83, 96
**SYST command
 (WS_FTP), 113**

T

**Tape Archive
 compression, 62**
.tar files, 62
television
 Cathouse FTP site,
 293-294
 Georgia Tech
 University FTP site,
 295
 Internet Wiretap FTP
 site, 294
 Rutgers University
 Archive FTP site, 295
 Widener University
 FTP site, 295
**telnet to Archie
 servers, 233-236**
**telnet command,
 233-236**
text files, *see* **ASCII
 files**
**Text Viewer dialog box
 (WS_FTP), 99**
**text viewers (Notepad)
 (WS_FTP), 98-99**

timeouts
 connections, 89
 profile settings, 117
**transcripts (Anarchie),
 167-168**
**Transfer dialog box
 (WS_FTP), 132**
**transfer protocols,
 226-230**
**Transfer Status dialog
 box (WS_FTP), 132**
transferring files, *see*
 **downloading files;
 uploading files**
troubleshooting
 connections to Archie
 servers, 127
 connections to FTP
 sites
 Anarchie, 162
 command line,
 214-216
**Trumpet software FTP
 site, 270**
**truncated names
 (downloaded files),
 102**
TV, *see* **television**

U

U.S. Army FTP site, 281
**U.S. Senate FTP site,
 287**
UMich FTP site, 273
**Uniform Resource
 Locators,** *see* **URLs**
**University of Illinois at
 Urbana-Champaign
 FTP site, 267-268**
**University of Maryland
 at College Park
 inforM FTP site, 293**
**University of Miami
 FTP site, 298**
**University of Michigan
 FTP site, 288-289**
**University of Minnesota
 FTP site, 270, 276**

Unzip utility, 174
uploading files
 America Online, 53
 Anarchie, 179-181
 command line, 230-231
 CompuServe, 48
 contacting
 administrators for
 permission, 180-181
 distribution
 restrictions, 178-179
 drag-and-drop method,
 105
 finding uploaded files,
 180
 multiple files, 106,
 179-181
 NetCruiser, 43
 to a specific directory,
 106, 180
 WS_FTP, 104-108
**URLs (Uniform
 Resource Locators),
 55, 250**
 copying (Anarchie),
 200
 creating lists, 257-258
 FTP sites, 251
UseNet newsgroups, 14
 UUNET FTP site, 278
 WinVN newsreader,
 270
**USER after logon
 firewalls, 145**
**USER FTP command
 (WS_FTP), 149**
**user IDs (profiles),
 112-113**
**User Preferences
 command (Options
 menu) (WSArchie),
 137**
**User Preferences dialog
 box (WSArchie), 137**
**USER with no logon
 firewalls, 145**
/util directories, 165
UUDecode, 174

X-Y-Z

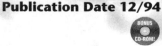

15 Hour Free Trial*

Internet access doesn't have to be expensive or difficult. Now you can enjoy **professional quality access** to the Internet for a **reasonable price.** We staff our network site **24 hours a day**, 7 days a week, 365 days a year to keep the network up and running.

We have also put together a collection of shareware programs for our Windows users to make getting started on the Internet a breeze. You'll get all the software you need and installation instructions when you subscribe.

Options for Every User

- Shell and SLIP accounts starting at $10.00 per month, with 120 hours per month included.

- Dedicated 14.4, 28.8, and 56K connections available.

- Dedicated T1 and T3 service available.

High-Speed Lines

All of our modems are 14.4kbps or faster. No waiting for a slow 9600-baud connection. We also have new 28.8K V.34 modem lines for the ultimate in SLIP PPP speed. ISDN service is also available. Call for details.

To Get an Account Now:

Call (317) 259-5050 or (800) 844-8649 and tell us you saw our ad in *Using FTP*.

We'll set up your account immediately and send you all the information and software you need so that you have your Internet access working with no hassles and no delays.

*Some restrictions apply. Call for details.

PLUG YOURSELF INTO...

MACMILLAN INFORMATION SUPERLIBRARY™

que   NRP
SAMS PUBLISHING   alpha books
Hayden Books   Brady
que COLLEGE   ADOBE PRESS

THE MACMILLAN INFORMATION SUPERLIBRARY™

Free information and vast computer resources from the world's leading computer book publisher—online!

FIND THE BOOKS THAT ARE RIGHT FOR YOU!

A complete online catalog, plus sample chapters and tables of contents give you an in-depth look at *all* of our books, including hard-to-find titles. It's the best way to find the books you need!

- **STAY INFORMED** with the latest computer industry news through our online newsletter, press releases, and customized Information SuperLibrary Reports.

- **GET FAST ANSWERS** to your questions about MCP books and software.

- **VISIT** our online bookstore for the latest information and editions!

- **COMMUNICATE** with our expert authors through e-mail and conferences.

- **DOWNLOAD SOFTWARE** from the immense MCP library:
  - Source code and files from MCP books
  - The best shareware, freeware, and demos

- **DISCOVER HOT SPOTS** on other parts of the Internet.

- **WIN BOOKS** in ongoing contests and giveaways!

TO PLUG INTO MCP: ➜

GOPHER: gopher.mcp.com
FTP: ftp.mcp.com

WORLD WIDE WEB: http://www.mcp.com

Home Page   What's New   Bookstore   Reference Desk   Software Library   Macmillan Overview   Talk to Us